ServiceStack 4 Cookbook

Over 70 recipes to create web services, build
message-based apps, and work with
object-relational mapping

Kyle Hodgson

Darren Reid

[PACKT] open source
PUBLISHING   community experience distilled

BIRMINGHAM - MUMBAI

ServiceStack 4 Cookbook

First published: January 2015

Production reference: 1190115

Published by Packt Publishing Ltd.
Livery Place
35 Livery Street
Birmingham B3 2PB, UK.

ISBN 978-1-78398-656-9

www.packtpub.com

Cover image by Jarosław Blaminsky (milak6@wp.pl)

Credits

Authors
Kyle Hodgson

Darren Reid

Reviewers
Phillip Haydon

Andreas Niedermair

Alex Pop

Jezz Santos

Commissioning Editor
Kunal Parikh

Acquisition Editor
Richard Brookes-Bland

Content Development Editor
Sumeet Sawant

Technical Editor
Vijin Boricha

Copy Editor
Sarang Chari

Project Coordinator
Danuta Jones

Proofreaders
Simran Bhogal

Maria Gould

Ameesha Green

Paul Hindle

Indexer
Mariammal Chettiyar

Graphics
Disha Haria

Production Coordinator
Alwin Roy

Cover Work
Alwin Roy

About the Authors

Kyle Hodgson is a software developer based in Toronto, Canada. He was working on full stack web development, but he fell in love with ServiceStack after finishing a large WCF project. He has led the development of several ambitious products for organizations ranging from small start-ups to Fortune 50 enterprises and has been invited to speak at several technology conferences about .NET and JavaScript. Having joined ThoughtWorks in 2012, Kyle is thrilled to be working with some of the smartest minds in software today. You can find his blog at http://www.kylehodgson.com.

I'd like to thank my wife, Lily, for her support during this project. I'd also like to thank ServiceStack creator Demis Bellot for his support while writing the book. Of course, I couldn't have done it without my friend and the book's co-author, Darren Reid.

Darren Reid is a .NET and JavaScript developer based in Canberra, Australia. He has worked primarily in large enterprise environments, building corporate web applications, and has also contributed to ServiceStack-related products. He received prizes for projects created for GovHack in 2012 and 2013, utilizing the ServiceStack framework. Darren is an accomplished open source advocate and blogger, and his work can be seen at www.layoric.org, where he blogs about advanced ServiceStack and AngularJS topics among other things.

I'd like to thank my wife, Kim, for her love and support. I'd also like to thank the book's co-author Kyle Hodgson for his tireless efforts, good advice, and encouragement during the writing of our book. A big thank you to ServiceStack creator Demis Bellot for making .NET developers' lives easier. Finally, thanks to the developers of my favorite games, which I intend to enjoy once this book is published.

About the Reviewers

Phillip Haydon is a Kiwi (New Zealander) who has spent the better part of the past 10 years traveling Asia during the day and coding furiously at night. He currently lives in Singapore, actively contributes to the NancyFX and SimpleAuthentication open source projects, and tries to maintain his own Sandra Snow blog engine.

> I would like to thank all the owners and contributors of NancyFX and ServiceStack, my two favorite projects with awesome teams that have taught me so much. Love you all!

Andreas Niedermair, a kid of the 1980s, got his hands dirty with QBasic and pressing "Refresh" in Netscape Navigator to review his websites, which later got enhanced by backend processing by PHP.

With the release of .NET he fell in love with the Microsoft stack, which he uses in his day job in the logistics industry.

Andreas lives in Austria and enjoys the outdoors, traveling, his guitars, and a good whisky in front of his *Kachelofen*. You can contact Andreas at `http://andreas.niedermair.name`.

Alex Pop is a professional software developer with a university degree in computer engineering and 12 years of commercial experience building .NET applications.

He has worked for ISVs, building enterprise resource planning applications, content management systems, and insurance and financial software products. He is currently working in the higher education sector as a web application developer.

His developer blog at `alexvpop.blogspot.co.uk` contains technical articles around .NET, JavaScript, and various software engineering topics.

I would like to thank my wife and daughter for their patient support.

Jezz Santos is a highly experienced developer, educator, coach, and mentor for software product delivery organizations and delivery teams. He began his career as a software research engineer at Nokia in Finland and then moved into software product development in start-ups in New Zealand, followed by over a decade at Microsoft in Western Europe and the USA. His broad focus at Microsoft was improving the output of product development teams, with a specific focus on development automation technologies and making team development a more sustainable, humanizing, and cooperative experience.

Now, he focuses on catalyzing excellence in product development by building high-performance, collaborative development teams that apply and continuously improve the application of the principles of craftsmanship, XP, and lean thinking. Jezz is currently doing all of that and still cutting code as a founder of Mindkin—a new, lean, Wellington-based product development start-up. Jezz is highly motivated to help establish New Zealand as a renowned worldwide leader in creating software development companies and products by growing and developing the huge potential of the people there.

You can reach out to Jezz through LinkedIn: `https://www.linkedin.com/in/jezzsa`.

See what Jezz Santos has to say about his experience with working on ServiceStack until now:

"After building numerous products and educating numerous teams of people on the full Microsoft web stack since .NET beta, the discovery of ServiceStack was just what test-first product developers want as a highly usable, testable, flexible, robust, and performant framework. Much like many other frameworks developed in the last few years, the experience of applying ServiceStack to real product development is to experience far less friction and higher productivity than applying any of the Microsoft web technologies. There is real "magic" in there and it's careful crafted to be highly usable by developers. Huge credit is deserved by the creators of ServiceStack, Demis Bellot et al and the entire ServiceStack community supporting it, making the experience for ServiceStack product developers such a fine and complete one."

"This book will be a real good guide for developers for getting up to speed, for revealing some of ServiceStack's, secrets and how to get more from it in your new products!"

www.PacktPub.com

Support files, eBooks, discount offers, and more

For support files and downloads related to your book, please visit www.PacktPub.com.

Did you know that Packt offers eBook versions of every book published, with PDF and ePub files available? You can upgrade to the eBook version at www.PacktPub.com and as a print book customer, you are entitled to a discount on the eBook copy. Get in touch with us at service@packtpub.com for more details.

At www.PacktPub.com, you can also read a collection of free technical articles, sign up for a range of free newsletters and receive exclusive discounts and offers on Packt books and eBooks.

https://www2.packtpub.com/books/subscription/packtlib

Do you need instant solutions to your IT questions? PacktLib is Packt's online digital book library. Here, you can search, access, and read Packt's entire library of books.

Why Subscribe?

- ▸ Fully searchable across every book published by Packt
- ▸ Copy and paste, print, and bookmark content
- ▸ On demand and accessible via a web browser

Free Access for Packt account holders

If you have an account with Packt at www.PacktPub.com, you can use this to access PacktLib today and view 9 entirely free books. Simply use your login credentials for immediate access.

Table of Contents

Preface

In recent times, web service APIs have become one of the most important parts of developing web applications. ServiceStack offers .NET developers a powerful set of tools that are thoughtfully architected with a core focus on simplicity, developer experience, and performance. With tools ranging from database access and HTML generation, to logging, serialization, caching, and more, ServiceStack gives developers a fantastic experience in developing web applications.

In this book, we address many of ServiceStack's features, including an introduction to using them and solving problems faced by .NET developers building web applications.

What this book covers

Chapter 1, Configuration and Routing, covers the various configuration options and ways to set up routing using the ServiceStack framework. We will also learn how to set up your solution and projects in a way that promotes testability and reuse and how to get the most out of ServiceStack's built-in IoC functionality.

Chapter 2, Services and Data Transfer Objects, says that these concepts (services and data transfer objects) are at the core of building web services with ServiceStack. This chapter teaches you techniques to produce clean, testable web services and gives examples of some common usages. You will also be shown how to use request/response filters for advanced request processing and integration.

Chapter 3, Testing and Logging, shows the integration of logging via ServiceStack LogManager, integration with popular testing frameworks as well as patterns for continuous integration.

Chapter 4, Object Relational Mapping (OrmLite), covers some of the functionality OrmLite provides while using practical patterns to keep your code clean and maintainable. OrmLite is a lightweight object relational mapping framework that focuses on simplicity and performance.

Chapter 5, HTML and Form Data, shows the different tools that the ServiceStack framework gives developers to handle HTML generation and specific interactions on web pages.

Chapter 6, Filters and Validators, shows the versatility of ServiceStack filters for different uses, including integration, as well as validators to assist with HTML forms or API error messages.

Chapter 7, Security and Authentication, shows ServiceStack OAuth and other built-in security functionality as well as how to deal with custom authentication and integration with commonly used frameworks/systems.

Chapter 8, Working with Redis, teaches you how to get the most out of the Redis client provided and ServiceStack integration as well as setting up Redis and using it in different environments.

Chapter 9, Integrating with Other Technologies, covers integration with popular and common frameworks and technologies to highlight ServiceStack's power when used in conjunction with existing systems. The chapter also covers how to handle introducing ServiceStack into an established ASP.NET MVC and WebForms project.

Appendix A, Getting Started, takes you through creating a ServiceStack solution, walking you through the different parts. This will be useful for readers who don't have access to use the ServiceStack Visual Studio extension, ServiceStackVS.

Appendix B, Testing Locally, is a short guide on how to use Fiddler2 to route traffic of a different domain to IIS Express. Depending on your environment restrictions, this might help debug OAuth providers. This isn't needed to complete the recipes in this book.

What you need for this book

While most examples simply require Visual Studio 2013 Community Edition or better, some recipes do use other technologies to illustrate integration with specific functionality within the ServiceStack framework. The following is a list of software required to use all the examples:

- ▶ Visual Studio 2013 Community Edition or better
- ▶ MS SQL Server 2008 R2 Express or later
- ▶ Redis 2.8
- ▶ MongoDB 2.6
- ▶ IIS8 or later

Who this book is for

If you are a .NET developer who is looking for a simpler way to build services, this is the book for you. It will show you how to write fast, maintainable APIs that are a pleasure to use and maintain, starting from the database to the client and everything in between.

Sections

In this book, you will find several headings that appear frequently (Getting ready, How to do it, How it works, There's more, and See also).

To give clear instructions on how to complete a recipe, we use these sections as follows:

Getting ready

This section tells you what to expect in the recipe, and describes how to set up any software or any preliminary settings required for the recipe.

How to do it...

This section contains the steps required to follow the recipe.

How it works...

This section usually consists of a detailed explanation of what happened in the previous section.

There's more...

This section consists of additional information about the recipe in order to make the reader more knowledgeable about the recipe.

See also

This section provides helpful links to other useful information for the recipe.

Conventions

In this book, you will find a number of text styles that distinguish between different kinds of information. Here are some examples of these styles and an explanation of their meaning.

Code words in text, database table names, folder names, filenames, file extensions, pathnames, dummy URLs, user input, and Twitter handles are shown as follows: "ServiceStack includes `ServiceStack.OrmLite`, which is much faster than Microsoft's own Entity Framework and most other ORMs."

A block of code is set as follows:

```
[Route("/hello/{Name}","GET")]
public class GreetingRequest
{
  public string Name { get; set; }
}
```

When we wish to draw your attention to a particular part of a code block, the relevant lines or items are set in bold:

```
public IEnumerable<Message> Where(
Expression<Func<Message, bool>> expression)
{
   using (var db = DbConnectionFactory.OpenDbConnection())
   {
     return db.Select(expression);
   }
}
```

Any command-line input or output is written as follows:

```
c:\projects>curl http://myserver/hello/world
Hello, world!
```

New terms and **important words** are shown in bold. Words that you see on the screen, for example, in menus or dialog boxes, appear in the text like this: " To get started, create an empty ASP.NET solution in Visual Studio. We'll name it **HelloWorldService**."

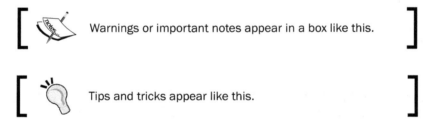

Warnings or important notes appear in a box like this.

Tips and tricks appear like this.

Reader feedback

Feedback from our readers is always welcome. Let us know what you think about this book—what you liked or disliked. Reader feedback is important for us as it helps us develop titles that you will really get the most out of.

To send us general feedback, simply e-mail feedback@packtpub.com, and mention the book's title in the subject of your message.

If there is a topic that you have expertise in and you are interested in either writing or contributing to a book, see our author guide at www.packtpub.com/authors.

Customer support

Now that you are the proud owner of a Packt book, we have a number of things to help you to get the most from your purchase.

Downloading the example code

You can download the example code files from your account at http://www.packtpub.com for all the Packt Publishing books you have purchased. If you purchased this book elsewhere, you can visit http://www.packtpub.com/support and register to have the files e-mailed directly to you.

Downloading the color images of this book

We also provide you with a PDF file that has color images of the screenshots/diagrams used in this book. The color images will help you better understand the changes in the output. You can download this file from: https://www.packtpub.com/sites/default/files/downloads/6569OS_ImageBundle.pdf.

Errata

Although we have taken every care to ensure the accuracy of our content, mistakes do happen. If you find a mistake in one of our books—maybe a mistake in the text or the code—we would be grateful if you could report this to us. By doing so, you can save other readers from frustration and help us improve subsequent versions of this book. If you find any errata, please report them by visiting `http://www.packtpub.com/submit-errata`, selecting your book, clicking on the **Errata Submission Form** link, and entering the details of your errata. Once your errata are verified, your submission will be accepted and the errata will be uploaded to our website or added to any list of existing errata under the Errata section of that title.

To view the previously submitted errata, go to `https://www.packtpub.com/books/content/support` and enter the name of the book in the search field. The required information will appear under the **Errata** section.

Piracy

Piracy of copyrighted material on the Internet is an ongoing problem across all media. At Packt, we take the protection of our copyright and licenses very seriously. If you come across any illegal copies of our works in any form on the Internet, please provide us with the location address or website name immediately so that we can pursue a remedy.

Please contact us at `copyright@packtpub.com` with a link to the suspected pirated material.

We appreciate your help in protecting our authors and our ability to bring you valuable content.

Questions

If you have a problem with any aspect of this book, you can contact us at `questions@packtpub.com`, and we will do our best to address the problem.

1

Configuration and Routing

In this chapter, we'll talk a bit about ServiceStack and we will present the following recipes:

- ▶ Up and running with ServiceStack
- ▶ Routing using data-transfer-object attributes
- ▶ Isolating web service routes from a web application
- ▶ Common ServiceStack plugins
- ▶ Writing a Custom Audit plugin
- ▶ Adding Routes via the API
- ▶ Structuring your project to avoid dependency issues
- ▶ Managing dependencies with Funq and **Inversion of Control** (**IoC**)
- ▶ Sharing and accessing configurations and common functionalities using Funq IoC

Introduction

ServiceStack is a .NET framework that makes it easy to write web services. It's fast, thoughtfully architected, and by our account, better to work with than Microsoft's own ASP.NET Web API and **Windows Communication Foundation** (**WCF**) frameworks. In this book, we'll show you what it's like to work with ServiceStack in a series of recipes that illustrate how to do things using the framework.

ServiceStack helps you to focus on modeling the messages your service will be exchanging with its clients by specifying **data transfer objects** (**DTO**). You might start by creating a `DTO` class to represent an expected HTTP request and provide an annotation on that class that specifies the expected route. A service will later be created that consumes these requests and returns a response DTO. This focus on the façade that your service presents allows you to easily manage the contract between your service and your consuming clients.

ServiceStack has sought out or created components that help it meet its goals of speed and simplicity. While in most cases, you can bring in your favorite frameworks, it provides several out of the box that are well supported:

▶ ServiceStack's JsonSerializer is much faster than both Microsoft Base Class Library and DataContractSerializer and faster than other competing open source serializers

▶ ServiceStack includes a slightly modified version of the open source Funq DI container known for its performance and simplicity

▶ ServiceStack includes `ServiceStack.OrmLite`, which is much faster than Microsoft's own Entity Framework and most other ORMs

Architecturally, ServiceStack favors a common pattern to develop what can be thought of as RESTful web services. REST is wildly popular today, and many consider it the best approach to a Services-oriented architecture.

Why REST?

Perhaps one of the most compelling reasons to use **Representational state transfer** (**REST**) is its focus on developing a design based on the concept of a remote resource. You could imagine that an application based on group messaging would require services where users could exchange messages; client applications would communicate by making HTTP connections to remote resources—the remote resource for a group called My Best Friends might be `/groups/MyBestFriends`. You could query to see what messages were available request by accessing that URL. You could send new messages to that group by sending an HTTP `POST` to it—the HTTP `POST` request could contain a JSON object with the sender's name, the text of the message, and other details. You could just as easily remove this group when it's no longer required by sending HTTP `DELETE` request to the same endpoint. You could specify that you need only JSON data by sending an `Accept` header set to `application/json` or specify that you want a web page by asking for `application/html`. The RESTful approach of designing a remote resource and then interoperating with that resource through simple HTTP calls naturally extends the Web.

ServiceStack's message-based approach often leads to a simpler service interface. SOAP, Microsoft WCF, and even WebAPI encourage a **remote procedure call** (**RPC**) style of programming, which encourages the creation of more and more methods—while a message-based approach encourages you to think about your API. We are aware of one project that took an RPC-based approach over two or three years and ended up with over seventy distinct methods being published. A redesign and the careful application of the message pattern reduced this to just two different REST resources. The result was far more manageable—it was also easier to extend, maintain, test, secure, and document.

While a full treatment of developing REST services is outside the scope of this book, the authors will purposefully take a RESTful approach to building services throughout the example. This is not by accident—and is made much easier when working with ServiceStack.

 Note: *REST in Practice* is a great practical book for getting started on the topic of building RESTful services.

Up and running with ServiceStack

Let's begin by creating our first service with ServiceStack.

How to do It...

To get started, create an empty ASP.NET solution in Visual Studio. We'll name it **HelloWorldService**. Next, install the ServiceStack nuget package. *Creating a ServiceStack solution with VisualStudio and NuGet* in *Appendix A, Getting Started* has more details on how. ServiceStack is capable of much more than Hello World Service, but doing something simple to start will help us explain some things.

Next, create the first class and call it `GreetingRequest`. Start by entering a single property `Name` as follows:

```
[Route("/hello/{Name}","GET")]
public class GreetingRequest
{
  public string Name { get; set; }
}
```

This class is now the entry point to our service. We're telling ServiceStack that it can expect HTTP GET requests to a URL /hello with a name parameter— such requests will be deserialized to an instance of the GreetingRequest class.

Next, let's create a service that knows how to handle GreetingRequest by adding another class to HelloWorldService—we can call it GreetingService. To register GreetingService with ServiceStack, we need to implement the IService marker interface. We could also extend the Service helper class, which implements IService and provides useful functionality, as follows:

```
using ServiceStack;
namespace HelloWorldService
{
    public class GreetingService : IService
    {
        public object Get(GreetingRequest request)
        {
            return "Hello, " + request.Name + "!";
        }
    }
}
```

What ServiceStack will do is run the GreetingService Get() method whenever an incoming GreetingRequest class requires processing.

ServiceStack's naming conventions for service methods is to name them in a way that indicates which HTTP verbs they expect to process. We could have named our method Any, for instance—if we had, ServiceStack would use our method for GET, POST, PUT, or DELETE requests. If we had named our method Post, our service would refuse to process a GET request, returning a 404 status code with a message that a handler for the request couldn't be found.

Next we'll build an ApplicationHost class that extends ServiceStack's AppHostBase class. You can think of ApplicationHost as a container—it handles the hosting details and dependency injection. If we wanted to quickly migrate our service from **Internet Information Services (IIS)** to a Windows service, we should only really need to change the ApplicationHost class.

This specific example will be hosted in an ASP.NET application, which is why we extend the AppHostBase class. However, ServiceStack services can be self-hosted, running as a command-line app or Windows service using AppSelfHostBase class.

We need one empty constructor that will pass in the name of the service and the assembly (or assemblies) that ServiceStack can discover your service classes in. It also expects that we'll pass in an IOC container with application configuration, but we don't need that yet, so we'll leave it blank, as follows:

```
using ServiceStack;
using System.Reflection;

namespace HelloWorldService
{
  public class ApplicationHost : AppHostBase
  {
    public ApplicationHost() : base("Greeting Service",
    typeof(GreetingService).Assembly)
    { }

    public override void Configure(Funq.Container container)
    { }
  }
}
```

One thing we need to handle is making sure our service gets started when the ASP.NET application boots. We wire that up by calling the `Init()` method on our `ApplicationHost` class in the `Application_Start` handler in `Global.asax`. First, we'll need to add `Global.asax` to our project—to do that, right-click the **HelloWorldService** project, then click on **Add**, and then click on **New Item**. Search for **Global**, choose **Global Application Class**, and then press **Add**, as follows:

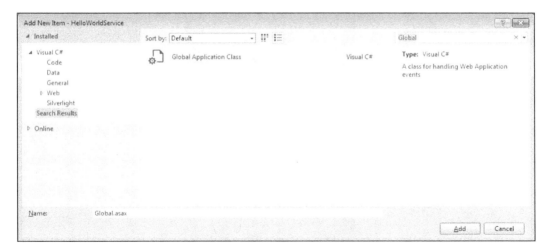

Visual Studio will bring up the template `Global.asax.cs` code—just add one line to `Application_Start` and delete the other methods. When it's done, your code looks like this:

```
public class Global : System.Web.HttpApplication
{
  protected void Application_Start(object sender, EventArgs e)
  {
    new ApplicationHost().Init();
  }
}
```

This tells ASP.NET to trigger our `ApplicationHost() Init()` method when starting this application.

Next, we need to add some configuration in `Web.config` to tell IIS about ServiceStack—we can do this by adding the following under the `<configuration>` element:

```
<system.webServer>
<validation validateIntegratedModeConfiguration="false"/>
  <handlers>
    <add path="*" name="ServiceStack.Factory"
      type="ServiceStack.HttpHandlerFactory, ServiceStack"
      verb="*" preCondition="integratedMode"
      resourceType="Unspecified" allowPathInfo="true"/>
  </handlers>
</system.webServer>
```

Note: these instructions work with IIS7. For instructions on how to make ServiceStack work with IIS6, the `https:// servicestack.net` site has further instruction.

At this stage, we should have a simple, basic service. From here, if you click *F5* in Visual Studio, a browser should open showing the default metadata page for a ServiceStack project—as you can see, it lists the different operations available. Clicking on the **JSON** link next to *GreetingRequest* will show instructions on how to use it, including an example HTTP request, as follows:

We can easily see our service in action by viewing the /hello/world endpoint. Try replacing **world** with your name, and the greeting should change too:

How it works...

When IIS starts our application, the Init() method on our ApplicationHost class will be called. Inherited from AppHostBase class, this method initializes our container, any plugins named, and the dependency injection configuration. As with any ASP.NET application, IIS bindings specify which requests will reach our application by specifying port, virtual host information, and so on.

The ServiceStack framework will attempt to deserialize any incoming requests into data transfer objects based on their composition and any routing configuration it has available. In this case, our Route attribute specifies that incoming GET requests with Name parameters should be deserialized into GreetingRequest class:

```
[Route("/hello/{Name}","GET")]
public class GreetingRequest
{
    public string Name { get; set; }
}
```

From there, ServiceStack will infer which method should process the DTO. Given that our example request is an HTTP GET request, our Greeting Service's Get() method will be called and presented with the incoming GreetingRequest object:

```
public object Get(GreetingRequest request)
{
    return "Hello, " + request.Name + "!";
}
```

It returns a string in this case, which will be presented to the user:

```
c:\projects>curl http://myserver/hello/world
Hello, world!
```

There's more...

We're beginning to build up some basic source code, but we don't have any tests yet. Let's see what that looks like:

```
[TestFixture]
public class GreetingServiceTest
{
  [Test]
  public void ShouldRespondToGreetingRequests()
  {

  }
}
```

 For basic information on how to get a testing environment running, check out the section *Integrating NUnit* in *Appendix A, Getting Started*.

The first thing our test will need is a test request. We can do that easily by creating `GreetingRequest` and filling in some basic values.

Before we can do that, we'll need to add a reference to the **HelloWorldService** project, as follows:

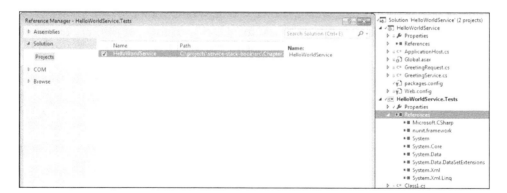

We'll pass this request in to our service so that we can make assertions on the response. If you've ever heard people talk about unit testing in terms of **Arrange-Act-Assert**, this is the Arrange section of the test. Your code might look like this:

```
[TestFixture]
public class GreetingServiceTest
{
  [Test]
  public void ShouldRespondToGreetingRequests()
  {
    var testRequest = new GreetingRequest { Name = "test value" };
    var target = new GreetingService();
  }
}
```

We can now execute our service (Act) and make assertions about the response. Let's start with a value that we know will fail to make sure that our test will catch the issue we're trying to find, as follows:

```
[TestFixture]
public class GreetingServiceTest
{
  [Test]
  public void ShouldRespondToGreetingRequests()
  {
    var testRequest = new GreetingRequest { Name = "test value" };
    var target = new GreetingService();
    var response = target.Get(testRequest);
    Assert.AreEqual("WRONG", response);
  }
}
```

This being our first test run, we expect the test to fail. You can see that **NUnit** is explaining to us exactly why it failed. Once we fix it by changing the "WRONG" string to "Hello, test value!", we'll expect it to pass, as follows:

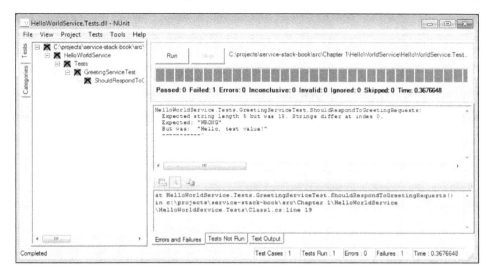

Fixing the test is as simple as writing the following code:

```
[Test]
public void ShouldRespondToGreetingRequests()
{
    var testRequest = new GreetingRequest { Name = "test value" };
    var target = new GreetingService();
    var response = target.Get(testRequest);
    Assert.AreEqual("Hello, test value!", response);
}
```

Here's a screenshot depicting the fixed test:

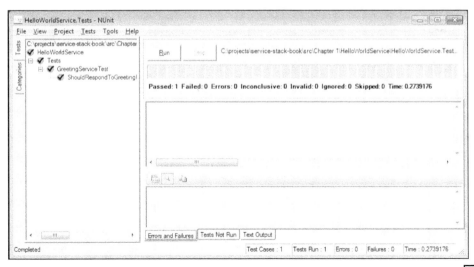

Now that we have a test in place for our service, we can have our IDE run this test (and others like it) frequently so that we can tell if the service stops doing what it's expected to do. The benefit of this can't be understated—bugs found moments after they are created are incredibly simple to fix, whereas bugs found in production can be very expensive to find and resolve.

Routing using data transfer object attributes

ServiceStack routes incoming HTTP requests to services by a number of mechanisms. Perhaps the most convenient is the `Route` attribute— simply annotate the class to indicate where ServiceStack should expect requests.

Getting ready

You'll need a request object. For instance, Reidson-Industries is interested in developing a group messaging application for use on the Web and on mobile devices. We could model an incoming request like this:

```
public class Message
{
  public string Body { get; set; }
  public string Sender { get; set; }
  public string GroupName { get; set; }
}
```

We might handle requests for this `Message` object with a `MessengerService` class, as follows:

```
public class MessengerService : Service
{
  static List<Message> _messages = new List<Message>();
  public MessageResponse Post(Message request)
  {
    _messages.Add(request);
    return new MessageResponse { Response = "OK" };
  }
}
```

In previous examples, our service methods have simply returned the object, with the service passing a string back. To add a bit more structure to our contract, a response might be modeled like this:

```
public class MessageResponse
{
  public string Response { get; set; }
}
```

How to do It...

To tell ServiceStack where to expect requests that contain `Message` objects, simply annotate the object with a `Route` annotation, as follows:

```
[Route("/message")]
public class Message
{
  public string Body { get; set; }
  public string Sender { get; set; }
  public string GroupName { get; set; }
}
```

How it works...

Now ServiceStack will accept `POST` requests containing either JSON data or form data at `http://yourserver/message` containing strings named `Body`, `Sender`, and `GroupName`. These requests will be deserialized in to an instance of the `Message` DTO. You can provide more information in the annotation as well— for instance, if you wanted to be able to provide an alternate URL format, you could do the following:

```
[Route("/message")]
[Route("/message/{GroupName}")]
public class Message
{
  public string Body { get; set; }
  public string Sender { get; set; }
  public string GroupName { get; set; }
}
```

Now, if ServiceStack sees a request for `http://yourserver/message/BestFriends`, it will assume that `Message` is destined for the `BestFriends` group. You can add multiple routes for the same request object by placing multiple `Route` annotations on the same object.

We'll need to retrieve messages too. We can do that by querying the `/group` endpoint. To do this, simply create a `request` object, as follows:

```
[Route("/group/{GroupName}")]
public class Group
{
  public string GroupName { get; set; }
}
```

We'll expand `MessengerService` to be able to handle this request:

```
public class MessengerService : Service
{
  static List<Message> _messages = new List<Message>();
  public MessageResponse Post(Message request)
  {
    _messages.Add(request);
    return new MessageResponse { Response = "OK" };
  }

  public GroupResponse Get(Group request)
  {
    return new GroupResponse
    {
      Messages = _messages.Where(
      message => message.GroupName.Equals(request.GroupName))
      .ToList()
    };
  }
}
```

The `GroupResponse` class is a simple DTO to model the expected response. In this example, the `GroupResponse` class has a single property `Messages` and simple `List<Message>` containing the messages that the user has requested:

```
public class GroupResponse
{
  public List<Message> Messages { get; set; }
}
```

 Note that the code in the previous example will work to get us started building a simple application, but storing all of our incoming messages in `static List<Message>` with no backing store isn't likely to work out well in practice. We'll refactor this into something more production-ready in a later recipe.

Once you start the app, you can send a form post to the `BestFriends` group with `curl`. A command-line HTTP utility, curl makes it easy to craft full-featured HTTP requests. It can specify headers and HTTP methods, send form data, and return any results on the command line.

We want to send an HTTP POST request with enough form data to provide a message to our service, and we'd like to see the response in JSON. We'll use curl with -H to specify the header, -X, to specify the HTTP method, and --data to specify the data to send. Put together, it looks like this:

```
curl -H "Accept: application/json" -X POST --data  \
    "Body=first post&Sender=Kyle&GroupName=BestFriends" \
    http://myserver/message
```

Then, you can read the messages that have been sent to the BestFriends group, as follows:

```
curl -H "Accept: application/json" \
    http://myserver/group/BestFriends
```

The result would be the JSON response, as follows:

```
{"Messages": [{"Body":"first post", "Sender":"Kyle",
"GroupName":"BestFriends"}]}
```

There's more...

Let's imagine that we wanted people to be able to search for a specific search term or possibly search for a term within a specified group. We could use the Route annotation to do this easily with one single request type. Implement it like this:

```
[Route("/message/search")]
[Route("/message/search/{Group}")]
public class Search
{
  public string Group { get; set; }
  public string Query { get; set; }
}
```

We'll easily expand our MessengerService class to be able to handle this request by adding a new method, as follows:

```
public GroupResponse Get(Search request)
{
    return new GroupResponse
    {
      Messages = _messages.Where(
        message => message.GroupName.Equals(request.Group)
        && message.Body.Contains(request.Query))
      .ToList()
    };
}
```

We could make use of this new endpoint with another `curl` command. First, we'll post a few messages so that we have something to search, as follows:

```
curl -H "Accept: application/json" -X POST \
    --data "Body=first post&Sender=Kyle"  \
    http://myserver/message/BestFriends
{"Response":"OK"}
curl -H "Accept: application/json" -X POST \
    --data "Body=second post&Sender=Kyle"  \
    http://myserver/message/BestFriends
{"Response":"OK"}
```

Then, we can easily search by sending a simple `GET` call:

```
curl -H "Accept: application/json" \
    http://myserver/message/search/BestFriends?query=second
{"Messages":
  [
    {"Body":"second post",
     "Sender":"Kyle",
     "GroupName":"BestFriends"}
  ]
}
```

Isolating web service routes from a web application

Until now, we've been talking about using ServiceStack in isolation, where it's the only thing handling all requests. It won't always be so simple, of course— sometimes you'll want to use ServiceStack in an existing MVC, WCF, or WebForms application. Here, we will learn different ways to isolate ServiceStack requests to ensure they don't get tangled up with requests from other frameworks.

Getting ready

For this example, let's keep building on `ReidsonMessenger` from the first recipe, but namespace the HTTP contract of our API by moving all of our service endpoints under a prefix. So, instead of making a `GET` call to `/group/BestFriends` to retrieve the messages from the `BestFriends` group, we'll be calling `/api/group/BestFriends`.

How to do It...

We'll need to configure the web server to facilitate our new prefix. We'll add the following to `Web.config`, just after the `system.web` section:

```
<location path="api">
  <system.web>
    <httpHandlers>
      <add path="*" type="ServiceStack.HttpHandlerFactory,
      ServiceStack" verb="*" />
    </httpHandlers>
  </system.web>

  <system.webServer>
    <modules runAllManagedModulesForAllRequests="true" />
    <validation validateIntegratedModeConfiguration="false" />
    <handlers>
      <add path="*" name="ServiceStack.Factory" type="ServiceStack.
      HttpHandlerFactory, ServiceStack" verb="*"
      preCondition="integratedMode" resourceType="Unspecified"
      allowPathInfo="true" />
    </handlers>
  </system.webServer>
</location>
```

After making this change, running our application might return an error message as we continue visiting `http://myserver/—` remember to add the `api` path at the end to see the usual metadata page you're expecting. We'll need to change the URLs we post to use curl too, as follows:

curl http://myserver/api/group/BestFriends

While not strictly necessary, one benefit of using the location element is the ability to remove other handlers, ensuring that ServiceStack is the only thing running on this path.

If it makes more sense to make this change in code, ServiceStack allows this to be changed within your `AppHost.Configure` method, as follows:

```
public override void Configure(Funq.Container container)
{
  SetConfig(new HostConfig
  {
    HandlerFactoryPath = "api"
  }
}
```

In your organization, if developers have a lot of control over deployment of code, it might make sense to control this in code, as then it can be more easily tested, and you might find it more expressive. However, if another team deploys your code or manages your application in production or if you want to be able to tune this location often, it might be preferable to specify the path in the `web config` file, as then changing it won't require a complete compile, test, and deploy cycle.

How it works...

When using any HTTP handlers with ASP.NET, a path must be registered to tell IIS how to handle requests of a specific path. ServiceStack provides its `HttpHandlerFactory` implementation, which is the initial *hook* into the rest of the framework.

By either changing the path in `web.config` or setting the path when your application starts, we can make a clear separation between our web services and other resources. There are important differences between the two methods.

By changing the path within the configuration, you'll notice that when you start up your web project, you are greeted with this:

HTTP Error 403.14 - Forbidden

The Web server is configured to not list the contents of this directory.

This is because ServiceStack is not actually handling your request and there is no default item within the solution that ASP.NET can serve.

By changing `HostConfig` and leaving `web.config path` as `"*"`, ServiceStack is serving all your other resources as well. So, as soon as you run your application, ServiceStack will default to your new web services path as follows:

The following screenshot shows you the metadata page:

Recipe 3 - Isolating Routes

The following operations are supported. For a formal definition, please review the Service XSD.

If you happen to be hosting files with uncommon file extensions, it's important to remember that if the ServiceStack handler path is configured as "*", ServiceStack needs to know what file types are able to be served.

For example, if you are writing your web client using something like Dart, which uses .dart files for it's source, both ASP.NET and ServiceStack need to know about this additional file type that is allowed. Perform the following steps towards this end:

1. ASP.NET will need to know about the appropriate file extension and MIME type, for example:

```
<staticContent>
  <remove fileExtension=".dart" />
  <mimeMap fileExtension=".dart"
  mimeType="application/dart" />
</staticContent>
```

2. ServiceStack will need to have the file extension added to the AllowFileExtensions property on HostConfig():

```
var hostConfig = new HostConfig();
hostConfig.AllowFileExtensions = {"dart"};
hostConfig.HandlerFactoryPath = "api";
SetConfig(hostConfig);
```

There's more...

ServiceStack can also be hosted in various environments including as a Windows service or even a simple console application. In this case, the initializer for the service is a call to the Start method on the AppHost, which accepts a parameter that represents the URL to bind to. If a prefix is required, it will need to be included into this urlBase parameter, as follows:

```
class Program
{
  const string ListeningOn = "http://*:1234/api/";
  static void Main(string[] args)
  {
    new AppHost()
    .Init()
    .Start(ListeningOn);

    Console.WriteLine("AppHost Created at {0}, " +
    "listening on {1}",
    DateTime.Now, ListeningOn);

    Console.ReadKey();
  }
}
```

Common ServiceStack plugins

There are some requirements that are very common when building web services. For instance, many sites need to validate user input, log requests, or manage the security of the application. ServiceStack comes with some plugins that are very simple to add and that provide advanced functionality through a simple interface. This recipe shows how these features can be added using some of the default plugins available.

How to do It...

There are quite a few plugins that ServiceStack v4.0 comes with, and they are all added the same way; some are standalone, some have dependencies, but they all implement the `IPlugin` interface. The following are a few examples showing how the required code is added to `AppHost` in the overridden `Configure` method:

`ValidationFeature` enables the use of *Fluent Validation* to construct easy to read rules. A common usage of these rules is validation of request values before ServiceStack executes the HTTP method of your service:

```
Plugins.Add(new ValidationFeature());
```

`RegistrationFeature` provides new web service endpoints to enable user registration. This feature is commonly used with `AuthFeature`:

```
Plugins.Add(new AuthFeature(() => new AuthUserSession(),
new IAuthProvider[]
{
    new BasicAuthProvider()
}));
Plugins.Add(new RegistrationFeature());
```

`CorsFeature` enables your web services to support **Cross-Origin Resource Sharing** (**CORS**). This allows JavaScript clients on other domains to use your web services:

```
Plugins.Add(new CorsFeature());
```

How it works...

The ServiceStack plugins object is just `List<IPlugin>` that is accessible from your `AppHost` class.

`CorsFeature` and `ValidationFeature` both utilize ServiceStack request filters to enable functionality for each request that is sent to your web services.

`AuthFeature` and `RegistrationFeature` create new endpoints to expose functionality as well as enable the use of `AuthenticateAttribute` to decorate your service classes. You can see this if you look at the metadata page of your application after adding `AuthFeature`; you'll notice the additional endpoints your application is now hosting.

The following screenshot depicts few of the plugins provided by the ServiceStack framework:

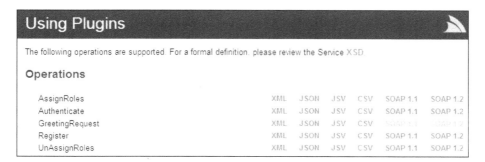

`AuthFeature` and `RegistrationFeature` have added four endpoints to enable functionality such as authenticating users and the registration of new ones. The implementation specifics of this depend on how these objects are created.

Plugins are a powerful way to expose reusable functionality across ServiceStack apps with minimal effort. The previous screenshot shows just a few of the plugins that the ServiceStack framework provides. It's easy to add the class implements `IPlugin`, it can be registered with ServiceStack and will be processed at start-up of the application.

Writing a custom audit plugin

In the ServiceStack framework, plugins are a great way to encapsulate completely independent functionality that can be reused between projects. ServiceStack itself bundles loads of useful packages this way, including authentication, validation, and others.

In this recipe, we will build a plugin to add an audit to our database's create and update methods—you might find this useful if your project requires auditing for changes to a data source. We'll make use of OrmLite features to do so.

How to do It...

Create a new class library project that will contain your plugin and all its required components—AuditFeaturePlugin.

Add ServiceStack and its dependencies as references to the new project.

Create an interface for objects you want to audit called IAuditable:

```
public interface IAuditable
{
    DateTime CreatedDate { get; set; }
    DateTime ModifiedDate { get; set; }
    string ModifiedByUserId { get; set; }
}
Create a class that implements IPlugin.
public class AuditFeature : IPlugin
{
  public IDbConnectionFactory DbConnectionFactory { get; set; }

  public void Register(IAppHost appHost)
  {
    if (OrmLiteConfig.DialectProvider == null)
    {
      throw new Exception(
      "AuditFeature requires the use of OrmLite and a DialectProvider
      must be first initialized.");
    }

    OrmLiteConfig.InsertFilter = AuditInsert;
    OrmLiteConfig.UpdateFilter = AuditUpdate;
  }

  private void AuditInsert(IDbCommand command, object rowObj)
  {
    var auditObject = rowObj as IAuditable;
    if (auditObject != null)
    {
      var now = DateTime.UtcNow;
      auditObject.CreatedDate = now;
      auditObject.ModifiedDate = now;
      // Modified by user running the process of
      the AppPool. Note: only works in Windows.
```

```
      auditObject.ModifiedByUserId
      =System.Security.Principal.WindowsIdentity.GetCurrent().Name;
    }
  }

  private void AuditUpdate(IDbCommand command, object rowObj)
  {
    var auditObject = rowObj as IAuditable;
    if (auditObject != null)
    {
      var now = DateTime.UtcNow;
      auditObject.ModifiedDate = now;
      // Modified by user running the process of
      the AppPool. Note: only works in Windows.
      auditObject.ModifiedByUserId
      =System.Security.Principal.WindowsIdentity.GetCurrent().Name;
    }
  }
}
```

Now that we have created a separate class library that contains our AuditFeature plugin, we can share it with the main project that is hosting the ServiceStack web services. Remember to add a reference to the main project so that both the IAuditable interface and the AuditFeature plugin itself are able to be used.

Register the plugin from within your ApplicationHost class:

```
public class ApplicationHost : AppHostBase
{
  public ApplicationHost()
  : base("Reidson Messenger",
  typeof(MessageRequest).Assembly)
  { }

  public override void Configure(Container container)
  {
    Plugins.Add(new AuditFeature());
  }
}
Add the IAuditable interface to a model class, like the Message
class:
public class Message : IAuditable
{
  //...
  public DateTime CreatedDate { get;set; }
```

```
        public DateTime ModfiedDate { get;set; }
        public string ModfiedByUserId { get;set; }
    }
```

How it works...

`IPlugin` that ServiceStack provides has one single method that ServiceStack calls when the framework is initializing.

In the case of the `AuditFeature` class, a check is made to make sure that OrmLite is being used in the project that is running the `AuditFeature` function by checking whether `DialectProvider` is currently being used with OrmLite.

Once this is done, it binds an *action* to both `InsertFilter` and `UpdateFilter` provided by OrmLite. These actions are fired whenever an insert or an update is processed using the OrmLite framework.

See also

  ▶ Using Ormlite filtering for custom actions on insert/update

Adding Routes via the API

This recipe covers the ability to add routes without using the provided `RouteAttribute` class. This technique might be needed if you have restrictions on your development environment or requirements that might prevent you from using `RouteAttribute`. In this situation where it's not ideal or possible to use the ServiceStack C# client, a client such as RestSharp with data transfer objects might be possible alternative.

Using the routing attributes gives you the advantages of more streamlined development when using the ServiceStack JsonClient and is the recommended way of managing your application's routes. The solution in this recipe is only intended for situations where this is not possible.

How to do It...

From the `AppHost` class, access the `Routes` property on the base `ServiceStackHost` class to add routes, passing the request object's type and the path to be used:

```
    public class AppHost : AppHostBase
    {
```

```
public AppHost()
: base("Adding Routes via AppHost",
typeof(AppHost).Assembly)
{ }

public override void Configure(Container container)
{
  Routes.Add<GreeterRequest>("/greetings/{Name}");
  Routes.Add<FarewellRequest>("/farewell/{Name}", "GET");
  Routes.Add<HowAreYouRequest>("/howareyou/{Name}",
  ApplyTo.Get);
  Routes.Add<IntroRequest>("/introducing/{0}/and/{1}",
  ApplyTo.Get,
  request => request.FirstName,
  request => request.SecondName);
  Routes.Add<IntroRequest>("/introducing/{0}/and/{1}/otherway",
  ApplyTo.Get,
  request => request.SecondName,
  request => request.FirstName);
  Routes.AddFromAssembly(typeof(ImFromRequest).Assembly);

}
}
```

How it works...

Using this recipe, routes are registered directly with the `ServiceStackHost` class using two methods.

▶ `Routes.Add<Type>(path)`: This is a single registration of a request type and a path, which will map the URL to the service associated with the request object, in this case `GreeterRequest` is associated with the URL `/greetings/{Name}`. The `{Name}` URL binds the value in the place of the path to the `Name` property of the request object.

▶ `Routes.Add<Type>(path, "GET, POST, DELETE")`: This is another way to register the route with the same passing of property values, but restricting the request to just the verb methods specified. If the verb isn't specified, it won't be available. If you try to access a route that hasn't been registered with the verb being requested, ServiceStack will respond with a 404 status code and default page advising you that the route was not found.

▶ `Routes.Add<Type>(path, ApplyTo.Get)`: This is the same as using a string of verbs to restrict the path, but can be useful when trying to avoid possible bugs from spelling mistakes in the list of verbs.

▶ `Routes.Add<Type>(pathWithFormater, ApplyTo.Get, propertyExpressions)`: This is an extension method to use for ordered variables to be used map properties to values within the path. This can be useful if you register different mappings with different verb restrictions or when dealing with complex routes that may have different binding behavior. In the example shown, by adding `otherway` to the end of the same route, we changed the binding behavior of the same service.

▶ `Routes.AddFromAssembly(assembly)`: This is a method that requires the use of `RouteAttribute` to find request objects with routes within a specified assembly.

▶ The add method also provides a way to register types that are only known at runtime with alternate methods such as `Routes.Add(myTypeInstance, path)`. This could be used in conjunction with standard .NET reflection methods such as `myObjectInstance.GetType()`, which can be used on any object.

There's more...

In versions of ServiceStack greater than 4.0.18.0, the `GetRouteAttributes(Type type)` method is virtual, allowing it to be overridden. This can allow the ability to source an array of `RouteAttribute` objects from custom locations or using custom logic.

For example, when the server's `AppHost` class is starting up, this method could check some custom configuration or even call external web services to work out what routes should be used. To achieve this, simply override the `GetRouteAttributes` method in a suitable place in your code.

Structuring your project to avoid dependency issues

When building up your project, it's important to choose a file structure that matches your architecture and simplifies your life as much as possible. For instance, projects that are considering an application with a service layer, a business model, and a repository layer might create a structure like this:

```
\CrudService
\CrudService\Models
\CrudService\Repositories
\CrudService\Services
\CrudService.Tests
\CrudService.Tests\Models
\CrudService.Tests\Repositories
\CrudService.Tests\Services
```

With ServiceStack and other frameworks that make use of strongly typed data transfer objects, it can make sense to have the DTOs themselves shared across both a client project, for instance, a ServiceStack C# client, and the server project, particularly when one team is in charge of both—this helps each project to immediately and automatically stay in sync on any changes to the DTOs.

We'll go into more depth on the C# client later in the *Integrating with ServiceStack using the C# client and NativeTypes* recipe in *Chapter 9, Integrating with Other Technologies*.

Getting ready

First make sure that your main project is broken up appropriately—creating folders for services and other layers for instance.

Secondly, create a new project within your solution for the data transfer objects. In our example, we'll call this project `ServiceModel`.

When that's done, we'll add a reference from the main project to the `ServiceModel` project.

When we create our client project after that, we'll add a reference only to the `ServiceModel` folder at that time, creating a clean line of separation between our projects. This leads to less coupling of our code and a more flexible interface.

While any unit test project will still require a reference to the main project, any integration test projects might not, depending on what all you're doing. Integration test projects will only require a reference to the `ServiceModel` project, as with our client.

How to do It

First, let's build on the service we created in the *Routing using data transfer object attributes* recipe, about the Route annotation. However, we'll refactor things a bit, creating a `Service` folder, and then creating a `ServiceModel` project. When you're finished, your project should look like this:

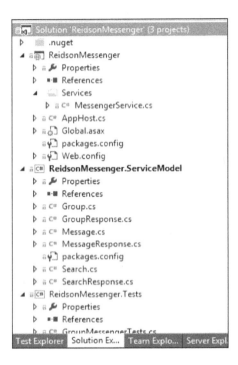

`MessengerService.cs` has been moved out to the `Service` folder, but nothing else has changed. Fix your namespaces, make sure things still build, and check that any tests still pass, as shown in the following screenshot:

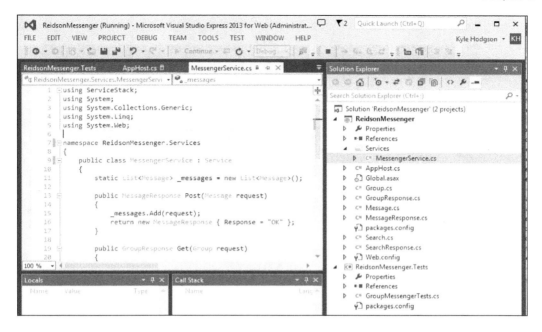

Once that's done, our next step is to create the `ReidsonMessenger.ServiceModel` project—a class library will do fine.

Next, we'll move all of our data transfer objects to `ServiceModel`. You can do it one at a time, or highlight all six of them and drag-and-drop. Make sure you get `Group.cs`, `GroupResponse.cs`, `Search.cs`, `SearchResponse.cs`, `Message.cs`, and `MessageResponse.cs` in the new project, and you can delete them from the old one.

Once you've done that, the project won't build anymore. To fix that, add a reference from the main project to the `ServiceModel` project:

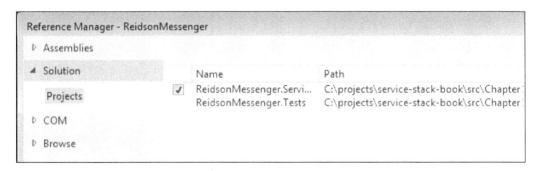

If you have any test projects, they'll need the reference too.

Once the references are in place, you need to add the `using` directives for each class that makes use of the DTOs. Once that's done, your project should build again, with tests still passing.

Now you can add a `client` project to your solution, and it would only need a reference to `ServiceModel`. To demonstrate, go ahead and add a `ServiceClient` project to the solution. Right-click the solution and choose **New Project**. Choose **Console Application** as the type, enter the name `ServiceClient`.

 Note that if you're using VisualStudio Express for Web, you can instead create a class library and then change the type to **Console Application** in the project properties.

You'll also need to add a reference to ServiceStack as usual.

Once the references are added, you could create a client as follows:

```
public class Program
{
  public static void Main(string[] args)
  {
    Console.WriteLine("Please enter your name:");
    var sender = Console.ReadLine();
    Console.WriteLine(
      "Please type the group name you'd like to post to:");
    var groupName = Console.ReadLine();
    Console.WriteLine("Please enter your message:");
    var body = Console.ReadLine();
    var message = new Message
    {
        Body = body,
        GroupName = groupName,
        Sender = sender
    };

    var client = new
    JsonServiceClient("http://localhost:2202");
    client.Post<MessageResponse>(message);
    Console.WriteLine(
      "Thank you. To read messages for " +
      groupName + ", please push any key.");
    Console.ReadKey();
```

Next up, we can query the service by calling `client.Get()`, passing in a request object, and specifying the response type we're looking for. We'll receive a response containing the messages we'd like to display. A simple `foreach` loop should do the trick of displaying them:

```
var messages = client.Get<GroupResponse>(
  new Group { GroupName = groupName });

Console.WriteLine("Displaying " +
messages.Messages.Count + " messages:");
foreach (var groupMessage in messages.Messages)
{
  Console.WriteLine(groupMessage.Sender + ": "
  + groupMessage.Body);
}
Console.ReadKey();
```

As you can see, with the one simple reference to `ServiceModel`, ServiceStack itself, and a starting URL, we can easily construct clients that can connect to the service without having any other references, reading documentation for the REST service, or needing to know the exact paths specified in the routes.

We'll describe the C# client in more detail in *Chapter 9, Integrating with Other Technologies*.

Managing dependencies with Funq and Inversion of Control (IoC)

Until now, `ReidsonMessenger` has stored all of its messages in a static `List<Message>` attached to `MessengerService`. This isn't a great design for a number of reasons—if our app restarts, all previous messages are lost. That's really just the beginning though; it's also not at all thread-safe. If two clients connect to our server and try to read or write messages at the same time, we're likely to see problems.

Let's refactor our code to fix the problem. The first thing we notice is that our existing implementation is a bit difficult to remove. We have a dependency on this static list—and all of our code in the `MessengerService` assumes that messages are stored in a `List<Message>` that we can access directly.

Let's start by making it easy to remove `static List<Message>` by wrapping it in a repository class. While we're at it, though, let's begin using Funq to inject this dependency to make our life easier—while we're experimenting with fixing the issue, we don't want to break the code.

This process of using IoC to replace an existing component with a new one while keeping the software working is sometimes referred to as "Branching by Abstraction". Instead of creating a separate feature branch of our software, we can keep working on the trunk, but get the benefits of creating our new implementation safely without interrupting production.

Getting ready

1. First, we'll write a test that illustrates the problem we're trying to solve—that the current implementation isn't thread-safe.

2. Since our theory is that the static list is at fault, we'll refactor the list so that it's not a field inside of our service anymore—we'll create a new class called `StaticMessagesRepository`, and move the static list into this new class. We'll make adjustments to our service to make calls to this class instead of accessing the list directly. We do this so that we can easily replace this working but flawed implementation with our new one.

3. We'll create an interface that covers the most important functionality for `StaticMessageRepository`—the method to Add new messages—and another method that accepts `Predicate<Message,bool>` and returns `IEnumerable<Message>`. This allows us to take a dependency on this interface, not the specific implementation, in our service. That makes it easier for us to swap it in the `AppHost.Configure` method, allowing us to keep control over which implementation to use in that central location.

4. Next, we'll start wiring up the messages repository with `Funq`. We'll set up our production `AppHost` class to wire up our existing but flawed `StaticMessagesRepository`, but we'll start working on a new implementation that leverages OrmLite. In our tests, we'll test the new `OrmMessagesRepository` until it solves the problem and is working. When we're through, we can simply change the `AppHost.Configure` method in our production `AppHost` class to use the newly tested implementation.

5. Once all of our tests pass, and we've been in production a little while, we can remove the old `StaticMessagesRepository` as it has outlived its usefulness.

 For more information on the *Branch by Abstraction* technique, the canonical article can be found on Martin Fowler's site at `http://martinfowler.com/bliki/BranchByAbstraction.html`.

How to do It...

1. Let's start by developing a unit test that shows the problem we're talking about. We can illustrate the problem with a simple `Parallel.ForEach` method that will run lots of commands against the list until it eventually throws an exception:

```
[Test]
public void ShouldBeThreadSafe()
{
  var service = new MessengerService();
  const string testGroupName = "Main";
  const int iterations = 200;

  Parallel.ForEach(
    Enumerable.Range(1, iterations),
    iteration =>
    {
      service.Post(new Message
      {
        Body = "Post {0}".Fmt(iteration),
        Sender = "Sender",
        GroupName = testGroupName
      });
      service.Get(new Search
      {
        Group = testGroupName,
        Query = "Post"
      });
    });

  var testGroup = service.Get(new Group
  {
    GroupName = testGroupName
  });

  var randomSearchString = "Post {0}".Fmt(
    new Random().Next(1, iterations));

  Assert.AreEqual(1, testGroupMessages
    .Messages
    .Count(m => m.Body.Equals(randomSearchString)));
}
```

On the author's machine, this test fails with this exception:

```
System.InvalidOperationException : Collection was modified;
enumeration operation may not execute.
```

This happens because the collection was modified by an `Add` method while we were trying to read from the collection, as expected.

2. Since we think that the `static List<Message>` is the problem, we'll make changes to the original service to isolate it for removal. Instead of just having `List<Message>` as a field on `MessengerService`, we'll wrap it in a class, and then use this new class for access. This class will implement an `IMessageRepository` interface in order to allow us to easily replace it later with a better implementation. The code for this procedure is as follows:

```
public interface IMessageRepository
{
   void Add(Message message);
   IEnumerable<Message> Where(Func<Message, bool> predicate);
}
public class StaticMessageRepository
   : IMessageRepository
{
   static List<Message> _messages = new List<Message>();

   public void Add(Message message)
   {
     _messages.Add(message);
   }

   public IEnumerable<Message> Where(Func<Message, bool> predicate)
   {
     return _messages.TakeWhile(predicate).ToList();
   }
}
```

3. Now we'll refactor our service to use the new wrapper class instead of directly accessing `static List<T>`. We call this change a *refactor* because the end result should be functionally equivalent; only the organization of the code has changed. We'll also change `MessengerService` to rely on Funq to provide `IMessageRepository` in the future:

```
public class MessengerService : Service
{
```

```
public IMessageRepository MessageRepository { get; set; }

public object Post(Message request)
{
  MessageRepository.Add(request);
  return new MessageResponse { Message = "OK" };
}

public object Get(Group request)
{
  return new GroupResponse
  {
    Messages = MessageRepository.Where(
      message => message
        .GroupName.Equals(request.GroupName))
      .ToList()
  };
}

public object Get(Search request)
{
  return new SearchResponse
  {
    Messages = MessageRepository.Where(
      message => message
        .GroupName.Equals(request.Group)
        && message.Body.Contains(request.Query))
      .ToList()
  };
}
}
```

4. Now, we'll create `BasicOrmMessageRepository`, a fresh, basic implementation using OrmLite, just enough to get it working. We can improve it with other refactoring later; it is important for now not to break our existing code. Here's how our code looks:

```
public class BasicOrmMessageRepository : IMessageRepository
{
  public IDbConnectionFactory DbConnectionFactory
  { get; set; }

  public void Add(Message message)
  {
```

```
    using (var db = DbConnectionFactory.OpenDbConnection())
    {
      db.Insert(message);
    }
  }


  public IEnumerable<Message> Where(
    Func<Message, bool> predicate)
  {
    using (var db = DbConnectionFactory.OpenDbConnection())
    {
      var allDatabase = db.Select<Message>();
      var results = new List<Message>();
      allDatabase.ForEach(m =>
      {
        if (predicate(m)) results.Add(m);
      });
      return results;
    }
  }
}
```

An astute reader might have noticed that the database code shown previously really isn't a great OrmLite implementation. It's quite likely that your database performance tests are going to notice a *big* slowdown with this implementation once the service has more than a few thousand messages as our search code simply fetches the entire database of messages into memory, loops them over, and checks them one by one for a match.

For now, we're forced into this implementation because we're trying to honor the existing contract, and OrmLite can't accept a raw predicate unlike our static list. OrmLite's `Select()` requires `Expression<Func<Message,bool>>` and not just `Func<Message,bool>`. This naive implementation gets us around that particular problem for now.

The good thing about this naive implementation is that it is completely compatible with the old one, so we can keep working on the new one while we coexist with the old implementation. We'll need to solve this performance problem, of course—we'll come back to this before the recipe is up, refactoring as we go.

5. Next, let's go into `TestFixtureSetUp` and wire up our new dependency. We'll also add code to a `SetUp` method that drops and recreates the table we'll use before any test. Once we're sure that the new implementation is better than our static list, we'll add similar code to `AppHost`:

```
[TestFixtureSetUp]
public void FixtureSetUp()
{
  _appHost = new BasicAppHost
  {
    ConfigureContainer =
      container =>
        {
          container.RegisterAutoWiredAs<
            BasicOrmMessageRepository, IMessageRepository>();
          container.RegisterAutoWired<
            MessengerService>();
          var dbFactory = new OrmLiteConnectionFactory(
            "~/App_Data/db.sqlite".MapHostAbsolutePath(),
            SqliteDialect.Provider);
          container.Register<IDbConnectionFactory>(
            dbFactory);
        }
  }.Init();
}

[SetUp]
public void SetUp()
{
  using (var db = _appHost.Resolve<IDbConnectionFactory>()
  .OpenDbConnection())
  {
    db.DropAndCreateTable<Message>();
  }
}
```

6. As soon as we drop this code in place, however, our tests start having problems. It turns out that OrmLite doesn't like our use of `.Equals()` in the predicate. We'll have to change `MessengerService` to accommodate that using `==` instead, which it can handle. Here's how the code for the procedure described in this paragraph looks:

```
public object Get(Group request)
{
  return new GroupResponse
```

```
    {
      Messages = MessageRepository
      .Where(message => message.GroupName == request.GroupName)
      .ToList()
    };
}


public object Get(Search request)
{
  return new SearchResponse
  {
    Messages = MessageRepository
        .Where(message => message.GroupName == request.Group
        && message.Body.Contains(request.Query))
      .ToList()
  };
}
```

7. With this code in place, the tests should now pass! Our `OrmMessageRepository` file solved the concurrency issue. Now it's time to go back and fix the performance issue.

8. Again, we'll start with a test to prove our theory that `BasicOrmMessageRepository` isn't fast enough. We'll create `TestFixtureSetup` that configures `BasicAppHost` to wire up `BasicOrmMessageRepository` and a `Setup` method that we'll run before each test and that creates a large database of records to test against. Our test can then search the repository for a random record and time it to see how long it takes. We'll set higher bounds of 150 milliseconds for now. Here's how the code for our test looks:

```
[TestFixture]
public class BasicOrmMessageRepositoryPerformanceTests
{
    const int LargeMessageCount = 100000;
    ServiceStackHost _appHost;

    [TestFixtureSetUp]
    public void FixtureSetUp()
    {
      _appHost = new BasicAppHost
      {
        ConfigureContainer =
          container =>
          {
            container.Register<IDbConnectionFactory>(
```

```
                new OrmLiteConnectionFactory(
                   "~/App_Data/db.sqlite".MapHostAbsolutePath(),
                   SqliteDialect.Provider));
              container
                 .RegisterAutoWired<BasicOrmMessageRepository>();
          }
       }.Init();
}

[SetUp]
public void SetUp()
{
  const string testDataFile =
  @"../../OrmMessageRepository_Performance_Test_Data.json";

  if (!File.Exists(testDataFile))
  {
    CreateTestFile(testDataFile, LargeMessageCount);
  }

  using (var db = _appHost
    .Resolve<IDbConnectionFactory>().OpenDbConnection())
  {
    db.DropAndCreateTable<Message>();
    var wholeList = File.ReadAllText(testDataFile)
      .FromJson<List<Message>>();
    db.InsertAll(wholeList);
  }
}

[TestFixtureTearDown]
public void FixtureTearDown()
{
  _appHost.Dispose();
}

[Test]
public void ShouldHandleLargeMessageCountEffeciently()
{
  var repo = _appHost.Resolve<BasicOrmMessageRepository>();

  var randomSearchString = "Message {0}".Fmt(
```

```
        new Random().Next(1, LargeMessageCount));

    var searchTimer = new Stopwatch();
    searchTimer.Start();
    var testSearchRecords = repo.Where(
      message => message
        .Body
        .Contains(randomSearchString));
    searchTimer.Stop();

    Assert.AreEqual(
      randomSearchString,
      testSearchRecords.First().Body);
    Assert.Less(searchTimer.ElapsedMilliseconds, 150);

  }
  void CreateTestFile(string fileName, int testRecords)
  {
    Console.WriteLine("Creating test data...");
    var tmp = new List<Message>();
    foreach (int iteration in
      Enumerable.Range(1, testRecords))
    {
      tmp.Add(new Message
      {
        Body = "Message {0}".Fmt(iteration),
        GroupName = "performance test group",
        Sender = "test sender"
      });

    }

    var wholeList = tmp.SerializeToString();
    File.WriteAllText(fileName, wholeList);
  }
}
```

Running this test should show a failure as with `BasicOrmMessageRepository`; we can't actually search through 100,000 records in less than 150 milliseconds. On my machine, it takes ~ 800 milliseconds, which will only get worse as we add messages.

9. Now that we have a failing test, again we can set out to fix the problem. The best way to do this is to allow OrmLite to run our predicate in the database engine instead of downloading the whole database and running the predicate in memory. However, as we know, OrmLite's `Select()` method requires `Expression<Func<Message,Bool>>`, and right now we only accept a `Func<Message,Bool>` function. Let's start by refactoring the interface and the basic static list, then refactoring `BasicOrmMessageRepository` to make it a bit smarter:

```
public interface IMessageRepository
{
  void Add(Message message);

  IEnumerable<Message> Where(
    Expression<Func<Message, bool>> predicate);
}
public class StaticMessageRepository : IMessageRepository
{
  static List<Message> _messages =
    new List<Message>();

  public void Add(Message message)
  {
    _messages.Add(message);
  }

  public IEnumerable<Message> Where(
    Expression<Func<Message, bool>> predicate)
  {
    return _messages.TakeWhile(predicate.Compile()).ToList();
  }
}
```

10. Now that we've changed the method signature on the interface and updated our `StaticMessageRepository` implementation, we need to update `BasicOrmMessageRepository` too or our code won't compile. Here's how we do that:

```
public class BasicOrmMessageRepository : IMessageRepository
{
  public IDbConnectionFactory
    DbConnectionFactory { get; set; }

  public void Add(Message message)
```

```
    {
      using (var db = DbConnectionFactory.OpenDbConnection())
      {
        db.Insert(message);
      }
    }

    public IEnumerable<Message> Where(
    Expression<Func<Message, bool>> expression)
    {
      using (var db = DbConnectionFactory.OpenDbConnection())
      {
        return db.Select(expression);
      }
    }
  }
}
```

11. With these changes, our original concurrency is solved, and so is our performance problem! Of course, our main service is still using StaticMessageRepository. Let's go back and wire it up in the production AppHost class:

```
public class AppHost : AppHostBase
{
  public AppHost() : base("Reidson Industries GroupMessenger",
  typeof(MessengerService).Assembly) { }
  public override void Configure(Funq.Container container)
  {
    var dbFactory = new OrmLiteConnectionFactory(
    "~/App_Data/db.sqlite".MapHostAbsolutePath(),
    SqliteDialect.Provider);

    container.Register<IDbConnectionFactory>(dbFactory);

    container.RegisterAutoWiredAs<
    BasicOrmMessageRepository,IMessageRepository>();

    using (var db = dbFactory.OpenDbConnection())
    {
      db.DropAndCreateTable<Message>();
    }
  }
}
```

How it works...

The basic pattern of this recipe is to build tests to prove the problem we're trying to solve, to build new implementations that pass the tests, then to use Funq IoC to switch implementations when new ones are ready. The previous code is a typical example of where we didn't necessarily plan ahead of time to make a component replaceable—we realized it as we recognized a problem. We showed realistic techniques to deal with this, making use of automated tests, interfaces, refactoring, and dependency injection.

While the *Branch by Abstraction* process might seem like it takes a little bit longer to get your code into the application, you reduce risk significantly by keeping your tests passing the whole time. You also reduce risk by not replacing something that works, albeit imperfectly, until your replacement is an actual improvement, all without needing to create a long-lived feature branch.

Sharing and accessing configuration and common functionality using Funq IoC

A pattern that ServiceStack encourages with its design is the use of IoC containers. While you can use most common IoC containers with ServiceStack, it defaults to Funq. Funq was adopted due to its excellent performance and memory characteristics, and it also exposes a simple, clean API.

In this recipe, we will look at sharing application settings and other common objects from our services with the use of the Funq IoC container. We will also look at how ServiceStack can help with accessing application settings in `web.config` or `app.config`.

Getting ready...

In ASP.NET, a common way to store configurations is by having those settings in either the `web.config` or the `app.config` file of your application. We will first need to have some configuration settings to store, which we are going to use in our code for various tasks. In this recipe, we are going to store the following:

- A connection string to our SqlLite database
- A list of e-mail addresses to identify administrators of the application
- Some environment-specific settings for integrated systems

These three examples will illustrate how to take advantage of some of the configuration's simple ways to access more complex settings using ServiceStack's appSettings functionality. Let's have a look at the appSettings section of our configuration:

```
<appSettings>
  <add key="sqlLiteConnectionString"
  value="~/App_Data/db.sqlite"/>
  <add key="AdminEmailAddresses"
  value="darren.reid@reidsonindustries.net,kyle.hodgson@reidsonindus
  tries.net"/>
    <add key="EmailSettings_Dev" value="{SMTPUrl:email-
    smtp.dev.reidsoninsdustries.net,SMTPPort:25}"/>
    <add key="EmailSettings_Test" value="{SMTPUrl:email-
    smtp.test.reidsoninsdustries.net,SMTPPort:25}"/>
    <add key="EmailSettings_Prod" value="{SMTPUrl:email-
    smtp.reidsoninsdustries.net,SMTPPort:25}"/>
    <add key="Environment" value="Dev"/>
</appSettings>
```

How to do It...

We are going to need a **Plain Old CLR Object** (**POCO**) to represent the e-mail settings:

```
public class EmailSettings
{
  public string SMTPUrl { get;set; }
  public int SMTPPort { get;set; }
}
```

Create a custom AppSettings class to help access specific configuration:

```
public class ReidsonAppSettings : AppSettings
{

public ApplicationEnvironment Environment
{
  get
  {
```

```
      return Get("Environment", ApplicationEnvironment.Dev);
    }
  }

  public EmailSettings EmailSettings
  {
    get
    {
      var settingsName =
          "EmailSettings_" + Environment;
      return Get<EmailSettings>(settingsName, null);
    }
  }

  public List<string> AdministratorEmails
  {
    get
    {
      return Get("AdminEmailAddresses", new List<string>());
    }
  }

    public enum ApplicationEnvironment
    {
      Dev,
      Test,
      Prod
    }
}
```

Create `AppSettings`, OrmLite Connection Factory, and the data repository objects:

```
public override void Configure(Container container)
{
container.RegisterAutoWired<ReidsonAppSettings>();
var appSettings = container.Resolve<ReidsonAppSettings>();
var dbFactory = new OrmLiteConnectionFactory(
    appSettings.Get(
    "sqlLiteConnectionString","").MapHostAbsolutePath(),
    SqliteDialect.Provider);

container.Register<IDbConnectionFactory>(dbFactory);

container.RegisterAutoWiredAs
```

```
    <ReidsonMessengerDataRepository,
    IReidsonMessengerDataRepository>();
//Other configuration...
}
```

In the web services, we will want to access all three objects that will be provided by the `Funq` container. To do this, declare public properties of the same types that are registered with the IoC container within your ServiceStack web service:

```
public ReidsonAppSettings ApplicationSettings
{ get; set; }
public IDbConnectionFactory DbConnectionFactory { get; set;
}
public IReidsonMessengerDataRepository DataRepository
{ get; set; }
```

How it works...

The custom settings object, `ReidsonAppSettings`, is a wrapper for accessing values within the `appSettings` section of `web.config`. This wrapper utilizes a few of the ServiceStack `appSettings` helper methods that let us store more complex information than just key/value pairs.

The list of administrator user e-mails are parsed as a comma-separated list and expressed in code as `List<string>`. This makes storing collections of values a lot simpler both in configuration and in code. `Get<Type>(key, defaultValue)` requires a type, key value, and default value if the setting is null.

Objects of key/value pairs can be read by `appSettings`. This requires the use of JSON-like object syntax, as seen in the previous example of application settings, but from code, it is all strongly typed configuration:

```
<add key="EmailSettings_Dev" value="{SMTPUrl:email-
smtp.dev.reidsoninsdustries.net,SMTPPort:25}"/>

public class EmailSettings
{
  public string SMTPUrl { get;set; }
  public int SMTPPort { get;set; }
}

this.Get<EmailSettings>("EmailSettings_Dev", null);
```

We are sharing this configuration and other objects by registering them in a few different ways using the Funq IoC container:

- `RegisterAutoWired<CustomType>();`
- `Register<Type>(instance);`
- `RegisterAutoWiredAs<CustomType,AsAnotherType>();`

These methods of the Funq container achieve the same result, but in different ways. `RegisterAutoWired<CustomType>` attempts to populate the public properties on `CustomType` that have the same declared type as objects that have already been registered with the Funq container. In the example of `ReidsonAppSettings`, we don't need to pass an instance to `RegisterAutoWired` as the Funq container will take care of any required instantiation. The order of registration is very important when dealing with IoC— `ReidsonAppSettings` also doesn't have any dependencies, so we can register this first.

Next, we registered an instance of `OrmLiteConnectionFactory`, specifying the interface `IDbConnectionFactory`. Since we used the `Register<AsAnotherType>` method to which we passed an instance, we don't get any auto-wiring for dependencies via a constructor or via public properties. This needs to be done manually when using the `Register<AsAnotherType>` method.

The registration of our data repository object used the `RegisterAutoWiredAs<Custom Type,AsAnotherType>` method that controls the construction of the object and, in this case, took care of the two public property dependencies, `IDbConnectionFactory` and `ReidsonAppSettings`, automatically.

If you want an instance of a registered type and you have access to the container, you can use the `Resolve<CustomType>` method.

> With Funq, as with any IoC, it's best practice to have control over all of your registrations and configurations in one place. As such, you want to avoid sharing the instance of the container with other classes—this will keep your code base easier to maintain.

There's more...

It is possible to use other IoC container implementations with ServiceStack with the use of custom adapters. A Ninject adapter is available on Nuget as an alternative. Otherwise, the `IContainerAdapter` interface is provided to create your own adapter to use with your IoC container of choice.

2
Services and Data Transfer Objects

In this chapter, we will cover the following topics:

- ▶ Creating a basic create/read/update/delete
- ▶ Splitting HTTP request methods
- ▶ Hosting services from different assemblies
- ▶ Utilizing the original HTTP request
- ▶ Overriding serialization of request object types
- ▶ Creating a simple admin service
- ▶ Intercepting requests and responses using attributes
- ▶ Making a basic proxy for existing web services
- ▶ Wrapping multiple existing services and exposing them through ServiceStack

Introduction

At the core of ServiceStack are the services you write and the contract that these services use. The contract is in the form of request-and-response data transfer objects or DTOs. DTOs are at the core of a message-based design that ServiceStack uses to construct typed clients end to end. In this chapter, we will go over creating a basic service to handle resources, structuring your services, and introduce some of the other ways we can extend the services we build through filters and authentication.

Creating a basic create/read/update/delete service

When you're building a REST service, it's important to make good use of the main tool available to you, HTTP. There are multiple books on the subject of what makes a good RESTful service, but here are some of the headlines:

- URL routes represent resources; they should be nouns, not verbs
- Services should act predictably to common verbs, for example, GET, POST, PUT, DELETE
- Use appropriate HTTP status codes for responses

In this recipe, we will build a simple service that will **Create, Read, Update, and Delete** (**CRUD**) entries from a database. For a deeper dive into some of the other concepts used in this example, please see the relevant recipes:

- The *Sharing and accessing configuration and common functionality using Funq IoC* recipe in *Chapter 1, Configuration and Routing*
- The *Using and accessing OrmLite* recipe in *Chapter 4, Object Relational Mapping (OrmLite)*
- The *Creating static validation rules using fluent syntax* recipe in *Chapter 6, Filters and Validators*
- The *Getting started with authentication, sessions, registration, and user repositories* recipe in *Chapter 7, Security and Authentication*

Getting ready

For this recipe, we will need to have ServiceStack already set up within a Visual Studio project. If you have ServiceStackVS installed, simply use one of the C# templates. Alternatively, see the section *Creating a ServiceStack solution with VisualStudio and NuGet* in *Appendix A, Getting Started* to help you to set up a ServiceStack solution.

When structuring your service application, there are a few common parts you'll find regardless of the application. Structuring your application correctly can make a big difference when the time comes to make changes. These parts are:

- Database model
- Service model
- Service interface
- Application host

Database models for use with our **Object-relational mapping** (**ORM**) will reflect what our database looks like. It's common for these classes to be in the same project as our service model.

Service models are the classes that represent our request and response objects of our service interface; it's encouraged that these exist in a project of relatively few dependencies as they are the most likely to be shared along with the database model classes.

The service interface is our RESTful contract that will usually contain logic that orchestrates our other abstractions, such as database access, business rules, and other isolated systems. It's the glue of the other moving parts of our system.

The application host specifies all the concrete implementations of the abstractions used by our service interfaces. This is usually done by an inversion of control container (IoC), which injects our services with any registered components. More information on the use of ServiceStack's default IoC container, Funq, can be found in the *Sharing and accessing configuration and common functionality using Funq IoC* recipe in *Chapter 1, Configuration and Routing*.

How to do it...

First, we want to structure our database model to match what we are storing in our SQL database. To interact with the database, we'll be using ServiceStack's OrmLite library. OrmLite is a lightweight and fast object-relational mapping library that maps your database tables to simple **Plain Old CLR Objects** (**POCOs**). In the example, our `Place` table only has three columns and is represented by the following class.

Create classes to represent our persisted model. These will be used by OrmLite for data access:

```
public class Place
{
    [Index]
    [PrimaryKey]
    [AutoIncrement]
    public long Id { get; set; }
    public string Name { get; set; }
    public string Description { get; set; }
}
```

This POCO maps to a table in our database, its properties map to specific columns, and the OrmLite specific attributes indicate to the underlying database various behaviors, such as `[AutoIncrement]` to automatically increase the `Id` value when a new value is inserted.

Create separate classes to represent our request-and-response objects. These objects will have attributes for the URL routes, which control how ServiceStack listens to incoming requests. They should also be created in a separate `ServiceModel` project to help us reuse these classes if needed in the future:

```
[Route("/places/{Id}", Verbs = "GET")]
public class PlaceToVisit : IReturn<PlaceToVisitResponse>
{
  public long Id { get; set; }
}


[Route("/places",Verbs = "GET")]
public class AllPlacesToVisit : IReturn<AllPlacesToVisitResponse>
{

}


[Route("/places", Verbs = "POST")]
public class CreatePlaceToVisit : IReturn<CreatePlaceToVisitResponse>
{
  public string Name { get; set; }
  public string Description { get; set; }
}


[Route("/places/{Id}", Verbs = "PUT")]
public class UpdatePlaceToVisit : IReturn<UpdatePlaceToVisitResponse>
{
  public long Id { get; set; }
  public string Name { get; set; }
  public string Description { get; set; }
}


[Route("/places/{Id}", Verbs = "DELETE")]
public class DeletePlaceToVisit
{
  public long Id { get; set; }
}


public class PlaceToVisitResponse
{
  public Place Place { get; set; }
}
```

```
public class AllPlacesToVisitResponse
{
  public List<Place> Places { get; set; }
}

public class CreatePlaceToVisitResponse
{
  public Place Place { get; set; }
}

public class UpdatePlaceToVisitResponse
{
  public Place Place { get; set; }
}
```

In the previous code sample, we explicitly use the `IReturn<T>` interface on our request objects. This actually isn't strictly needed if the naming conventions of your request-and-response objects follows the pattern of `MyDto` and `MyDtoResponse`. ServiceStack will infer from the use of a class in a service method, such as `Get(MyDto request)`, that a class named `MyDtoResponse` is the corresponding response DTO.

Create `PlaceService` to expose our `Place` resource using appropriate HTTP verbs. These services should be created in a separate `ServiceInterface` project, as this helps with testing our services and enables reuse when different hosting configurations are required:

```
public class PlaceService : Service,
    IGet<PlaceToVisit>,
    IGet<AllPlacesToVisit>,
    IPost<CreatePlaceToVisit>,
    IPut<UpdatePlaceToVisit>,
    IDelete<DeletePlaceToVisit>
{
    public object Get(PlaceToVisit request)
    {
        if (!Db.Exists<Place>(x => x.Id == request.Id))
        {
            throw HttpError.NotFound("Place not found");
        }
        return new PlaceToVisitResponse
        {
            Place = Db.SingleById<Place>(request.Id)
        };
    }
```

```
public object Get(AllPlacesToVisit request)
{
    return new AllPlacesToVisitResponse
    {
        Places = Db.Select<Place>().ToList()
    };
}

public object Post(CreatePlaceToVisit request)
{
    var place = request.ConvertTo<Place>();
    Db.Insert(place);
    return new PlaceToVisitResponse
    {
        Place = place
    };
}

public object Put(UpdatePlaceToVisit request)
{
    if (!Db.Exists<Place>(x => x.Id == request.Id))
    {
        throw HttpError.NotFound("Place not found");
    }

    var place = request.ConvertTo<Place>();
    Db.Update<Place>(place);
    return new PlaceToVisitResponse
    {
        Place = place
    };
}

public object Delete(DeletePlaceToVisit request)
{
    if (!Db.Exists<Place>(x => x.Id == request.Id))
    {
        throw HttpError.NotFound("Place not found");
    }
    Db.DeleteById<Place>(request.Id);
    base.Response.StatusCode = (int)HttpStatusCode.NoContent;
    return null;
}
}
```

Previously, in the `PlacesService` class, we leveraged some defaults from the ServiceStack `Service` base class. The `Db` property used to access our database is `IDbConnectionFactory` injected by our IoC container, Funq. The concrete implementation of `IDbConnectionFactory` is registered in the application host, as follows:

```
var dbFactory = new OrmLiteConnectionFactory(
    "~/App_Data/db.sqlite".MapHostAbsolutePath(),
    SqliteDialect.Provider);
container.Register<IDbConnectionFactory>(dbFactory);
```

Using the `Db` property resolves and opens a database connection automatically. If you need more control over the database connection, you can simply declare a `public` property within the `Service` class with both public `get` and `set`. ServiceStack will inject the registered `IDbConnectionFactory` into this property before the request is processed.

If we try out our `PlaceService` class, we can see that we have a basic CRUD service that is ready to be expanded on with business-specific rules, authentication, caching, and so on.

The example with this recipe is a simple HTML page to try out our CRUD `PlacesToVisit` service, as follows:

Read all places

Get All Places

Output

Read all successful
{"Places":[{"Id":1,"Name":"Canberra","Description":"Capital city of Australia"},
{"Id":2,"Name":"Toronto","Description":"Provincial capital of Ontario"},
{"Id":3,"Name":"Auckland, New Zealand","Description":"A city in the north island"}]}

Create a place

Name

Description

Create

How it works...

In this recipe, we went through an example of a simple CRUD service to show how this is done using ServiceStack and how we might structure the code to help maintain the separation of concerns for easier maintenance as the project changes in the future.

In the first step, we created our classes for use with OrmLite; these are kept separate from the classes created for our requests and response objects created in the second step. It is good practice to keep the request objects separate from our database model even though it is common that these structures look very similar. This separation is driven by the want to make our code easier to read and understand what objects are responsible for different aspects of your system.

One of the responsibilities of the request objects is to control the service routes which, for example, should have nothing to do with indexes on your database. Even though the property `type` and `name` values are the same and represent the same model, they have two distinct responsibilities. If your service interface has to change to meet a business or usability requirement, for example, there is a good chance you don't want those changes directly effecting your database model.

After we have our routes, requests, and response objects set up the way we want them, we can move on to writing our actual services.

The service itself, you'll notice, implements the `IGet<T>`, `IPost<T>`, `IPut<T>`, and `IDelete<T>` interfaces. These are *not required* as ServiceStack will bind requests to the appropriate methods by the naming convention and the DTO argument type. These interfaces, however, can help you write the service if you like to be more explicit about your writing your services.

We take advantage of a few different parts of ServiceStack to make the code within our service methods concise:

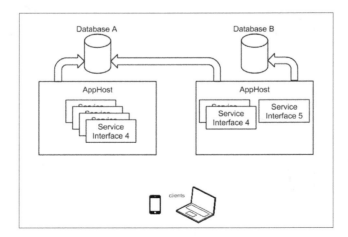

The previous figure shows the different parts of the recipe project in relation to the database and clients and how it is structured. This pattern can be followed to create what are essentially structured monolithic applications that can be easily split up and hosted in different combinations. ServiceStack encourages this structure to not only try and strike a balance and create the flexibility of creating standalone micro services if required, but also to allow you to composite them in a single application by reusing the `ServiceModel` and `ServiceInterface` projects. This allows the developer to choose how they want to composite these different parts in a single application host or to break them up into separate application hosts.

In this recipe, we wrote a service with examples of the most basic parts that most of your data-collection-centric services will have. In my experience, the layering and separation of concerns that ServiceStack encourages make enhancements and future development a much more fiction-free task. So, although there is a lot of structure for relatively little code, this structure is important. Trying to maintain multiple thousands of lines of logic for a request in one method leads to many problems and code that very few people will want to pick up and maintain. The functionality ServiceStack provides is vast, but the clean development practices it encourages are what makes this framework so productive to work with.

There's more...

In the example, a simple use of validation and authentication is added to show how these might be used. Just like our `IDbConnectionFactory`, we need to register our authentication and validation-related objects with our IoC container.

Authentication requires a few additional steps; further description of these can be found in the *Getting started with authentication, sessions, registration, and user repositories* recipe in *Chapter 7, Security and Authentication*:

```
var userRep = new OrmLiteAuthRepository(container.Resolve<IDbConnecti
onFactory>());
container.Register<IUserAuthRepository>(userRep);
Plugins.Add(
    new AuthFeature(() =>
    new AuthUserSession(),
    new IAuthProvider[] {
    new CredentialsAuthProvider(),
}));
```

We also need to initialize the user authentication schema in our database. This can be done using the `InitSchema` method on the `IUserAuthRepository` object or the `DropAndReCreateTables` method. The `DropAndReCreateTables` method is used in this recipe to make it easy to run and test out; this should *not* be used in a production application, else you will lose all your information when your application starts.

For validation, we need to ensure that the validation plugin has been added to our host; this is done in our `AppHost.Configure` method, as follows:

```
Plugins.Add(new ValidationFeature());
container.RegisterValidators(typeof(CreatePlaceValidator).Assembly);
```

Once this feature is added, we can write validation classes for our requests. ServiceStack uses Fluent Validation; we can associate our validators and request objects using the `AbstractValidator<T>` class. Rules are declared in the constructor of the validator. Once registered, these rules will run automatically for every request of the associated DTO:

```
public class CreatePlaceValidator :
AbstractValidator<CreatePlaceToVisit>
{
    public CreatePlaceValidator()
    {
        RuleFor(r => r.Name).NotEmpty();
        RuleFor(r => r.Name.Length).GreaterThan(2);
    }
}

public class UpdatePlaceValidator :
AbstractValidator<UpdatePlaceToVisit>
{
    public UpdatePlaceValidator()
    {
        RuleFor(r => r.Id).NotEmpty();
        RuleFor(r => r.Name).NotEmpty();
    }
}

public class DeletePlaceValidator :
AbstractValidator<DeletePlaceToVisit>
{
    public DeletePlaceValidator()
    {
        RuleFor(r => r.Id).NotEmpty();
    }
}
```

See also

In this example, we also used a `CredentialsAuthProvider` method for simple username and password authentication. If your service or application needs authentication, this topic is important enough to deserve consideration for what is right for your application. See *Chapter 7, Security and Authentication*, for more in-depth details on how ServiceStack works with its various options for security and authentication.

Other chapters that also have more in-depth details on topics this recipe has touched on are listed below:

- The *Routing using data transfer object attributes* recipe in *Chapter 1, Configuration and Routing*
- The *Structuring your project to avoid dependency* issues recipe in *Chapter 1, Configuration and Routing*
- The *Sharing and accessing configuration and common functionality using Funq IoC* recipe in *Chapter 1, Configuration and Routing*
- The *Using and accessing OrmLite* recipe in *Chapter 4, Object Relational Mapping (OrmLite)*
- The *Creating static validation rules using fluent syntax* recipe in *Chapter 6, Filters and Validators*
- The *Getting started with authentication, sessions, registration, and user repositories* recipe in *Chapter 7, Security and Authentication*

Splitting HTTP request methods

When you're building a REST service, it's good practice to make efficient use of the HTTP protocol to assist you in your design. While full coverage of what makes for good RESTful design is outside the scope of this book, we will cover how to use ServiceStack's built-in tools to help you reuse code.

 I recommend *REST in Practice, O'Reilly*, and *APIs: A Strategy Guide, O'Reilly*, for more on designing effective RESTful web services.

One project I am acquainted with started out with an RPC-style design. The service owner realized that they had well over 65 endpoints, such as `/createNewGroup`, `/renameGroup`, and so on, making it hard for developers to remember the exact name of the endpoint for the function they need. This was overhauled, and the RESTful approach was applied. The end result had only four endpoints and still served the same user base with the same functionality. The end result was a much simpler service that was easier to learn, deploy, and debug—but the process created a lot of churn for the teams that consumed that service to get to that end goal.

Basically, this redesign consisted of replacing endpoints that facilitated only small operations to a more RESTful design based on resources. The *R* in REST stands for *Resource*. The idea is to design an API that provides different resources and then allows consuming teams to perform different operations on that resource. This cleans up our API considerably—instead of `/getMessagesFromGroup`, `/createNewGroup`, and `/renameGroup`, you would just have `/groups`. Our service can infer from the type of request being sent to the resource what the client is requesting. This has many benefits—less code, greater code reuse, and importantly, an easy-to-use API for clients.

Let's take the `ReidsonMessenger` service that we built up in the *Routing using data transfer object attributes* recipe in *Chapter 1, Configuration and Routing*. It currently expects to find HTTP `GET` requests that contain a `Group` object from the `ServiceModel` project. Currently, this specific endpoint returns all the messages from the specified group. What if you also wanted to allow a `New Group` functionality? We could create a `/newGroup` endpoint that accepts HTTP `POST` messages with a new `ServiceModel` type, but then we're starting to have a proliferation of endpoints and message types. It's better to design our services to avoid this proliferation.

How to do it...

We'll start out with the `ReidsonMessenger` service where we left off, but we'll make some changes to facilitate the new group creation functionality that we need. Since we're refactoring some of our existing code, let's start with a test, as follows:

```
[Test]
public void ShouldCreateNewGroupsOnRequest()
{
    var service = new MessengerService();
    var response = service.Post(
    new Group
    {
        GroupName = "NewGroup",
        Creator = "Me"
    });
    Assert.That(response.Name.Equals("NewGroup"));
}
```

We're specifying that we'd like the service to expect a `Group` message arriving as an HTTP `POST`. It will contain a new `Creator` property that's a string containing the user who wants to create the group. At the moment, if we try to run this test, it won't even compile—we need to create the `Creator` property, and we need to handle the `Post` method on `MessengerService`. Let's do those two things next.

Changing the `Group` model is a simple refactor; we should end up with code that looks like the following:

```
[Route("/groups/{GroupName}")]
public class Group
{
  public string GroupName { get; set; }
  public string Creator { get; set; }
}
```

Next up, we'll add a new `Post` method to `MessengerService` that accepts `Group` objects. We can implement this fairly simply for now by just placing a message in our `_messages` list with `GroupName` set to that of the request and `Sender` set to the string specified in the `Creator` property.

Let's take a look at both of the methods that deal with `Group` requests in `MessengerService` after providing this implementation:

```
public object Get(Group request)
{
  return new GroupResponse {
      Messages = _messages.Where(message =>
      message.GroupName.Equals(request.GroupName))
      .ToList()
  };
}
public object Post(Group request)
{
  _messages.Add(new Message
  {
    Sender = request.Creator,
    GroupName = request.GroupName,
    Body = request.Creator + " created " + request.GroupName + "
    group."
  });
  return new GroupResponse
  {
    Name = request.GroupName,
    Messages = _messages.Where(
    message => message.GroupName.Equals(request.
    GroupName))
    .ToList()
    };
  }
}
```

Our tests should pass now, and our new functionality is ready. However, if we check the metadata that ServiceStack generates for this new functionality, we'll see the following for the `Group` message type:

What's happened is that the service will now accept the GET or POST messages at /groups/{GroupName}—an unintended side effect. We wanted GET /groups/bestfriends to get all the messages on the bestfriends group, but we didn't want to enable posting to /groups/newGroupName necessarily. This is easy to fix—we simply need to fix the [Route] annotation on the Group object so that it only works on GET methods and add another route to handle both, like this:

```
[Route("/groups/")]
[Route("/groups/{GroupName}","GET")]
public class Group
{
    public string GroupName { get; set; }
    public string Creator { get; set; }
}
```

Now, if we check our service metadata, we'll see what we were expecting—the /group endpoint accepts all HTTP verbs, but /groups/{GroupName} only accepts HTTP GET, which is depicted in the following screenshot:

There's more...

We could easily make use of this pattern to create new service methods that would allow the deletion of a group by calling the /groups endpoint with an HTTP DELETE call.

Hosting services from different assemblies

The output of a .NET project is typically an assembly. This applies to ServiceStack projects also. These assemblies can be in the form of a DLL, which could be used by other programs or by a program itself. In this example, we'll show how you can create and reuse assemblies.

In this example, we'll take the ReidsonMessenger service we've been creating, refactor it a bit to be more modular, and then create a new project to host it.

Getting ready

When we last left off with the **ReidsonMessenger service**, it had the following structure:

We'll refactor the solution by moving `MessengerService` out to its own project, which will leave only the hosting details, `AppHost` and `Global.asax`, in the main project. Then, we'll create an entirely new solution that hosts the messenger in a console project instead of IIS and add the `MessengerService.ServiceModel` and `MessengerService.ServiceInterface` DLLs to it as references.

How to do it...

Right-click on the solution and choose **Add New Project**.

Choose **Class Library** and name it `ReidsonMessenger.ServiceInterface`.

Move `ReidsonMessenger` in to this project, and resolve the resulting reference issues by installing ServiceStack and adding a reference to `ReidsonMessenger.ServiceModel`:

- ▶ Tests will need references to ServiceStack, `ServiceInterface`, and `ServiceModel`

- ▶ `ServiceModel` needs a reference to ServiceStack

- ▶ `ServiceInterface` needs references to ServiceStack and `ServiceModel`

- ▶ `ServiceClient` needs references to ServiceStack and `ServiceModel`

- ▶ `ReidsonMessenger` needs references to ServiceStack, `ServiceInterface`, and `ServiceModel`

Rebuild the solution and make sure your tests pass—we now have a fairly well-structured solution with components that could be hosted in a variety of different ways.

The new structure should look like this:

Now that we have cleaned up our project structure, let's create a new hosting project. We'll call it `ConsoleHostedMessneger`. Choose the **Console Application** project type.

 If you're using VisualStudio Express 2013 for Web, you can create a class library and then change the Output Type to **Console Application** in the **Solution properties**.

Add an `AppHost` class that extends `AppSelfHostBase` instead of `AppHostBase`, as follows:

```
class ConsoleAppHost : AppSelfHostBase
{
  public ConsoleAppHost()
      : base("ReidsonIndustries Console Messaging Service",
        typeof (MessengerService).Assembly)
  { }

  public override void Configure(Funq.Containercontainer)
  { }
}
```

Now that we have an `AppHost` class suitable for self-hosting, we can change our program class' `Main` method to initialize the service, as follows:

```
public class Program
{
  static void Main(string[] args)
  {
    var listeningOn = "http://localhost:2202/";
    new ConsoleAppHost()
        .Init()
        .Start(listeningOn);
    Console.WriteLine("Listening on {0}", listeningOn);
    Console.WriteLine("Push any key to stop.");
    Console.ReadKey();
  }
}
```

The resulting service should look like this:

```
file:///C:/projects/service-stack-book/src/Chapter 2/Recipe3/te
Listening on http://localhost:2202/
Push any key to stop.
_
```

How it works...

Adding the assembly reference to the `ServiceInterface` project gives our new solution access to the `MessengerService` service from the other project just by referencing the DLL. Adding the assembly reference to the `ServiceModel` project gives our new solution access to the different types required to use the `ServiceModel project`. We can then easily host these services in an entirely new way by creating a custom `AppHost`.

ServiceStack's `AppSelfHostBase` gives us access to `HttpListener` and a high-performance self-hosting option that doesn't require IIS. We could just as easily have used this technique to add `ReidsonMessager` to an entirely different solution to add the services to the new solution.

This provides a flexible way to reuse services in other solutions.

There's more...

There is an important difference between different hosts regarding threading. The ASP.NET host, `AppHostBase`, leaves the thread creation up to the web server. ServiceStack does not create any new threads. The `AppHostHttpListenerBase class`, which is used by `AppSelfHostBase`, creates a single new thread on startup. These different concurrency models should be taken into consideration when deciding which host to use for different tasks.

Utilizing the original HTTP request

There are a few types of situations when you might need to access the original ASP.NET `HttpRequest`. You might be migrating to ServiceStack from a large existing WCF code base or another framework where this object was used a lot. You might be required to integrate with a legacy or custom services/clients that are unable to be changed, and your web service endpoints must adhere to a specific set of requests and responses. In this recipe, we will go over some of the options you have when using the ServiceStack framework—the access and use of the original HTTP request object as well as some ways you can leverage how ServiceStack binds values to your request data transfer objects.

Getting ready

You'll need to have your ServiceStack project up and running; please see *Creating a ServiceStack solution with VisualStudio and NuGet* in *Appendix A, Getting Started*.

How to do it...

Accessing the original ASP.NET `HttpRequest` is very simple to do as it's exposed from your web service that inherits from `Service`, as follows:

```
var originalRequest = this.Request.OriginalRequest as HttpRequest;
```

As you can see, it's really straightforward to get access to the underlying ASP.NET `HttpRequest`. This could make transitioning or integration with some existing applications easier, but something important to note is the `Request` object itself in the previous code.

How it works...

The `IRequest` object that `Service` exposes in the `Service` base class wraps and exposes many of the same properties with some helpful extension methods to try and make your life a bit easier. If you need to deal with the specific implementation of the original `Request` object, it can be used as shown previously, but the type of the original request might not always be an `HttpRequest` object. ServiceStack helps with this abstraction by providing useful methods that work with the different original requests.

The following are some really simple examples of common tasks you might perform, most of which are the same or very close to how developers interact with the original request. This makes picking up ServiceStack more straightforward for developers who are well-versed at writing *classic* ASMX HTTP handlers or WCF services, as follows:

```
string queryStringValue = this.Request.
QueryString["CustomQueryString"];
string formData = this.Request.FormData;
string body = this.Request.GetRawBody();
string headerValue = this.Request.Headers["CustomHeader"];
IHttpFile[] files = this.Request.Files;
```

If you do have some experience with dealing with the ASP.NET `HttpRequest` object, most of the preceding code should look pretty familiar. If you don't and, for example, just the data in bolded lines is inserted in your custom request DTO, you're in luck!

If your request DTO has property names that match that of the query string, form data entry, or key/value pair in the body of a request, ServiceStack will automatically bind these values.

For example, if there was an unchangeable requirement that every request object can only be populated by query string values, as long as those keys match, ServiceStack will automatically bind these values, as follows;

```
public class LegacyHelloWorld : Service
{
    public object Get(LegacyHelloWorldRequest request)
```

```
    {
        return "Hello, " + request.Name;
    }
}
[Route("/hello")]
[Route("/hello/{Name}")]
public class LegacyHelloWorldRequest
{
    public string Name { get; set; }
}
```

If we perform a GET request in a browser to hit this service, /hello/Reader will result in the expected value of Hello, Reader. However, since we have added the Route("/hello") route, it will process the same request with /hello?Name=Reader, and we will get the same Hello, Reader message back. This is the same for FormData as well! If we were processing a POST request, the body of the request would also be processed to populate this value.

You might be in the situation that the query strings, form data, or the body of the request might have characters you really don't want to have in your code. For example, if the same request and service has to bind to a HttpRequest with a JSON request that had users_ friendly_name_1 as the Name property value, and you can't change what the client is sending, you can let ServiceStack know the name to bind to through the .NET DataContract and DataMember attributes, as follows:

```
[Route("/hello")]
[Route("/hello/{Name}")]
[DataContract]
public class LegacyHelloWorldRequest
{
    [DataMember(Name = "user_friendly_name_1")]
    public string Name { get; set; }
}
```

Now, if we send {"user_friendly_name_1":"Reader"} via Postman, we get Hello, Reader back, which we were expecting!

> Postman is a free extension for the Chrome browser, which can be easily used with ServiceStack thanks to the PostmanFeature() plugin. Postman allows developers to easily create HTTP requests to test web services. The ServiceStack plugin exposes an endpoint for Postman to automatically import all the types of valid requests that can be used with your services.
>
> Postman is available from the Chrome Web Store.

The following screenshot depicts an example of the Postman feature plugin:

 When using the `DataContract` and `DataMember` attributes, remember that you have to use both and that the original `Name` property still binds. Even though this allows you to potentially support new and old clients, be aware of possible collisions with other property names.

There's more...

If you do need access to IIS and Windows-specific properties like `LogonUserIdentity` for example, you will also need to make sure the service to which your host `AppPool` is configured is done correctly and ServiceStack has been enabled to resolve this correctly.

See also

The *Accessing Windows identity information from ServiceStack for an intranet application* recipe in *Chapter 7, Security and Authentication*.

Overriding serialization of request object types

ServiceStack's fast serialization of requests and responses is at the center of how its clients and services interact. Sometimes, however, there might be a need to have your request objects structured differently on the server than the client. In this recipe, we will cover how this can be handled within the ServiceStack framework.

Getting ready

First, we'll need a project with ServiceStack references to be up and running. To do this, please see *Creating a ServiceStack solution with VisualStudio and NuGet* in *Appendix A, Getting Started*.

Although ServiceStack has a simple way of aliasing properties for a request object, sometimes there might be more control needed around how your request-and-response objects serialize and deserialize.

 In this recipe, we are looking at only JSON serialization; some of these concepts can be converted into the other formats ServiceStack supports, such as JSV and CSV.

How to do it...

So, in this example, we are migrating from an old system, and we have to support the old clients, which only accept a very specific naming convention in their JSON payload, and beyond the URLs they hit, we are unable to change how they consume the responses from the server. So, one way we might handle this is having another host that reuses our code from the main project, but control how some of the domain objects are serialized, as follows:

```
public override void Configure(Funq.Container container)
{
    //Configuration code...
    JsConfig<Place>.RawSerializeFn = (place) =>
{
        return place.SerializeForOldClient();
};
}
public static class PlaceSerializer
{
    public static bool HasCountryInName(this Place place)
    {
        //If comma, client expects a country name
        return place.Name.Contains(',');
```

```
    }

    public static string SerializeForOldClient(this Place place)
    {
        if (place.HasCountryInName())
        {
            string[] nameCountry = place.Name.Split(',');
            return "{\"0_Name\":\"" + nameCountry[0].Trim() + "\",\"1_
            CountryName\":\"" + nameCountry[1].Trim() + "\",\"2_
            Description\":\"" + place.Description + "\"}";
        }

        return "{\"0_Name\":\"" + place.Name + "\",\"1_
        Description\":\"" + place.Description + "\"}";
    }
}
```

Another requirement for this old client might be that the service must return all names in capitalized text. Due to a matching routine, we no longer have the ability to change. A delegate for a different method is used for this kind of modification. Here's how this can be done:

```
JsConfig<Place>.RawSerializeFn = (place) =>
{
    place = JsConfig<Place>.OnSerializingFn(place);
    return place.SerializeForOldClient();
};
JsConfig<Place>.OnSerializingFn = (place) =>
{
    place.Name = place.Name.ToUpper();
    return place;
};
```

How it works...

The `JsConfig` object is a part of ServiceStack. This means that text that is responsible for all the JSON serialization. The generic T passed is used to isolate the functions you register to apply only to the type specified. Once registered, any serialization or deserialization performed on the specified type will run your registered functions.

The previously used serialize examples also have deserialize counterparts, which are used to convert back to the typed object on the request to your services. So, if your client was also responsible for updating data, you might consider using `OnDeserializedFn` and/or `RawDeserializeFn` to handle these requirements.

Creating a simple admin service

ServiceStack's heavy use of DTOs in the form of Plain Old CLR Objects (POCOs) enables developers to expose data in very simple, elegant ways. A common service you might want to add to your API or web services is an admin interface where you might want to list all your users to administrators. In this recipe, we will see how, using various parts of the ServiceStack framework, this can be achieved in a very readable and concise way.

Getting ready

First, we'll need a project with ServiceStack references to be up and running. To do this, please see *Creating a ServiceStack solution with VisualStudio and NuGet* in *Appendix A, Getting Started*.

We are also going to have some basic authentication, settings, and OrmLite set up to work in our application, as follows:

```
var dbFactory = new OrmLiteConnectionFactory(
            "~/App_Data/db.sqlite".MapHostAbsolutePath(),
            SqliteDialect.Provider);
container.Register<IDbConnectionFactory>(dbFactory);
var userRep = new OrmLiteAuthRepository(dbFactory);
container.Register<IUserAuthRepository>(userRep);

Plugins.Add(new PostmanFeature());
Plugins.Add(
    new AuthFeature(() =>
        new AuthUserSession(),
        new IAuthProvider[]
        {
```

```
            new CredentialsAuthProvider(),
    }));
```

```
userRep.DropAndReCreateTables();
CreateUsers(userRep);
```

 For more information on the AuthFeature plugin, see the *Getting started with authentication, sessions, registration, and user repositories* recipe in *Chapter 7, Security and Authentication*.

How to do it...

First, we need to create a request object to handle the request for registered users in our application, as follows:

```
[Route("/admin/users")]
public class RegisteredUsers
{

}
```

This request object doesn't need any properties as authentication, and the session will be able to identify who is making the request and if they are authenticated. For this example, we are just attributing an object to wire it up to the following service. The Authenticate and RoleRequired attributes are used with ServiceStack's authentication. Marking the class with these attributes means that only authenticated users with the role of Admin can access the service methods within. The *Getting started with authentication, sessions, registration, and user repositories* recipe in *Chapter 7, Security and Authentication*, shows an isolated look at how these can be used:

```
[Authenticate]
[RequiredRole("Admin")]
public class RegisteredUsersService : Service
{
    public object Get(RegisteredUsersRequest request)
    {
        var response = new
        {
            UserAuths = Db.Select<UserAuth>()
        };
        //nulled out for security
        response.UserAuths.ForEach(x => x.PasswordHash = null);
        response.UserAuths.ForEach(x => x.Salt = null);
```

```
                response.UserAuths.ForEach(x => x.DigestHa1Hash = null);

                return response;
        }
    }
```

The `response` object being returned here is an anonymous type that contains a property called `UserAuths`, which is being populated from the `UserAuth` table. This `UserAuth` table was set up by the use of `OrmLiteAuthRepository`, which is an implementation of `IUserAuthRepository`.

The result of this request shows the currently registered users with our application:

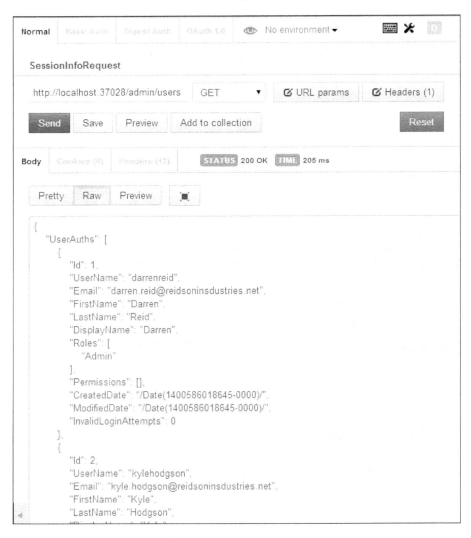

How it works...

Since ServiceStack allows developers to return any POCO from these services and serializes it into the appropriate requested format, we are able to simply return the `UserAuth` objects and let ServiceStack take care of the rest. Anything returned from a service will be automatically serialized into the required format, including anonymous types.

 If the support of SOAP is required, objects need to be attributed correctly with `System.Data` attributes, `DataContract` for classes, and `DataMember` for properties. See the ServiceStack wiki at `https://github.com/ServiceStack/ServiceStack/wiki` for more information.

This service also has the `Authenticate` attribute and `RequiresRole` attribute to ensure that only authenticated users with the `Admin` role are able to access this service. If no credentials are provided, the service will return a **401 Unauthorized** response, as follows:

If we then log in with the guest user by posting credentials to `/auth/credentials?format=json`, we will have an authenticated session, a glimpse of which is shown in the following screenshot:

However, if the guest user attempts to access this endpoint, they will receive a **403 Invalid Role** error due to the required role `Admin` marked on the service, as shown in the following screenshot:

See also

The *Getting started with authentication, sessions, registration, and user repositories* recipe in *Chapter 7*, *Security and Authentication*

Intercepting requests and responses using attributes

In many situations, you might have a need to rewrite HTTP requests and even HTTP responses. For instance, you might have certain parts of your API publically accessible and certain parts that require an API key for access. In this case, you wouldn't want to copy and paste this logic all over your service. ServiceStack supports this in the framework in a number of ways—one way that this author is fond of is using custom attributes. You can use these attributes to inject filters, which will be executed prior to executing a service rendering a response. In this recipe, we'll extend the Reidson Industries Messenger to show how to do that.

How to do It...

First, we'll develop a custom request attribute that verifies that an API key is correct. We'll create it as an attribute and have it extend `RequestFilterAttribute`, as follows:

```
public class ValidateApiKeyAttribute : RequestFilterAttribute
{
  public override void Execute(
      IRequest req, IResponse res, object requestDto)
  {
    if (InvalidApiKey(req.Headers["MessengerServiceApiKey"]))
    {
```

```
      throw HttpError.Unauthorized("Unauthorized");
    }
  }

  private static bool InvalidApiKey(string apiKey)
  {
    return !TokenService.ValidTokens.Contains(apiKey);
  }
}
```

Now that we've implemented it, we can use our attribute to decorate a specific request method on the service. Let's imagine we wanted to require an API key for requests to create a new group:

```
[ValidateApiKey]
public object Post(Group request)
{
  // create the group
}
```

How it works...

When ServiceStack encounters a request matching the pattern specified in the DTO, ServiceStack will note the annotation and execute the filter before calling our service implementation. Inside the filter, we override the `Execute` method, which expects an `IRequest req` request object, an `IResponse res` response object, and the `requestDTO` object.

We can then inspect the request object, looking for an API key header in this case. When we find that a request does not contain a valid key, we throw an exception that ServiceStack will map to a **401 Unauthorized** HTTP response.

There's more...

ServiceStack supports placing these attributes on a service method or an entire `Service` class—placing the annotation at the class level will inject the filter on every request handled by that service. You could also place the annotation only on a single request DTO, as shown in the following code:

```
[ValidateApiKey]
[Route("/group/")]
[Route("/group/{GroupName}","GET")]
public class Group
```

```
    {
      public string GroupName { get; set; }
      public string Creator { get; set; }
    }
```

To be more specific, in this case, ServiceStack would call the filter on every call specified by that DTO, including all calls to /group that do not have {GroupName} provided in the URL.

You can also provide filters to handle response objects specifically. For instance, you might want to add a response header to certain HTTP responses. You could implement that as follows :

```
    public class CustomResponseAttribute : ResponseFilterAttribute
    {
      public override void Execute(
        IRequest req, IResponse res, object responseDto)
        {
          if (req.Headers["CustomResponseHeaderRequired"] == "true")
          {
            res.AddHeader("CustomResponseHeader","response value");
          }
        }
    }
```

Once you implement this response filter, you can now use the [CustomResponse] attribute in annotations. For instance, you could decorate the entire service as follows:

```
    [CustomResponse]
    public class MessengerService : Service
```

Making a basic proxy for existing web services

From time to time, it might be useful to build a proxy for a web service that already exists. Maybe this is because you have an internal service that wasn't designed for consumer use. You'd love to expose it, but you'd need to change it first, and for some reason you cannot. The proxy technique can come in handy here—build a new service that connects to the old service and proxies requests to the old service. In this recipe, we'll build an example of doing just that using the Twitter API as an example of a service you'd like to wrap.

Let's imagine that we wanted users of our group messaging app to search for keywords so that they could find pictures that they could post as messages to their friends. We could leverage an existing provider, such as Flickr, and proxy the service through our application.

How to do It...

First we'll use `JsonServiceClient` to access Flickr. We can create a `FlickrSearch` class to help with that, as follows:

```
[Route("/services/rest/")]
public class FlickrSearch
{
    public string api_key { get; set; }
    public string text { get; set; }
    public string method { get; set; }
    public string format { get; set; }
    public string nojsoncallback { get; set; }

    public FlickrSearch (string term)
    {
      this.text = term;
      this.api_key = "your api key goes here";
      this.method = "flickr.photos.search";
      this.format = "json";
      this.nojsoncallback = "1";
    }
}
```

We won't use this request type directly as a service endpoint, but when we pass the C# client a `FlickrSearch class`, it'll know how to construct requests for the Flickr API. You can sign up for your own Flickr API key at their website `https://www.flickr.com/services/api/`. The next thing we need to model is the response that Flickr sends back, as follows:

```
public class FlickrSearchResponse
{
  public FlickrPhotos photos { get; set; }
  public string stat { get; set; }
}

public class FlickrPhotos
{
  public List<FlickrPhoto> photo { get; set; }
  public string page { get; set; }
  public string pages { get; set; }
  public string perpage { get; set; }
  public string total { get; set; }
}
```

```
public class FlickrPhoto
{
  public string id { get; set; }
  public string owner { get; set; }
  public string secret { get; set; }
  public string server { get; set; }
  public string farm { get; set; }
  public string title { get; set; }
  public string ispublic { get; set; }
  public string isfriend { get; set; }
  public string isfamily { get; set; }

  public string MakeImageUrl()
  {
    return String.Format(
            "http://farm{0}.staticflickr.com/{1}/{2}_{3}.jpg",
             this.farm, this.server, this.id, this.secret);
  }
}
```

Now that we have modeled Flickr, we can use `JsonServiceClient` to access it. Let's write a test to make sure that this is working:

```
[Test]
public void ShouldGetPhotos()
{
  var client = new JsonServiceClient(
  "https://api.flickr.com/");
  var flickrSearchRequest = new FlickrSearchRequest(
  "algonquin");
  var response = client.Get<FlickrSearchResponse>(
  flickrSearchRequest);
  var imageUrl = response.photos.photo
                  .FirstOrDefault()
                  .MakeImageUrl();

  Assert.Greater(response.photos.photo.Count, 0);
  Assert.IsTrue(imageUrl.Contains("staticflickr"));
}
```

Now that we have a working client, it's a simple matter of wiring it up with its own service interface. Our new endpoint will need a request object, as follows:

```
[Route("/images/{Keyword}")]
public class ImageRequest
{
  public string Keyword { get; set; }

  public ImageRequest(string keyword)
  {
    this.Keyword = keyword;
  }
}
```

This request object will be handled by a new service method, as follows:

```
public object Get(ImageRequest request)
{
  var flickrClient = new JsonServiceClient(
  "https://api.flickr.com/");
  var flickrSearchRequest = new FlickrSearchRequest(
  request.Keyword);
  var response = flickrClient.Get<FlickrSearchResponse>(
  flickrSearchRequest);

  return response.ToList();
}
```

As you can see, when we visit /image/ endpoint, we'll get back a list of JPG images from Flickr, as follows:

How it works...

We are using `JsonServiceClient`, which ServiceStack provides as a way to connect to other services. We could have used JSON.Net or even a SOAP client. The client connects to Flickr, sends a request, receives a response, and then converts it to a list of URLs.

Once we have this logic working, it's a simple matter of creating a service interface for the client as a proxy. You could easily add caching, authentication, and other logic as required.

Wrapping multiple existing services and exposing them through ServiceStack

In the previous recipe, we showed how we can use the C# client to act as a proxy for services where we don't have control of the source code. We'll continue with that concept in this recipe, adding the capability to send SMSes so that our messaging app can send text messages to users when new messages are sent. Being able to wrap multiple existing services allows you as a software developer to mix in powerful components quickly instead of needing to build everything yourself. This time, we'll add the concept of SMS messaging by referencing the popular *Twilio* API.

Twilio, for a small fee, will send and receive text messages and also send and receive phone calls in addition to a number of other services. You can check out `https://www.twilio.com/docs/` for more information.

How to do it...

We'll start with Reidson Messenger from the previous recipe. We'll add Twilio to our mash-up this time in order to support sending text messages to users when new messages are sent. Twilio's API doesn't accept JSON over `POST` requests; it's looking for form data instead—so, we can't use `JsonServiceClient` that we've used in the past. We'll make use of the `PostToUrl` extension method, which specializes in sending form data with a `POST` request. Here's what the Twilio client looks like:

```
public class TwilioClient
{
  private static string _accountSid = "your account secret";
  private static string _authToken = "your auth token";
  private static string _accountNumber = twilio phone number";

  public string SendTextMessage(string toNumber, string message)
  {
    var url = String.Format(
```

```
            "https://api.twilio.com/2010-04-01/Accounts/{0}/SMS/
            Messages.json",
            _accountSid);

            var auth = String.Format("Basic {0}", GetAuthstring());

            var response = url.PostToUrl(
                    new
                    {
                        From = _accountNumber,
                        To = toNumber,
                        Body = message
                    },
                    requestFilter:
                    request =>
                    request.Headers.Add("Authorization",auth))
                    .FromJson<TwilioSmsResponse>();
        return response.status;
    }

    private static string GetAuthstring()
    {
        return Convert.ToBase64String(
                Encoding.ASCII.GetBytes(
                String.Format("{0}:{1}",
                _accountSid, _authToken)));
    }
}
```

`TwilioClient` has one public method, `SendTextMessage`, that knows how to work with `PostToUrl`. We assemble a `url` variable containing the URL we need to post to, and an `auth` variable that contains our authentication header. Twilio is expecting HTTP basic authentication, which `GetAuthString` implements.

`PostToUrl` is an extension method on the string type. It assumes that you want to post the HTTP data payload to the URL contained in the string and optionally provides a request filter. In this case, the request filter allows us to change the HTTP request object before it's sent off to the remote URL. Here, we're adding the authentication header with the HTTP basic authentication data.

The anonymous object contains our payload data; the phone number the SMS is being sent from, the phone number it's being sent to, and the body of the SMS itself.

The `FromJson<T>` extension method to `string` then parses the JSON and returns a `TwilioSmsResponse` object, which is simply a DTO that models Twilio's response, as follows:

```
public class TwilioSmsResponse
{
  public string sid { get; set; }
  public string date_updated { get; set; }
  public string date_sent { get; set; }
  public string account_sid { get; set; }
  public string to { get; set; }
  public string from { get; set; }
  public string body { get; set; }
  public string status { get; set; }
  public string direction { get; set; }
  public string api_version { get; set; }
  public string price { get; set; }
  public string price_unit { get; set; }
  public string uri { get; set; }
  public string num_segments { get; set; }
}
```

Now that we have `TwilioClient` to connect to Twilio and send a text message, it's simple to wire it up inside `MessengerService`. We'll use IoC to inject an instance of `wilioClient` into `MessengerService` on a variable called `SmsService`, as follows:

```
public object Post(Message request)
{
  _messages.Add(request);
  SubscribersFor(request.GroupName).Each(
  phoneNumber => SmsService.SendTextMessage(
  phoneNumber, request.Body));

  return new MessageResponse { Response = "OK" };
}
```

You can imagine that `SubscribersFor` knows how to fetch the list of subscribers to a specific group and return them in `IEnumerable`. For each of those, we'll simply call `SendTextMessage`.

In the end, you could easily put together a service that mashes up any number of existing APIs. ServiceStack includes many tools that make it easier to develop service clients that can communicate with different kinds of endpoints, which can be very helpful in building service proxies.

3
Testing and Logging

In this chapter, we will cover the following topics:

- ▶ Unit testing ServiceStack applications
- ▶ Integration testing with the ServiceStack C# client
- ▶ Functional contract testing ServiceStack services
- ▶ Accessing the request-and-response object with the JsonServiceClient
- ▶ Continuous integration with TeamCity and self-hosted services
- ▶ Logging with a choice of frameworks
- ▶ Writing a logger to monitor exceptions via e-mail

Introduction

Some of the most important advances in the field of software development over the last decade have involved an increased reliance on automated techniques to test code code. While the concept of automated testing isn't new, systems are growing larger and more complicated—so these techniques are fast becoming the skill that separates novice programmers from professionals.

In this chapter, we will go over some of the techniques and patterns that can be used with ServiceStack to help you write maintainable web services. The patterns will help you write unit and integration tests as well as figure out how you might use these in local development with a continuous integration server such as TeamCity.

Many software developers subscribe to the theory of a **Testing pyramid**. The idea is that unit tests form the base of the pyramid—there should be more of them than any other kind of test. Integration tests form the middle, and functional tests form the top:

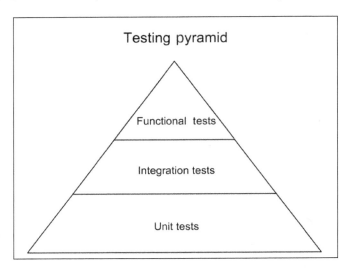

Let's discuss the ideas behind the Testing pyramid:

- ▶ While functional tests provide great value in actually testing the application the way a user uses it, they are the most expensive tests to develop and run. Often a functional suite might take hours or even days to run—so there's a diminishing return in adding too many of them.

- ▶ Functional tests are often seen as brittle in that small changes to the UI might break several or all of your functional tests. If such a UI design change does break several tests, there isn't much value in the failing tests either—you already know your UI changed.

- ▶ Integration tests are good for situations where you need to test the way you're using something; a common situation might be to have a class that's applying some business logic to the retrieval of data from a repository—in this case, an integration test that holds the service, the ORM, and some seed data under test might be useful to prove that the logic works as expected with the given ORM.

- ▶ Integration tests can go wrong when a team begins writing lots of tests that simply prove some framework or library they interact with work as expected. There's little value in writing tons of tests mostly against your ORM as one would hope that the team that develops it is already doing that.

- ▶ With an integration test, when the integration boundary you're testing against does change, you'll know what in your code is impacted; integration tests do provide value. However, they don't really pinpoint what class has issues.

- Unit tests can run much more quickly—most unit tests can be run in under 10 milliseconds by convention. Developers who are adept at the process can have hundreds or thousands of inexpensive unit tests that can run in a few seconds and often have the tests run continuously. This results in much faster time to spot issues and resolve them.

- When a unit test fails, it often points directly to the source of a problem. When an integration or functional test fails, you often have to wade in and try to figure out which class has an issue.

- There are different approaches to unit testing. With any approach, it's important to attempt to write tests that verify the outward behavior of the class and not the internal implementation of how it works; otherwise, perfectly valid changes to the implementation will cause the test to fail:

  - The *mockist* style applies a very literal lens to the unit testing concept. The developer will work to develop test doubles, fakes, stubs, and mocks to isolate the unit being tested from the classes surrounding it. This style is useful in that it tests only the mocks and the unit under test, but the mocking activities themselves can become expensive over time.

  - The *classic* style is where a unit test might end up exercising code in more than one unit, but the tests focus on the capabilities of the specific unit under test. This style isn't quite as "clean room" as the mockist style, but it avoids the penalty associated with developing mocks that continue to increase in complexity.

Often developers experienced with automatic testing will strive for a balance of techniques in order to gain confidence that the application under test is of sufficient quality—the test pyramid is one guideline on the balance you should be aiming for.

We will also go over ServiceStack's logging with some practical examples of how you can switch logging implementations and how to write your own ServiceStack logging factory.

Unit testing ServiceStack applications

In this recipe we'll focus on simple techniques to test individual units of code within a ServiceStack application. We will use the ServiceStack testing helper `BasicAppHost` as an application container, as it provides us with some useful helpers to inject a test double for our database. Our goal is small; fast tests that test one unit of code within our application.

Getting ready

We are going to need some services to test, so we are going to use the `PlacesToVisit` application. If you are starting your own project from the beginning, refer to *Creating a ServiceStack solution with Visual Studio and NuGet* in *Appendix A, Getting Started* for information on how to get ready with Visual Studio and ServiceStack. This also covers basic usage of `NUnit`, the unit testing framework we will be using in this recipe.

How to do it...

1. Create a new testing project. It's a common convention to name the testing project `<ProjectName>.Tests`—so in our case, we'll call it `PlacesToVisit.Tests`. Create a class within this project to contain the tests we'll write—let's name it `PlacesServiceTests` as the tests within it will focus on the `PlacesService` class. Annotate this class with the `[TestFixture]` attribute, as follows:

```
[TestFixture]
public class PlaceServiceTests
{
```

2. We'll want one method that runs whenever this set of tests begins to set up the environment and another one that runs afterwards to tear the environment down. These will be annotated with the `NUnit` attributes of `TestFixtureSetUp` and `TextFixtureTearDown`, respectively. Let's name them `FixtureInit` and `FixtureTearDown`.

   In the `FixtureInit` method, we will use `BasicAppHost` to initialize our `appHost` test container. We'll make it a field so that we can easily access it in each test, as follows:

```
ServiceStackHost appHost;

[TestFixtureSetUp]
public void FixtureInit()
{
  appHost = new BasicAppHost(typeof(PlaceService).Assembly)
  {
    ConfigureContainer = container =>
    {
      container.Register<IDbConnectionFactory>(c =>
        new OrmLiteConnectionFactory(
          ":memory:", SqliteDialect.Provider));
      container.RegisterAutoWiredAs<PlacesToVisitRepository,
        IPlacesToVisitRepository>();
    }
  }.Init();
}
```

The `ConfigureContainer` property on `BasicAppHost` allows us to pass in a function that we want `AppHost` to run inside of the `Configure` method. In this case, you can see that we're registering `OrmLiteConnectionFactory` with an in-memory SQLite instance. This allows us to test code that uses a database without that database actually running. This useful technique could be considered a classic unit testing approach—the mockist approach might have been to mock the database instead.

The `FixtureTearDown` method will dispose of `appHost` as you might imagine. This is how the code will look:

```
[TestFixtureTearDown]
public void FixtureTearDown()
{
  appHost.Dispose();
}
```

3. We haven't created any data in our in memory database yet. We'll want to ensure the data is the same prior to each test, so our `TestInit` method is a good place to do that—it will be run once before each and every test run as we'll annotate it with the `[SetUp]` attribute, as follows:

```
[SetUp]
public void TestInit()
{
  using (var db = appHost.Container
      .Resolve<IDbConnectionFactory>().Open())
  {
    db.DropAndCreateTable<Place>();
    db.InsertAll(PlaceSeedData.GetSeedPlaces());
  }
}
```

As our tests all focus on `PlaceService`, we'll make sure to create `Place` data.

4. Next, we'll begin writing tests. Let's start with one that asserts that we can create new places. The first step is to create the new method, name it appropriately, and annotate it with the `[Test]` attribute, as follows:

```
[Test]
public void ShouldAddNewPlaces()
{
```

Next, we'll create an instance of `PlaceService` that we can test against. We'll use the Funq IoC `TryResolve` method for this:

```
    var placeService = appHost.TryResolve<PlaceService>();
```

5. We'll want to create a new place, then query the database later to see whether the new one was added. So, it's useful to start by getting a count of how many places there are based on just the seed data. Here's how you can get the count based on the seed data:

```
var startingCount = placeService
                .Get(new AllPlacesToVisitRequest())
                .Places
                .Count;
```

6. Since we're testing the ability to handle a `CreatePlaceToVisit` request, we'll need a test object that we can send the service to. Let's create one and then go ahead and post it:

```
var melbourne = new CreatePlaceToVisit
{
   Name = "Melbourne",
   Description = "A nice city to holiday"
};
placeService.Post(melbourne);
```

7. Having done that, we can get the updated count and then assert that there is one more item in the database than there were before:

```
var newCount = placeService
                .Get(new AllPlacesToVisitRequest())
                .Places
                .Count;
Assert.That(newCount == startingCount + 1);
```

8. Next, let's fetch the new record that was created and make an assertion that it's the one we want:

```
var newPlace = placeService.Get(new PlaceToVisitRequest
{
   Id = startingCount + 1
});
Assert.That(newPlace.Place.Name == melbourne.Name);
}
```

With this in place, if we run the test, we'll expect it to pass both assertions. This proves that we can add new places via `PlaceService` registered with Funq, and that when we do that we can go and retrieve them later as expected.

9. We can also build a similar test that asserts that on our ability to update an existing place. Adding the code is simple, following the pattern we set out previously. We'll start with the *arrange* section of the test, creating the variables and objects we'll need:

```
[Test]
public void ShouldUpdateExistingPlaces()
{
    var placeService = appHost.TryResolve<PlaceService>();

    var startingPlaces = placeService
        .Get(new AllPlacesToVisitRequest())
        .Places;
    var startingCount = startingPlaces.Count;


    var canberra = startingPlaces
        .First(c => c.Name.Equals("Canberra"));

    const string canberrasNewName = "Canberra, ACT";
    canberra.Name = canberrasNewName;
```

10. Once they're in place, we'll act. In this case, the `Put` method on `placeService` has the responsibility for *update* operations:

```
placeService.Put(canberra.ConvertTo<UpdatePlaceToVisit>());
```

11. Think of the `ConvertTo` helper method from ServiceStack as an auto-mapper, which converts our `Place` object for us. Now that we've updated the record for Canberra, we'll proceed to the *assert* section of the test, as follows:

```
var updatedPlaces = placeService
    .Get(new AllPlacesToVisitRequest())
    .Places;
var updatedCanberra = updatedPlaces
    .First(p => p.Id.Equals(canberra.Id));
var updatedCount = updatedPlaces.Count;

Assert.That(updatedCanberra.Name == canberrasNewName);
Assert.That(updatedCount == startingCount);
}
```

How it works...

These unit tests are using a few different patterns that help us write concise tests, including the development of our own test helpers, and with helpers from the `ServiceStack.Testing` namespace, for instance `BasicAppHost` allows us to set up an application host instance without actually hosting a web service. It also lets us provide a custom `ConfigureContainer` action to mock any of our dependencies for our services and seed our testing data, as follows:

```
appHost = new BasicAppHost(typeof(PlaceService).Assembly)
{
  ConfigureContainer = container =>
  {
    container.Register<IDbConnectionFactory>(c =>
      new OrmLiteConnectionFactory(
      ":memory:", SqliteDialect.Provider));

    container.RegisterAutoWiredAs<PlacesToVisitRepository,
    IPlacesToVisitRepository>();
  }
}.Init();
```

To test any ServiceStack service, you can resolve it through the application host via `TryResolve<ServiceType>()`. This will have the IoC container instantiate an object of the type requested. This gives us the ability to test the `Get` method independent of other aspects of our web service, such as validation. This is shown in the following code:

```
var placeService = appHost.TryResolve<PlaceService>();
```

In this example, we are using an in-memory SQLite instance to mock our use of OrmLite for data access, which `IPlacesToVisitRepository` will also use as well as seeding our test data in our `ConfigureContainer` hook of `BasicAppHost`. The use of both in-memory SQLite and `BasicAppHost` provide fast unit tests to very quickly iterate our application services while ensuring we are not breaking any functionality specifically associated with this component. In the example provided, we are running three tests in less than 100 milliseconds. If you are using the full version of Visual Studio, extensions such as NCrunch can allow you to regularly run your unit tests while you make changes to your code. The performance of ServiceStack components and the use of these extensions results in a smooth developer experience with productivity and quality of code.

There's more...

In the examples in this recipe, we wrote out tests that would pass, ran them, and saw that they passed (no surprise). While this makes explaining things a bit simpler, it's not really a best practice. You generally want to make sure your tests *fail* when presented with wrong data at some point. The authors have seen many cases where subtle bugs in test code were causing a test to pass that should not have passed. One best practice is to write tests so that they fail first and then make them pass—this guarantees that the test can actually detect the defect you're guarding against. This is commonly referred to as the red/green/refactor pattern.

Integration testing with the ServiceStack C# client

In this recipe, we'll look at one option for integration testing with ServiceStack. In this case, we'll use a specific approach to integration testing where we develop a separate `AppHost` Class for the purpose of testing. It's worth pointing out that this approach shouldn't be thought of as an end-to-end test as it doesn't make any guarantees about what will happen when the code is integrated with `AppHost`, and it also doesn't use the same database software as the production service does.

While there are several approaches you can take to test your ServiceStack app, this approach allows the developer to test validation code, request-and-response filters, and other techniques that change the way ServiceStack will handle HTTP requests and responses that `BasicAppHost` won't, as they would require actual HTTP communication.

Getting ready

First, we need some services to test. Let's make use of the `PlaceToVisit` application from previous recipes. We'll write tests that perform various actions, verifying that the objects are successfully being added, updated, and removed. If you are setting up your own project or need guidance on how to use NUnit, please go to *Creating a ServiceStack solution with Visual Studio and NuGet* in *Appendix A, Getting Started* for help with setting up a new project.

How to do it...

Now that we have some services to test, we are going to need these services available for the C# client to call via HTTP for integration testing. As mentioned previously, we are going to self-host these services in the process, allowing them to run the tests themselves:

1. First we need to create our custom `TestAppHost` class. We'll extend the `AppSelfHostBase` class to make use of its `Start()` method, which will start `HttpListener` for us. We'll also borrow techniques from `BasicAppHost`, where we'll create a `ConfigureContainer` property of type, `Action<Container>`, which allows our test fixture to provide a specific configuration to the `TestAppHost` class. Also, like `BasicAppHost`, we'll expose the `ResponseFilters` property, which will allow us to pass in any filters we want to run in our integration tests, as follows:

```
public class TestAppHost : AppSelfHostBase
{
    public Action<Container> ConfigureContainer { get; set; }

    public List<Action<IRequest, IResponse, object>>
            ResponseFilters { get; set; }

    public TestAppHost()
            : base("Test Container for PlaceToVisit Service",
            typeof(PlaceService).Assembly)
    { }

    public override void Configure(Container container)
    {
        if (ConfigureContainer != null)
            this.ConfigureContainer(container);

        if (ResponseFilters != null)
            this.GlobalResponseFilters.AddRange(ResponseFilters);
    }
}
```

2. Next, we'll set up `TestFixture`. Let's call it `PlaceIntegrationTests`. We'll need a URL to pass to the `Start()` method, and we can use the same URL to configure our connections to the listener later, as follows:

```
[TestFixture]
public class PlaceIntegrationTests
{
    const string URLBase = "http://localhost:28193/";
```

3. Next, we'll create a field for our `appHost`—our `TestFixtureSetUp()` method will create it, and our `TestFixtureTearDown()` method will call the `Dispose()` method, as follows:

```
ServiceStackHost appHost;
```

4. In this case, the filter we want to test can be accessed on our production `AppHost` class. We'll prepare a list containing the filter so that we can pass it in to the `TestAppHost` class, as follows:

```
[TestFixtureSetUp]
public void FixtureSetUp()
{
  var responseFilters =
    new List<Action<IRequest, IResponse, object>>
      {AppHost.ETagResponseFilter};
```

5. The `AppHost.ETagResponseFilter` simply injects an `ETag` in to the HTTP response from the service. Injecting it here will allow us to make assertions about its behavior later. As we've done previously, we'll pass in a configuration suitable for testing, including an in-memory SQLite implementation linked to OrmLite. We'll also pass in `responseFilters` we just created. Once we've instantiated `TestAppHost`, we can initialize it and start `HttpListener`. Here's the code that does what we just explained:

```
appHost = new TestAppHost
{
  ConfigureContainer = container =>
  {
    container.Register<IDbConnectionFactory>(
    new OrmLiteConnectionFactory(":memory:",
    SqliteDialect.Provider));
    container.RegisterAutoWiredAs<
    PlacesToVisitRepository, IPlacesToVisitRepository>();
    container.RegisterAutoWired<PlaceService>();
  },
  ResponseFilters = responseFilters
}
.Init()
.Start(URLBase);
```

6. Each test will need fresh seed data, so we'll build a `TestSetUp()` method and annotate it with the `[SetUp]` attribute, as follows:

```
[SetUp]
public void TestSetUp()
{
  using (var db = appHost.Container
```

```
                              .Resolve<IDbConnectionFactory>().Open())
    {
      db.DropAndCreateTable<Place>();
      db.InsertAll(PlaceSeedData.GetSeedPlaces());
    }
}
```

7. Now, let's build up our test. We'll create an instance of `JsonServiceClient` and pass in the URL that `TestAppHost` is configured to listen on. `JsonServiceClient` is a HTTP client provided by ServiceStack that is aware of ServiceStack endpoints. Here's the code for what we just explained:

```
[Test]
public void ShouldAddNewPlaces()
{
    var client = new JsonServiceClient(URLBase);
```

8. `JsonServiceClient` allows us to pass in a `ResponseFilter`. The `ResponseFilter` property allows us to run code against the HTTP response that our service provides. In this case, we're expecting our service to return `ETag` in the response headers—so we can pass in an assertion for this. Later, when the client executes our request, that assertion will fire. This is how the code looks:

```
client.ResponseFilter = resp =>
        Assert.IsNotNull(resp.Headers[HttpHeaders.ETag]);
```

9. Next, we'll create a test place and post it to the service under test, with a simple assertion that the service returns the values expected:

```
var testPlace = new CreatePlaceToVisit
{
  Name = "Halifax",
  Description = "Very friendly Atlantic city"
};

var response = client.Post(testPlace);

Assert.AreEqual(testPlace.Name, response.Place.Name);
```

Our first assertion, passed into the client's `ResponseFilter` property, will execute when we `Post(testPlace)` after the client receives the response. The second assertion fires at the end of the test as expected.

10. It's important to make sure that we include the `TestFixtureTearDown` method. If we try to create `AppHost` in a subsequent test, we'll have failing tests unless we call `Dispose()` on `TestAppHost`, as follows:

```
[TestFixtureTearDown]
public void TearDown()
{
   appHost.Dispose();
}
```

How it works...

In this case, we want to actually make sure that specific HTTP headers are present when we send a specific request. While `BasicAppHost` allows us to pass in a testing configuration and `ResponseFilter`, it doesn't provide `HttpListener`. We've combined the techniques in `BasicAppHost` that allow us to pass in configuration and response filters with the `HttpListener` capability of `AppSelfHostBase`. Since we want to put it all together and test the interaction between client and server, we need an actual interaction to inspect the HTTP response from ServiceStack. Extending `AppSelfHostBase` allows us such an interaction. For this purpose, the following is what your code will look like:

```
public class TestAppHost : AppSelfHostBase
{
  public Action<Container> ConfigureContainer { get; set; }

  public List<Action<IRequest, IResponse, object>>
  ResponseFilters { get; set; }

  public TestAppHost()
    : base("Test Container for PlaceToVisit Service",
    typeof(PlaceService).Assembly)
  { }

  public override void Configure(Container container)
  {
    if (ConfigureContainer != null)
      this.ConfigureContainer(container);

    if (ResponseFilters != null)
      this.GlobalResponseFilters.AddRange(ResponseFilters);
  }
}
```

When you instantiate `TestAppHost` and call the `Start()` method, our test harness will start a ServiceStack service listening on the URL we pass in. We've configured this container with an in-memory SQLite instance connected to OrmLite and passed in the same response filters that our production container uses so that we can test those interactions. This is what our code looks like:

```
[TestFixtureSetUp]
public void FixtureSetUp()
{
  var responseFilters = new
      List<Action<IRequest, IResponse, object>>
      {AppHost.ETagResponseFilter};

  appHost = new TestAppHost
  {
    ConfigureContainer = container =>
    {
      container.Register<IDbConnectionFactory>(
      new OrmLiteConnectionFactory(":memory:",
      SqliteDialect.Provider));
      container.RegisterAutoWiredAs<
          PlacesToVisitRepository, IPlacesToVisitRepository>();
      container.RegisterAutoWired<PlaceService>();
    },
    ResponseFilters = responseFilters
  }
  .Init()
  .Start(URLBase);
}
```

Later, in our tests, we use `JsonServiceClient` to connect to the service and send a JSON request, passing in an assertion for the client to run when it receives the response looking for the HTTP header that we're expecting, as follows:

```
var client = new JsonServiceClient(URLBase);
client.ResponseFilter = resp =>
        Assert.IsNotNull(resp.Headers[HttpHeaders.ETag]);

var testPlace = new CreatePlaceToVisit
{
  Name = "Halifax",
  Description = "Very friendly Atlantic city"
};

var response = client.Post(testPlace);
Assert.AreEqual(testPlace.Name, response.Place.Name);
```

There's more...

While the techniques in this recipe are definitely towards the top of the testing pyramid, they can be useful in circumstances where we need actual HTTP communication to take place in order to verify that things are working correctly. However, it's worth noting that these tests run much more slowly than the unit testing technique shown in the previous recipe. While the unit tests run quickly, between 5 and 50 milliseconds, the single integration test shown here takes ten times longer to run on my computer. 500 milliseconds might not seem like much, and it might be worthwhile for a few specific cases, but you'll want to make sure that most of your tests run using a faster technique, most likely making use of `BasicAppHost`.

Functional contract testing ServiceStack services

While integration tests can combine several layers of our software, they are not definitive tests of all of your application from the outside in. If your team is publishing a service that only your team depends on, and you have an existing UI functional suite, then this is likely to be sufficient, and the techniques that we will explain now won't be required.

However, if your team publishes a service that is used by several other groups, you might find yourself wanting to build a functional test suite for the actual API of your service, enforcing the contract between the API consumer and the maintainer of the API.

While we can usually use `JsonServiceClient` to test a ServiceStack endpoint, the fact that it automatically picks up any changes to routes will work against us when we do functional testing. If a service's routes change unintentionally, and a service no longer responds to `PUT` in the way that it did in the past, the C# `JsonServiceClient` class might just go with the flow and send the right DTO in accordance to the change, not noticing that the service no longer fits your published specification. The change might break your clients, and you wouldn't know. In this recipe, we'll show techniques that will detect just this situation.

Getting ready

Luckily, ServiceStack also includes a number of useful lower-level HTTP utilities that we can make use of to perform functional contract testing. Let's say you needed to validate that a specific URL continued to respond to a `GET` request; we could make use of the `GetJsonFromUrl()` method. Then, we'll use the `FromJson()` method to convert the JSON result to a C# object matching the response DTO.

 Note that these lower-level HTTP utilities were originally provided as clients to use third-party services, but they happen to be very useful in this case as well.

We'll use this technique to test the `PlacesToVisit` service, picking up where we left off in previous recipes. However, we'll need a way to start our service and have it listen in on a specified URL so that we can make assertions about how the service will react to different HTTP requests. Like with the previous recipe, we will extend `AppSelfHostBase`. We'll borrow a technique from `BasicAppHost` of providing a way to pass in a `Configure()` method by providing an anonymous function, as follows:

```
public class TestAppHost : AppSelfHostBase
{
  public TestAppHost(String serviceName, Assembly assembly) :
    base(serviceName, assembly)
  { }

  public Action<Container> ConfigureContainer { get; set; }

  public override void Configure(Container container)
  {
    if (this.ConfigureContainer == null)
      return;
    this.ConfigureContainer(container);
  }
}
```

With this in place, we can create a `TestFixtureSetUp` function just as we did before. However, by overloading the `AppSelfHostBase` class, we can now instruct our application host to start up and listen in on a specific URL, as follows:

```
[TestFixture]
public class PlacesToVisitContract
{
  private const string URLBase = "http://localhost:28192/";
  ServiceStackHost appHost;
  PlaceService targetPlaceService;

  [TestFixtureSetUp]
  public void TestFixtureInit()
  {
    appHost = new TestAppHost("Places to Visit Service",
                              typeof(PlaceService).Assembly)
    {
      ConfigureContainer = container =>
      {
```

```
container.Register<IDbConnectionFactory>(
new OrmLiteConnectionFactory(":memory:",
SqliteDialect.Provider));

    container.RegisterAutoWiredAs<
    PlacesToVisitRepository, IPlacesToVisitRepository>();
    container.RegisterAutoWired<PlaceService>();
  }
}.Init()
.Start(URLBase);

targetPlaceService = appHost.TryResolve<PlaceService>();
}
```

We'll also need seed data, but unlike `AppHost`, which we want to initialize once for all the tests, we want to drop and recreate the seed data for every test. Here's how we do that:

```
[SetUp]
  public void TestSetup()
{
  using (var db =
      appHost.Container.Resolve<IDbConnectionFactory>().Open())
  {
    db.DropAndCreateTable<Place>();
    db.InsertAll(PlaceSeedData.GetSeedPlaces());
  }
}
```

How to do it...

Now that we have an app host that will start listening for HTTP requests on a specified URL, we can begin using the HTTP utilities to connect and make assertions. First, we'll test that a `GET` request to the URL `/places` returns a **200 status code** and a content body containing a JSON object with a place for each of our seed data items:

```
[Test]
public void GetSlashPlacesShouldReturnJsonWithAllPlaces()
{
  var placesData = (URLBase + "/places")
    .GetJsonFromUrl(responseFilter: response =>
    Assert.AreEqual(HttpStatusCode.OK,
    response.StatusCode))
    .FromJson<PlaceToVisitResponse>();
```

```
   Assert.IsTrue(
     placesData.Places.Any(p => p.Name.Equals("Sydney")));
   Assert.IsTrue(
     placesData.Places.Any(p => p.Name.Equals("Toronto")));
}
```

How it works...

GetJsonFromUrl() is an extension method on the string type. It will connect to the URL specified in the string and then send it to the following request:

```
GET http://localhost:28192/places HTTP/1.1
Accept: application/json
Accept-Encoding: gzip,deflate
```

We don't have to tell the method to send the accept header specifying the JSON format as you would imagine given that the name of the method is GetJsonFromUrl. The string returned by the service looks like this, as you might imagine:

```
{"Places":[{"Id":1,"Name":"Canberra","Description":"Capital city
of Australia"},{"Id":2,"Name":"Sydney","Description":"Largest city
in Australia"},{"Id":3,"Name":"Ottawa","Description":"Capital city
of Canada"},{"Id":4,"Name":"Toronto","Description":"Most populated
city in Canada"}]}
```

This JSON will be passed into the method FromJson<T>, and we'll pass in the type of the response DTO we're expecting, which is PlaceToVisitResponse, in this case. FromJson<T> will return an instance of our DTO populated with the JSON result.

We can then make assertions on the results as you'd expect. One thing to note, however, is that if you want to make assertions on the actual HTTP response, you need to pass an anonymous function in to the GetJsonFromUrl call as we do here:

```
var placesData = (URLBase + "/places")
    .GetJsonFromUrl(responseFilter: response =>
        Assert.AreEqual(HttpStatusCode.OK,
        response.StatusCode))
    .FromJson<PlaceToVisitResponse>();
```

We can also specify a specific document that we want back using this fluent style, like in the following code:

```
[Test]
public void GetSlashPlacesWithIdInUrlShouldReturnSpecificJson()
{
```

```
var shouldBeToronto = (URLBase + "/places/{0}")
    .Fmt(4)
    .GetJsonFromUrl(responseFilter: response =>
                    Assert.AreEqual(HttpStatusCode.OK,
                    response.StatusCode))
    .FromJson<PlaceToVisitResponse>();

Assert.AreEqual("Toronto",
    shouldBeToronto.Place.Name);
Assert.AreEqual("Most populated city in Canada",
    shouldBeToronto.Place.Description);
}
```

The `Fmt` extension method can be used with a string that accepts any object and replaces parameters in the string with the values found there; in this case we are requesting the `/places/4` document.

Until now, we only looked at functionally testing our `Get` methods with the help of some of ServiceStack's extension and utility functions. Since there are different conventions and rules behind each HTTP method, we can test each one using slightly different techniques. Let's have a look at testing some of the other HTTP verbs.

Testing POST

As you might imagine, ServiceStack provides several other similar tools to test `HTTP PUT`, `HTTP POST`, and `HTTP DELETE`. We can test a URL that accepts `POST` using `PostJsonToUrl`, as follows:

```
[Test]
public void PostingJsonToPlacesShouldRCreateAndReturnNewPlace()
{
  var placeToPost = new Place
  {
    Name = "London",
    Description = "Capital of UK"
  };

  var postedPlace = (URLBase + "/places")
      .PostJsonToUrl(placeToPost, responseFilter:
        response => Assert.AreEqual(HttpStatusCode.OK,
        response.StatusCode))
      .FromJson<PlaceToVisitResponse>();
  Assert.AreEqual(
    placeToPost.Name, postedPlace.Place.Name);
}
```

As with the other HTTP utilities, `PostJsonToUrl()` is an extension method that helps us to form a fluent syntax to send `POST` requests to a URL. It accepts a parameter where we can provide the DTO, which it will convert to JSON for us and `POST` to the URL. Just as it did earlier, `FromJson<T>` converts the JSON response to our strongly typed DTO that we can make assertions against.

Here's what would be sent on the wire for this test:

```
POST http://localhost:28192/places HTTP/1.1
Content-Type: application/json
Accept: application/json
Accept-Encoding: gzip,deflate
Host: localhost:28192
Content-Length: 54
Expect: 100-continue

{"Id":0,"Name":"London","Description":"Capital of UK"}
```

Testing PUT

Testing a URL that expects `PUT` uses a similar pattern:

```
[Test]
public void PutJsonToPlaceShouldUpdateExistingPlace()
{
  var placeToReplaceWith = new UpdatePlaceToVisit
  {
    Id = 3,
    Description = "Capital city of Kansas",
    Name = "Ottawa"
  };

  var receivedPlace = (URLBase + "/places/{0}")
      .Fmt(3)
      .PutJsonToUrl(placeToReplaceWith, responseFilter:
          response => Assert.AreEqual(HttpStatusCode.OK,
          response.StatusCode))
      .FromJson<PlaceToVisitResponse>();

      Assert.AreEqual(
        placeToReplaceWith.Description,
        receivedPlace.Place.Description);
}
```

If we looked at this test on the wire, we'd see the following:

```
PUT http://localhost:28192/places/3 HTTP/1.1
Content-Type: application/json
Accept: application/json
Accept-Encoding: gzip,deflate
Host: localhost:28192
Content-Length: 63
Expect: 100-continue


{"Id":3,"Name":"Ottawa","Description":"Capital city of Kansas"}
```

Testing DELETE

DeleteFromUrl allows us to perform DELETE actions. Delete differs in that we don't provide a request body to the method because in the HTTP specification DELETE is not allowed a body; it's just an action sent to a specific URL. Here's how DELETE can be used:

```
[Test]
public void DeleteShouldDeletePlace()
{

  (URLBase + "/places/{0}")
    .Fmt(2)
    .DeleteFromUrl(responseFilter: response =>
        Assert.AreEqual(HttpStatusCode.NoContent,
        response.StatusCode))
    .FromJson<PlaceToVisitResponse>();


  var placesAfterDelete = (URLBase + "/places")
      .GetJsonFromUrl(responseFilter: response =>
        Assert.AreEqual(HttpStatusCode.OK, response.StatusCode))
      .FromJson<PlaceToVisitResponse>();

  Assert.IsFalse(
    placesAfterDelete.Places.Any(p => p.Name.Contains("Sydney")));
}
```

DeleteFromUrl sends the following across the wire:

```
DELETE http://localhost:28192/places/2 HTTP/1.1
Accept: */*
Accept-Encoding: gzip,deflate
Host: localhost:28192
```

Another thing that's different about this example is that ServiceStack doesn't return a **200 OK** on a `DELETE` call—it returns a **204 No Content** response. Make sure the response filter you pass in to `GetJsonFromUrl` takes that in to account.

Using these `HTTP` utilities allows us to have fine-grained control over how we test.

Accessing the request-and-response object with the JsonServiceClient

ServiceStack provides many tools that allow a developer to access `REST` services. These tools can be very useful in building automated tests that can increase developer confidence with the solution being developed.

From time to time, you might need to test for the presence of a specific header in a response or to simulate a client that provides a specific header in a request. `JsonServiceClient` allows you to customize a request header before sending it and to access the raw response object as it is received in order to make assertions about the status of the request and response.

Getting ready

While this technique is easy once you know the trick, it can take a bit of hunting around. We can show the power of request and response filters in a simple testing scenario. We'll start off with a `JsonServiceClient` object like in the following code:

```
var client = new JsonServiceClient(
  "http://localhost:28192");
```

How to do it...

From there, we can hook in to a `RequestFilter` property on the client. `RequestFilter` is a kind of `Action<WebRequest>` class that will run once the client has created the request but prior to firing it off. We can add a simple one like this:

```
var client = new JsonServiceClient(
               "http://localhost:28192")
           {
             RequestFilter =
```

```
            request =>
            request.Headers.Add("REIDSON-CUSTOM-HEADER",
            "FLUX-CAPACITOR-PRESENT")
    };
```

This code adds a custom header with an associated value to the headers, but we could have done anything else that you would want to do with a request.

How it works...

What ServiceStack's `JsonServiceClient` class does under the covers is that it executes our action on `WebRequest`, which it builds up just before connecting to the remote server. The actual HTTP request that is sent shows you the result:

```
GET http://localhost:28192/places HTTP/1.1
Accept: application/json
User-Agent: ServiceStack .NET Client 4.020
Accept-Encoding: gzip,deflate
REIDSON-CUSTOM-HEADER: FLUX-CAPACITOR-PRESENT
Host: localhost:28192
Connection: Keep-Alive
```

There's more...

Additionally, you can also tap in to HTTP responses that `JsonServiceClient` receives to inspect them closely—for instance, to look for a specific response header or debug something that isn't being deserialized properly. `ResponseFilter` works in a manner similar to `RequestFilter`, except that it expects `HttpWebResponse` instead of `WebRequest`. The code looks similar too, as follows:

```
string responseHeader = null;
var client = new JsonServiceClient("http://localhost:28192")
            {
                ResponseFilter =
                    resp =>
                    responseHeader = resp.Headers.Get("Content-type")
            };
var response = client.Get(new AllPlacesToVisitRequest());
Assert.AreEqual("application/json; charset=utf-8",
responseHeader);
```

The code here passes in `<HttpWebResponse>` that analyzes the content-type header of the response and captures the value so that we can make assertions on it later.

Continuous Integration with TeamCity and self-hosted services

When more than one programmer is writing code in a project, it's possible that one person will make changes to the source code that will conflict with the changes that the second person is making. In the past, teams would often have a person dedicated to just building the code. This seems like a foreign concept today, thanks to Continuous Integration systems, such as ThoughtWorks's open source Go Continuous Delivery and JetBrains's TeamCity, and classic open source systems like Jenkins. Today, teams can easily access the benefits of **Continuous Integration** (**CI**)—a known, up-to-date, and controlled build environment that is distinct from the ones developers have so that a team can have confidence that the solution still works in other environments, getting past most "it works on my machine" problems. In this recipe, we'll show you how to get started with Continuous Integration on your project using JetBrains's popular TeamCity.

Getting ready

TeamCity has two basic components: a server process and a build agent. Build agents check out code, run build steps, such as MSBuild and MSTest, report progress, and then wait in a queue for more requests.

The server process hosts a dashboard where you can monitor builds, keeps the configuration, and manages build agents, licensing, and administration.

What we'll do is install both and then configure our build to check out some code and build it.

To grab the latest version of TeamCity, you can go to `http://www.jetbrains.com/teamcity` and download the latest version. You can install it on Mac, Windows, and Linux; we'll stick to Windows in this recipe though.

You'll need a central integration repository. Even when using **Distributed Current Version Systems** (**DCVS**), such as Git and Mercurial, it's common for a team to have a single central repository that they push code to when they want the Continuous Integration system to validate the new build.

You will also need a machine to run TeamCity. You can use a VM on your PC, a cloud host, or just run TeamCity directly on your primary development machine. In a team environment, it's wise to install TeamCity on a server that all the developers can connect to.

While it's possible to run the Build Agent on the same machine with the server process, it's good to keep in mind that your Continuous Integration system can only build new source code when a Build Agent isn't busy. If it takes twenty minutes to check out your code, build it, and run your test suite, and developers are pushing once per hour, you're in good shape. If that ratio goes the wrong way, you'll be able to tell, as your Build Agent won't be finishing builds fast enough. At that point, it might be smart to add more agents.

How to do it...

Once you've downloaded TeamCity, run its installer. It will install the server process and the Build Agent. It's best to create a new administrative user for the Build Agent, and configure TeamCity to run as that user as running a Build Agent as the system account will mean that its PATH and other environment variables will be hard to manage.

If you receive an error message about your administrative user not having permission to Logon as a service, run `secpol.msc`, and grant the right to the user in question, as follows:

1. Configure the server and note the port it's listening in on. When configuring the Build Agent, make sure that the server address includes the correct port and application root.

2. Visit the admin site on the server process with a web browser, where you'll be prompted through a first-visit configuration, including setting up usernames for each developer and agreeing to the licensing.

3. You can then create a new project to start building some code. You can choose **Project by URL** to have TeamCity autoconfigure certain aspects of this process. For instance, add `https://github.com/Reidson-Industries/places-to-visit.git` and accept the defaults.

4. Next we'll configure the build steps. TeamCity can auto-detect build steps, picking up your solution file, and auto-building any projects inside it.

5. If your project uses NuGet, you can instruct TeamCity to first update any NuGet packages it finds. You can configure TeamCity to either search through the solution file or reference your `packages.config` files.

6. Viewing the dashboard will show you that TeamCity has checked out your code, updated the system with the NuGet packages it found, and processed your build steps as you configured it.

Here's how the resultant screen looks:

How it works...

The TeamCity server process monitors your remote integration repository looking for changes. When it sees them, it sends information to a Build Agent waiting in the queue—the Build Agent then checks out your code and runs any steps necessary.

In complex environments, it's possible to have agents that run Windows building and testing Windows software while Linux agents build and test other projects. TeamCity gracefully handles most languages and frameworks and even includes integration with several useful plugins that perform code analysis—you can even configure your server to fail the build if your cyclomatic complexity gets too high.

There's more...

It's important to keep in mind that having a CI system automatically run your build and tests doesn't mean that developers don't need to perform the tests locally before committing changes. It can be very detrimental to team velocity when a developer checks in code that breaks the build. Developers should still be building and running their test suites locally on their computers before pushing to the integration repository.

Logging with a choice of frameworks

In this recipe, we will look at a few ways ServiceStack allows you to perform logging in your application. There are lots of options to choose from in log frameworks in .NET, and a lot of developers have specific frameworks they prefer. ServiceStack provides a couple of simple interfaces to enable developers to make their own choice while still providing simple implementations for developers who just want to get something logging. Let's have a look at some of our choices.

Note that evolving your logging strategy over time might require looking at several different concepts—auditing, tracing, access logs, error logs, and others included. We'll cover a simple scenario to get you started down this path in this recipe—a full exploration is outside of the scope of this book.

Getting ready

First, we need some services to log from. We are going to use the `GreetingsService` class to show a simple example of how we can incorporate logging into our ServiceStack application. If you are setting up your own project, please go to *Creating a ServiceStack solution with Visual Studio and NuGet* in *Appendix A, Getting Started* for help with setting up a new project.

ServiceStack provides several adapters for different logging implementations:

- **Log4Net**: This adapter handles binding to the popular Log4Net framework. This is included in the `ServiceStack.Logging.Log4Net` NuGet package.
- **EventLog**: This adapter handles logging to the Windows `EventLog`. This is only appropriate for Windows-based hosts.
- **ELMAH**: The `ServiceStack.Logging.ELMAH` NuGet package provides integration with the popular **Error Logging Modules and Handlers** (**ELMAH**) framework.
- **Console Log**: This is included in the base ServiceStack packages. This logs messages to a terminal.
- **Debug Log**: This is included in the base ServiceStack packages and is intended for development time.

For the purpose of this recipe, we'll use the EventLog adapter.

How to do it...

Now that we have some services, let's start with some of the loggers ServiceStack provides. If you are using Visual Studio Express 2013 for Web with IIS express, the simplest logger that ServiceStack provides to get working is the event logger.

To log something, you will need an instance of an `ILog` object, which `ILogFactory` provides via the `GetLogger` function that takes any type.

There are two common ways you could access your `ILogFactory` instance from your service or elsewhere in your application. The first way is using the static `LogManager` class and the registered `LogFactory` property, as follows:

```
LogManager.LogFactory = new EventLogFactory(
"Recipe 6 via LogManager");
```

This should be registered in the constructor of your application host:

```
public AppHost()
    : base("Recipe 6 - Logging with your favorite logger",
    typeof(GreetingService).Assembly)
{
    LogManager.LogFactory = new EventLogFactory(
    "Recipe 6 via LogManager");
}
```

Once it has been registered, this can be accessed the same way from your services:

```
var logManagerLogger = LogManager.GetLogger(GetType());
logManagerLogger.Info("Greeting sent to - " + request.Name);
```

Now, we can log different levels of information, such as `Debug`, `Error`, `Fatal`, `Info`, and `Warn`, via their respective function names provided by the `ILog` interface.

The second way is leveraging inversion of control to provide the service with `ILog` or `ILogFactory`, as follows:

```
container.Register<ILogFactory>(
new EventLogFactory("Recipe 6 via IoC"));
container.Register<ILog>(
container.Resolve<ILogFactory>().GetLogger(GetType()));
```

We can then log from our service using any of these methods of providing the `ILog` instance:

```
public class GreetingService : Service
{
  public ILog IoCLogger { get; set; }
```

```
public ILog LogManagerLogger { get; set; }

public GreetingService()
{
  LogManagerLogger = LogManager.GetLogger(GetType());
}

public object Get(GreetingRequest request)
{
  //Created from Funq container
  IoCLogger.Debug("Greeting sent to - " + request.Name);

  //Created from LogManager as needed
  var logManagerLogger = LogManager.GetLogger(GetType());
  logManagerLogger.Error("Greeting sent to - " + request.Name);

  //LogManager wrapped in a property
  LogManagerLogger.Fatal("Greeting sent to - " + request.Name);
  return "Hello, " + request.Name + "!";
}
}
```

After you hit the service, we can now expect lots of logging on each request. To see it, open up **Event Viewer** in Windows, and check the **Application** log. Close to the top, you should find events for each log event raised, as follows:

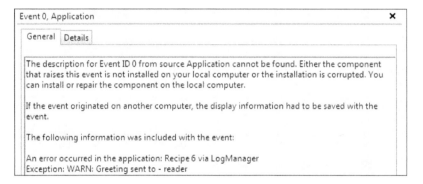

How it works...

This example is just the use of one of the loggers that ServiceStack supports. What is great about this approach is that regardless of which logger implementation you choose, the use and registration of an `ILogFactory` and `ILog` instance are the same.

`EventLogFactory` is obviously not suitable for larger-scale applications that might need more control over its logging. ServiceStack also has wrappers for the more popular and feature-rich loggers, such as `Log4Net`, `Elmah`, and `NLog`.

There's more...

Let's have a quick look at how we can incorporate a simple `Log4Net` file logger to our application. We will first need the correct configuration for `Log4Net` for `RollingFileAppender` to support this functionality. Within the `configuration` element of `web.config`, add the following:

```
<configSections>
  <section name="log4net" type="log4net.Config.
Log4NetConfigurationSectionHandler, log4net" />
</configSections>
<log4net>
  <appender name="RollingFileAppender" type="log4net.Appender.
  RollingFileAppender">
    <file value="log.txt" />
    <appendToFile value="true" />
    <rollingStyle value="Size" />
    <maxSizeRollBackups value="10" />
    <maximumFileSize value="250KB" />
    <staticLogFileName value="true" />
    <layout type="log4net.Layout.PatternLayout">
      <conversionPattern value="%date [%thread] %-5level %logger
      [%property{NDC}] - %message%newline" />
    </layout>
  </appender>
  <root>
    <level value="INFO" />
    <appender-ref ref="RollingFileAppender" />
  </root>
</log4net>
```

This provides the `Log4Net` library enough information to log information to a specified file `log.txt`. Since a path is not absolute, it will be relative to the application, for example, one directory up from the `bin` folder of the application.

Now, we will need to register `Log4netFactory` with `LogManager` or inject it into our `IoC` container just like we did for `EventLogFactory`:

```
LogManager.LogFactory = new Log4NetFactory(true);
container.Register<ILogFactory>(new Log4NetFactory(true));
```

This is how the resultant screen looks:

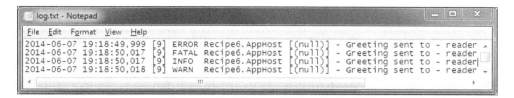

The code in our service remains the same due to ServiceStack providing the single interface for logging.

Writing a logger to monitor exceptions via e-mail

In this recipe, we will look at creating a simple way to make sure you're aware of any exceptions your web services are throwing. We will write our own implementation of `ILog` and `ILogFactory` that ServiceStack provides as a generic way of logging information.

We have had mixed experiences with e-mail loggers in large-scale production environments—it's not a great practice unless a significant amount of sophisticated logic goes into figuring out which errors constitute something interesting, and which don't. Having said that, it's still a useful technique for smaller applications and makes a great example for how to structure your own logger.

Getting ready

First, we will need some services to work with. In this example, we will use `GreetingService`, so we can focus on how we can incorporate our e-mail logger to the application. If you are starting from a new project, please read *Creating a ServiceStack solution with Visual Studio and NuGet* in *Appendix A, Getting Started* on how to get the application up and running.

How to do it...

Since we want e-mails when an exception is thrown, we will have to register a function with the ServiceStack host to let us know when our service throws an exception.

 Your services should try to handle errors and throw the appropriate `HttpError` so that you have more control over throwing the appropriate error code.

What we need to do is create a method that we can add to the
ServiceExceptionHandlers collection. The following method has the right signature:

```
public object EmailExceptions(IRequest httpReq, object request,
Exception ex)
{
    var logger = LogManager.GetLogger(GetType());
    logger.Error(ex.Message, ex);
    return DtoUtils.CreateErrorResponse(request, ex);
}
//… in the constructor of the AppHost
this.ServiceExceptionHandlers.Add(EmailExceptions);
```

Now we need to create our ILogFactory and ILog implementations for e-mailing. We will
create a wrapper around .NET's e-mail-related classes, as follows:

```
public class EmailLogFactory : ILogFactory
{

    SmtpClient smtpClient;
    string emailFrom;
    string emailTo;
    public EmailLogFactory(SmtpClient client, string emailFrom,
    string emailTo)
    {
        this.smtpClient = client;
        this.emailFrom = emailFrom;
        this.emailTo = emailTo;
    }

    public ILog GetLogger(string typeName)
    {
        return new EmailLogger(smtpClient, emailFrom, emailTo);
    }

    public ILog GetLogger(Type type)
    {
        return new EmailLogger(smtpClient, emailFrom, emailTo);
    }
}
```

`EmailLogFactory` must return an `ILog` implementation from its `GetLogger` functions:

```
public class EmailLogger : ILog
{
    SmtpClient smtpClient;
    string emailFrom;
    string emailTo;
    public EmailLogger(
            SmtpClient client,string emailFrom, string emailTo)
    {
        this.smtpClient = client;
        this.emailFrom = emailFrom;
        this.emailTo = emailTo;
    }

    public void Debug(object message, Exception exception)
    {
        MailMessage mailMsg = new MailMessage(emailFrom, emailTo);
        mailMsg.Subject = "DEBUG: " + message.ToString();
        mailMsg.Body = "DEBUG: " + message.ToString() +
                    Environment.NewLine + exception.StackTrace;
        smtpClient.Send(mailMsg);
    }

    public void Debug(object message)
    {
        MailMessage mailMsg = new MailMessage(emailFrom, emailTo);
        mailMsg.Subject = "DEBUG: " + message.ToString();
        smtpClient.Send(mailMsg);
    }

    public void DebugFormat(string format, params object[] args)
    {
        throw new NotImplementedException();
    }

    public void Error(object message, Exception exception)
    {
        MailMessage mailMsg = new MailMessage(emailFrom, emailTo);
        mailMsg.Subject = "Error: " + message.ToString();
        mailMsg.Body = "Error: " + message.ToString() +
```

```
                    Environment.NewLine + exception.StackTrace;
        smtpClient.Send(mailMsg);
    }

    public void Error(object message)
    {
        MailMessage mailMsg = new MailMessage(emailFrom, emailTo);
        mailMsg.Subject = "Error: " + message.ToString();
        smtpClient.Send(mailMsg);
    }

    public void ErrorFormat(string format, params object[] args)
    {
        throw new NotImplementedException();
    }

    public void Fatal(object message, Exception exception)
    {
        MailMessage mailMsg = new MailMessage(emailFrom, emailTo);
        mailMsg.Subject = "Fatal: " + message.ToString();
        mailMsg.Body = "Fatal: " + message.ToString() +
        Environment.NewLine + exception.StackTrace;
        smtpClient.Send(mailMsg);
    }

    public void Fatal(object message)
    {
        MailMessage mailMsg = new MailMessage(emailFrom, emailTo);
        mailMsg.Subject = "Fatal: " + message.ToString();
        smtpClient.Send(mailMsg);
    }

    public void FatalFormat(string format, params object[] args)
    {
        throw new NotImplementedException();
    }

    public void Info(object message, Exception exception)
    {
        MailMessage mailMsg = new MailMessage(emailFrom, emailTo);
        mailMsg.Subject = "Info: " + message.ToString();
        mailMsg.Body = "Info: " + message.ToString() +
```

```
        Environment.NewLine + exception.StackTrace;
        smtpClient.Send(mailMsg);
    }

    public void Info(object message)
    {
        MailMessage mailMsg = new MailMessage(emailFrom, emailTo);
        mailMsg.Subject = "Info: " + message.ToString();
        smtpClient.Send(mailMsg);
    }

    public void InfoFormat(string format, params object[] args)
    {
        throw new NotImplementedException();
    }

    public bool IsDebugEnabled
    {
        get { return true; }
    }

    public void Warn(object message, Exception exception)
    {
        MailMessage mailMsg = new MailMessage(emailFrom, emailTo);
        mailMsg.Subject = "Warn: " + message.ToString();
        mailMsg.Body = "Warn: " + message.ToString() +
        Environment.NewLine + exception.StackTrace;
        smtpClient.Send(mailMsg);
    }

    public void Warn(object message)
    {
        MailMessage mailMsg = new MailMessage(emailFrom, emailTo);
        mailMsg.Subject = "Warn: " + message.ToString();
        smtpClient.Send(mailMsg);
    }

    public void WarnFormat(string format, params object[] args)
    {
        throw new NotImplementedException();
    }
}
```

In our `AppHost` class, we want to create and register `ILogFactory`:

```
public AppHost()
  : base("Recipe 7 - Monitoring service exceptions via emails",
    typeof(GreetingService).Assembly)
{
  this.ServiceExceptionHandlers.Add(EmailExceptions);
}

public object EmailExceptions(IRequest httpReq,
object request, Exception ex)
{
  Container.Resolve<EmailLogFactory>()
    .GetLogger(GetType())
    .Error(ex.Message, ex);
  return DtoUtils.CreateErrorResponse(request, ex);
}

public override void Configure(Funq.Container container)
{
  var smtpClient = new SmtpClient();
  smtpClient.Host = "smtp.example.com";
  smtpClient.Credentials = new NetworkCredential(
  "email", "password");
  var emailLogger = new EmailLogFactory(
  smtpClient, "system@example.com", "reader@example.com");

  container.Register(emailLogger);

  ILog logger = new EventLogger("Application",
  "Recipe 7 - Monitoring service exceptions via emails");
  container.Register(logger);
}
```

In our service, we will have a simple check that will generate an exception for us to e-mail, as follows:

```
public object Get(GreetingRequest request)
{
    if (request.Name == null || request.Name.Length < 2)
    {
        throw new HttpError(400, "Name is too short");
    }
    return "Hello, " + request.Name + "!";
}
```

One more thing we will need to do to test this our services and make sure our new e-mail monitoring will behave as expected. We don't want to send real e-mails to a real server when testing locally, we first want to see whether the e-mails being generated have the right content and are formatted as expected. The easiest way to do this is to configure the application to save these e-mails to folder somewhere. To do this, add the following to your `web.config` or `app.config` files accordingly. Remember to check or change the folder location to somewhere that exists on your local computer:

```
<system.net>
  <mailSettings>
    <smtp deliveryMethod="SpecifiedPickupDirectory">
      <specifiedPickupDirectory pickupDirectoryLocation="C:\Temp"/>
    </smtp>
  </mailSettings>
</system.net>
```

If we try to send a `GET` request to `/hello/z`, we get the following response:

Response Status

Error Code   Name is too short

Message   Name is too short

Stack Trace

[GreetingRequest: 8/06/2014 6:37:56 AM]: [REQUEST: {Name:z}]
ServiceStack.HttpError: Name is too short at
Greetings.ServiceInterface.GreetingService.Get(GreetingRequest
request) in c:\projects\service-stack-book\src\Chapter 3\Recipe
6\Greetings.ServiceInterface\GreetingService.cs:line 14 at
lambda_method(Closure , Object , Object) at
ServiceStack.Host.ServiceRunner`1.Execute(IRequest request,
Object instance, TRequest requestDto)

We also get the following e-mail saved in our location that has the following content:

Sun 8/06/2014 4:38 PM
system@example.com
Error: ServiceBase<TRequest>::Service Exception

To   reader@example.com

Error: ServiceBase<TRequest>::Service Exception
  at Greetings.ServiceInterface.GreetingService.Get(GreetingRequest request) in c:\projects\service-stack-book\src\Chapter 3\Recipe 6\Greetings.ServiceInterface\GreetingService.cs:line 14
  at lambda_method(Closure , Object , Object)
  at ServiceStack.Host.ServiceRunner`1.Execute(IRequest request, Object instance, TRequest requestDto)

How it works...

ServiceStack provides the `ILog` and `ILogFactory` interfaces as a way to abstract how your services log information. This allows us to create our own logger relatively simply, and if we had code elsewhere in the application, none of that would need to change with the introduction of a new logger.

To deal with exceptions from our services, ServiceStack also provides a delegate so that we can listen to these events.

There are logging frameworks that offer e-mail logging as a part of their suite, such as `Log4Net`, and the techniques in this recipe can be adapted to handle exceptions the same way.

There's more...

A pattern that can prove useful in the case of custom logging is writing a custom implementation of `ILog` and `ILogFactory` to encapsulate requirements around logging itself. For example, if you inherit a system that you are migrating to ServiceStack, there might be some custom logic and classes around logging that might be quite difficult to rewrite into a sophisticated logging framework, such as `Log4Net`, but can be wrapped quite easily using the interfaces provided.

Another example is that you might want simple behavior from multiple existing loggers. It might be easier to create a decorator implementation around them in your own `ILogFactory` and `ILog` interfaces rather than move to another framework.

Object Relational Mapping (OrmLite)

In this chapter, we will cover the following topics:

- Modeling your database with types and attributes
- Using and accessing OrmLite
- Using OrmLite filters to create audit functionality
- CRUD and other common operations
- Utilizing stored procedures using OrmLite
- Mapping custom queries using POCOs
- Starting with an existing database with the OrmLite and T4 templates
- Working with Entity Framework and ServiceStack

Introduction

One of the great components of ServiceStack is OrmLite. In this chapter, we will cover some of the functionality OrmLite provides while using practical patterns to keep your code clean and maintainable. OrmLite is a lightweight object-relational mapping framework that focuses on simplicity and performance. We will look at how you can use OrmLite in your application along with some of the common syntax to make queries, including the use of stored procedures and strongly typed SQL expressions. We will also show you how your database can be modeled with POCOs and its attributes, and use OrmLite T4 templates to quickly prototype against an existing database.

Modeling your database with types and attributes

OrmLite provides several attributes that you can use to annotate your data types—several of these allow you to control the underlying table schema. For instance, you can assert that a specific field be indexed to auto-increment integers and assign primary and foreign key relationships. In this recipe, we'll show you how.

Getting ready

In this recipe, we'll start with a basic data model using SQLite and OrmLite. We'll build up our types and view the schema that OrmLite creates. Then, we'll apply various attributes and see how the schema changes. To get started, you'll need a new project created either using a template from the ServiceStackVS extension or by following the section *Creating a ServiceStack solution with Visual Studio and NuGet* in *Appendix A, Getting Started*.

How to do it...

1. Install the `Sqlite.OrmLite` NuGet package to your application. This will be needed whenever you register `IDbConnectionFactory` with `ServiceStackHost`, usually your `AppHost` class. The following code will do the trick:

    ```
    Install-Package ServiceStack.OrmLite.Sqlite.Windows
    ```

2. Create some classes in your `ServiceModel` project that will be used to persist data to our SQLite database:

    ```
    public class UserGreeting
    {
      public string Greeting { get; set; }
    }
    public class UserLanguage
    {
      public string Language { get; set; }
    }
    ```

3. Add an `Id` property of the type `int` to both `UserGreeting` and `UserLanguage`, and attribute this property with the `[AutoIncrement]` attribute. The code can also be written in the following manner:

    ```
    public class UserGreeting
    {
        [AutoIncrement]
    ```

```
    public int Id { get; set; }
    public string Greeting { get; set; }
}
```

4. Use `[References(typeof(UserLanguage))]` in the `UserGreeting` class to create a foreign-key relationship with `UserLanguage`, as follows:

```
public class UserGreeting
{
    [AutoIncrement]
    public int Id { get; set; }
    public string Greeting { get; set; }

    [References(typeof(UserLanguage))]
    public int UserLanguageId { get; set; }

    [Reference]
    public UserLanguage Language { get; set; }
}
```

5. Create and register `IDbConnectionFactory`, which uses the SQLite provider in your `AppHost.Configure()` method:

```
var dbFactory = new OrmLiteConnectionFactory(
  "~/App_Data/db.sqlite".MapHostAbsolutePath(),
  SqliteDialect.Provider);
container.Register<IDbConnectionFactory>(dbFactory);
```

6. Also, in your `AppHost.Configure()` method, create the `UserGreeting` and `GreetingUsage` tables and seed some greetings, as follows:

```
using(var dbConnection = dbFactory.OpenDbConnection())
{
    dbConnection.DropAndCreateTable<UserGreeting>();
    dbConnection.DropAndCreateTable<UserLanuage>();
}

using (var dbConnection = dbFactory.OpenDbConnection())
{
    dbConnection.Insert(
        new UserLanguage {Language = "English"});

    dbConnection.Insert<UserGreeting>(new UserGreeting
    {
        Greeting = "Hello, {0}",
        UserLanguageId = 1
```

```
        });

        dbConnection.Insert<UserGreeting>(new UserGreeting
        {
            Greeting = "G'day, {0}"
        });
        dbConnection.Insert<UserGreeting>(new UserGreeting
        {
            Greeting = "Howdy, {0}!"
        });
    }
```

7. Create a request-and-response object to be used with `GreetingsService`:

```
[Route("/greetings/{Id}/sayto/{Name}")]
public class GetUserGreeting
{
    public int Id { get; set; }
    public string Name { get; set; }
}


public class GetUserGreetingResponse
{
    public string Result { get; set; }
}
```

8. Create a service that will return the greeting with the name provided:

```
public class GreetingsService : Service
{
    public object Any(GetUserGreeting request)
    {
        var userGreeting =
        Db.SingleById<UserGreeting>(request.Id);
        if (userGreeting == null)
        {
            throw HttpError.NotFound("Greeting not found");
        }

        return new GetUserGreetingResponse
        {
            Result = userGreeting.Greeting.Fmt(request.Name)
        };
    }
}
```

How it works...

Initially, we started with two very basic classes: `UserLanguage`, to model the concept of a language and `UserGreeting` to model the concept of a greeting. In this basic example, you can simply store the language in the greeting, but this design will allow each concept to evolve on its own. Also, OrmLite naturally creates one table per class, so in this design we'll end up with two tables, which is useful for showing how foreign-key relationships work.

If we ran the application with `UserGreeting` and `UserLanguage` how they were after step two, then we can inspect the schema and see the following basic tables. As you can see, OrmLite has elected to create a primary key constraint on the only possible field:

```
sqlite> .schema
CREATE TABLE "UserGreeting"
(
   "Greeting" VARCHAR(8000) PRIMARY KEY
);
CREATE TABLE "UserLanguage"
(
   "Language" VARCHAR(8000) PRIMARY KEY
);
```

OrmLite provides a range of attributes to help us model our database; we will be looking at the following attributes:

- ▶ PrimaryKey
- ▶ Reference
- ▶ AutoIncrement
- ▶ Index

PrimaryKey attribute

We can now add an `Id` property to our models. This is a very common practice when dealing with relational databases and very useful for many reasons. Here's how the `Id` property can be added to our models:

```
public class UserGreeting
{
    public int Id { get; set; }
    public string Greeting { get; set; }
}
public class UserLanguage
```

```
    {
        public int Id { get; set; }
        public string Language { get; set; }
    }
```

Now, when we inspect the schema, we can tell that OrmLite has elected to treat our new Id fields as the primary key, as follows:

```
sqlite> .schema
CREATE TABLE "UserGreeting"
(

  "Id" INTEGER PRIMARY KEY,
  "Greeting" VARCHAR(8000) NULL
);
CREATE TABLE "UserLanguage"
(

  "Id" INTEGER PRIMARY KEY,
  "Language" VARCHAR(8000) NULL
);
```

It did this based on convention—OrmLite looks for a field named Id. If it doesn't find that, it will select the first suitable field. If OrmLite doesn't find a property named Id or usage of the [PrimaryKey] attribute, it will simply use the first property in the class. If the property you want to be used as the primary key doesn't follow the convention, the use of the [PrimaryKey] attribute takes precedence. Here's how you can write the code for this bit of information:

```
    public class UserLanguage
    {
      public int CountryCode { get; set; }
      [PrimaryKey]
      public int CID { get; set; }
      public string Language { get; set; }
    }
```

Since our intended CID field isn't named Id, and it isn't the first field, marking it as [PrimaryKey] ensures that OrmLite will set it up correctly, as follows:

```
sqlite> .schema
CREATE TABLE "UserLanguage"
(

  "CountryCode" INTEGER NOT NULL,
```

```
  "CID" INTEGER PRIMARY KEY,
  "Language" VARCHAR(8000) NULL
);
```

AutoIncrement attribute

It's easy to make sure that an integer field has an auto-incrementing value. You can simply annotate that field with the [AutoIncrement] attribute, as follows:

```
public class UserLanguage
{
  [AutoIncrement]
  public int Id { get; set; }
  public string Language { get; set; }
}
```

OrmLite will comply and make sure that the underlying table supports this:

```
sqlite> .schema
CREATE TABLE "UserLanguage"
(
  "Id" INTEGER PRIMARY KEY AUTOINCREMENT,
  "Language" VARCHAR(8000) NULL
);
```

References attribute

If you'd like to model a foreign-key relationship, the References attribute supports this. The argument you provide is the type that the foreign key relates to. For instance, to create a foreign-key relationship between UserLanguage and UserGreeting, we can represent that with the References attribute, as follows:

```
public class UserLanguage
{
  [AutoIncrement]
  public int Id { get; set; }
  public string Language { get; set; }
}
public class UserGreeting
{
  [AutoIncrement]
  public int Id { get; set; }
```

```
    public string Greeting { get; set; }

    [References(typeof(UserLanguage))]
    public int LanguageId { get; set; }
}
```

Thanks to the `References` attribute mentioned previously, OrmLite will create tables with a corresponding foreign key, as follows:

```
sqlite> .schema
CREATE TABLE "UserGreeting"
(

  "Id" INTEGER PRIMARY KEY AUTOINCREMENT,

  "Greeting" VARCHAR(8000) NULL,

  "LanguageId" INTEGER NOT NULL,


  CONSTRAINT "FK_UserGreeting_UserLanguage_LanguageId" FOREIGN KEY
  ("LanguageId") REFERENCES "UserLanguage" ("Id")
);
CREATE TABLE "UserLanguage"
(

  "Id" INTEGER PRIMARY KEY AUTOINCREMENT,

  "Language" VARCHAR(8000) NULL
);
```

There's more...

Whenever you create your tables using OrmLite, OrmLite will represent the classes it's given in the underlying database technology—in this example SQLite. Value type properties, such as `int`, `string`, and so on, will be represented by database fields, while complex properties that are not used in an existing relationship will be serialized automatically and stored as JSON. Depending on the database, complex fields might have different types depending on their level of JSON support. For example, let's create a table to store the usage of each greeting. It will have a foreign-key relationship to `UserGreeting`, but store the language as a serialized blob. Create the table in the following manner:

```
public class GreetingUsage
{
    [AutoIncrement]
    public int Id { get; set; }

    [References(typeof(UserGreeting))]
    public int UserGreetingId { get; set; }

    [Reference]
    public UserGreeting UserGreeting { get; set; }

    public UserLanguage Language { get; set; }
}

public object Any(GetUserGreeting request)
{
    var userGreeting =
        Db.LoadSingleById<UserGreeting>(request.Id);
    if (userGreeting == null)
    {
        throw HttpError.NotFound("Greeting not found");
    }

    Db.Insert(
        new GreetingUsage
        {
            UserGreetingId = userGreeting.Id,
            Language = userGreeting.Language
        });

    return new GetUserGreetingResponse
    {
        Result = userGreeting.Greeting.Fmt(request.Name)
    };
}
```

We are using the `[References(typeof(UserGreeting))]` attribute for our `UserGreetingId` relationship combined with the `UserGreeting` property with the `[Reference]` attribute. The `[Reference]` attribute lets OrmLite know that this property is used in an existing foreign-key relationship. The `UserGreeting` complex type will not be blobbed and will remain null when used with `Db.SingleById<GreetingUsage>()`. If we use a `Db.Load*` query, complex type properties with the attribute `[Reference]` will be populated base on a foreign key relationship of the same type. If a complex type property exists without the `[Reference]` attribute, it is automatically serialized and stored as previously explained:

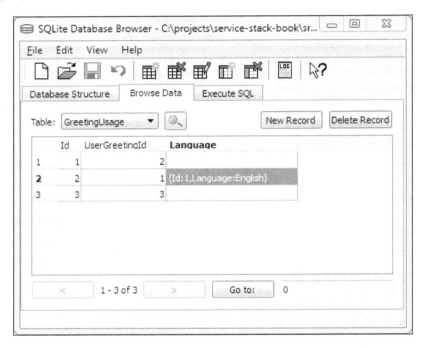

Using and accessing OrmLite

When writing applications for the Web, it's almost inevitable that some kind of persistence of data will be required. Object-relational mapping is a technique that enables us to handle tables, columns, and rows and match them to objects in your application. There are many ORM frameworks in .NET, such as Entity Framework, Lightspeed, NHibernate, and others. ServiceStack has its own ORM framework that follows a lot of the same design principles as the rest of the stack: simplicity and performance. OrmLite is really fast, simple, and supports many of the most popular database technologies, but it is different than the others listed as it is what's known as a **micro ORM** framework.

OrmLite doesn't try to solve all data-access problems in one framework, which makes the others complicated and sometimes hard to use, but it does make the most common tasks simple and fast. In this recipe, we will have a look at a simple use case to show how we can use and access OrmLite from our web services.

Getting ready

In this example, we will create a simple service that greets users in different ways based on a string format stored in the database. To get started, you'll need a new project created either using a template from the ServiceStackVS extension or by following the section *Creating a ServiceStack solution with Visual Studio and NuGet* in *Appendix A, Getting Started*.

How to do it...

1. Starting from a project template from ServiceStackVS or using the section *Creating a ServiceStack solution with Visual Studio and NuGet* in *Appendix A, Getting Started*, install the SQLite specific OrmLite package using the **Package Manager Console** and the following command:

   ```
   Install-Package ServiceStack.OrmLite.Sqlite.Windows
   ```

2. Create `OrmLiteConnectionFactory` with a local SQLite file connection string and the OrmLite SQLite provider, as follows:

   ```
   var dbFactory = new OrmLiteConnectionFactory(
       "~/App_Data/db.sqlite".MapHostAbsolutePath(),
       SqliteDialect.Provider);
   container.Register<IDbConnectionFactory>(dbFactory);
   ```

3. Register `IDbConnectionFactory` with the IoC container:

   ```
   container.Register<IDbConnectionFactory>(dbFactory);
   ```

4. Create our `UserGreeting` class, which will represent a table in our database:

   ```
   public class UserGreeting
   {
       [PrimaryKey]
       [AutoIncrement]
       public int Id { get; set; }
       public string Greeting { get; set; }
   }
   ```

5. Create and seed the `UserGreeting` table using OrmLite:

```
using(var dbConnection = dbFactory.OpenDbConnection())
{
    dbConnection.DropAndCreateTable<UserGreeting>();
}

using(var dbConnection = dbFactory.OpenDbConnection())
{
    dbConnection.Insert<UserGreeting>(new UserGreeting
    {
        Greeting = "Hello, {0}"
    });
    dbConnection.Insert<UserGreeting>(new UserGreeting
    {
        Greeting = "G'day, {0}"
    });
    dbConnection.Insert<UserGreeting>(new UserGreeting
    {
        Greeting = "Howdy, {0}"
    });
}
```

 The `DropAndCreate <T>` method is being used in this example to make it easy to try out and modify the example. The `CreateIfNotExists<T>` method would be a more appropriate method once changes to your database model are less frequent.

6. Create a request DTO to be used to handle the greeting request, as follows:

```
[Route("/greetings/{Id}/sayto/{Name}")]
public class UserGreeting
{
    public int Id { get; set; }
    public string Name { get; set; }
}
```

7. Create the greeting service to handle the request:

```
public class GreetingsService : Service
{
    public object Any(UserGreetingRequest request)
    {
        var userGreeting =
        Db.SingleById<UserGreeting>(request.Id);
```

```
        if (userGreeting == null)
        {
            throw HttpError.NotFound("Greeting not found");
        }

        return userGreeting.Greeting.Fmt(request.Name);
    }
```

How it works...

After installing the OrmLite framework, first we create `new OrmLiteConnectionFactory` class, which needs to be told what kind of database we are using. In this case, we will be using a SQLite database, so we will need to specify `SqliteDialect.Provider` as the `OrmLiteDialectProvider` class that is passed to the constructor of `IOrmLiteConnectionFactory` along with a connection string.

A dialect provider is the specific implementation that translates queries to OrmLite to the specific SQL query for the underlying database technology. This pattern used by OrmLite allows us to swap from SQLite to PostgresSQL simply by changing the dialect provider when instantiating `IDbConnectionFactory`.

> Different database technologies have varying support for different features, so not all queries translate in a one-to-one fashion. A good way to check what the result of an OrmLite query in the specific SQL syntax is to use `Db.GetLastSql()`. This to return a string of the last SQL statement generated by an OrmLite query.

To construct the connection string, we use the `.MapHostAbsolutePath()` method to provide the full filesystem path to our project and `App_Data` folder.

Once we have created the connection factory, we will need to register it using the inversion of control (IoC) container, as follows:

```
container.Register<IDbConnectionFactory>(dbFactory);
```

Now, we have a database connection, but we still don't have any tables in the database that will represent our object. We need to create our object, and with the use of some attributes this will specify what the table will look like. This is how we create an object and specify the table attributes:

```
public class UserGreeting
{
    [PrimaryKey]
    [AutoIncrement]
```

```
        public int Id { get; set; }
        public string Greeting { get; set; }
    }
```

Now in `AppHost`, we want to make sure this table is created. For this example, we will drop and create the table at the start of the application; however, as you can see in the commented out code, you can simply create the table when it doesn't yet exist.

Once created and seeded, our table has the structure and data in SQLite as shown in the following screenshot:

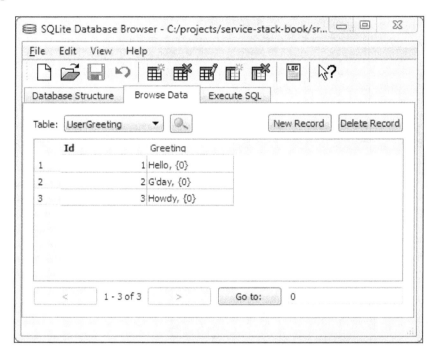

 A handy tool to work with SQLite database files can be found on Github and is now called SQLite Database Browser.

In the example service, we access the database via OrmLite using the syntax `Db.SingleById<UserGreeting>(request.Id)`. There are a few things to go over as to how this works.

The `Db` property is available from the ServiceStack base `Service` class from which services inherit, this is a helper property that creates `IDbConnection` to use when accessed. This property exposes a database connection that can be used from a service to a simply query using `IDbConnectionFactory`, which was registered in `AppHost`. In this example, a SQLite connection factory was registered using the following code:

```
var dbFactory = new OrmLiteConnectionFactory(
    "~/App_Data/db.sqlite".MapHostAbsolutePath(),
    SqliteDialect.Provider);
container.Register<IDbConnectionFactory>(dbFactory);
```

 Like a lot of components in ServiceStack, properties are injected using the IoC container. To use properties on the base `Service` class, you must register them with the IoC container. For example, the `Db` property requires that `IDbConnectionFactory` is registered, so the connections can be generated from the factory when the `Db` property is used.

If you want more control over the opening and closing of database connections, you can create a public `IDbConnectionFactory` property in your services to have your registered connection factory injected and available to use, as follows:

```
public IDbConnectionFactory DbConnectionFactory { get; set; }

using (var dbConnection = DbConnectionFactory.OpenDbConnection())
{
    userGreeting =
    dbConnection.SingleById<UserGreeting>(request.Id);
}
```

Like a lot of ORM frameworks, one of the benefits of writing code in this way is you can change the underlying SQL database technology without having to change your queries. This is done by specifying a different provider when `IDbConnectionFactory` is created. The SQL is generated using the specified dialect provider and information inferred from type information, attributes, and, when used, the `SqlExpression` builder.

The following code is an example of the main operations that can be performed with OrmLite to query SQL databases:

```
dbConnection.Insert<UserGreeting>(new UserGreeting
{
    Greeting = "Hello, {0}"
});
dbConnection.Update<UserGreeting>(new UserGreeting
{
    Greeting = "Hello, {0}"
```

```
});

List<UserGreeting> allRows = dbConnection.Select<UserGreeting>();

//Returns all UserGreetings that start with 'Hello'
List<UserGreeting> queryUsingLambaSyntax =
dbConnection.Select<UserGreeting>(
    dbConnection.From<UserGreeting>().Where(
    x => x.Greeting.StartsWith("Hello")
    ));
```

See also

▶ Refer to the *Mapping custom queries to POCOs* recipe

Using OrmLite filters to create audit functionality

This recipe will cover the use of OrmLite filters and how they can be used to audit what is being added, updated, and deleted in your database. We will also go over the creation of `ResultFilter` for OrmLite and how this could be incorporated into your own project. In *Chapter 1, Configuration and Routing* we wrapped this functionality into a plugin, while focusing on the plugin interface. In this recipe we will have a closer look at OrmLite filters.

Getting ready

In this example, we will use the `PlacesToVisit` domain to show how OrmLite filters can be used to help with requirements such as auditing or protecting sensitive information coming out of your database. To get started, you'll need a new project created either using a template from the ServiceStackVS extension or by following the section *Creating a ServiceStack solution with Visual Studio and NuGet* in *Appendix A, Getting Started*.

How to do it...

1. If we want our model objects to be auditable, first we will create an interface for them to implement, as follows:

```
public interface IAuditable
{
    DateTime Created { get; set; }
    DateTime Modified { get; set; }
}
```

2. Then, we can apply the interface to our `Place` model, as follows:

```
public class Place : IAuditable
{
    [Index]
    [PrimaryKey]
    [AutoIncrement]
    public int Id { get; set; }
    public string Name { get; set; }
    public string Description { get; set; }

    public DateTime Created { get; set; }

    public DateTime Modified { get; set; }
}
```

3. Now that our database knows how to store the additional information in our `Place` table, we need to populate those values with data at the time of an insert or update SQL command, as follows:

```
//Hook insert filter
OrmLiteConfig.InsertFilter = (dbCmd, rowObj) =>
{
    var auditObject = rowObj as IAuditable;
    if (auditObject != null)
    {
        var now = DateTime.UtcNow;
        auditObject.Created = now;
        auditObject.Modified = now;
    }
};

//Hook update filter
OrmLiteConfig.UpdateFilter = (dbCmd, rowObj) =>
{
    var auditObject = rowObj as IAuditable;
    if (auditObject != null)
    {
        var now = DateTime.UtcNow;
        auditObject.Modified = now;
    }
};
```

How it works...

Filters are functions that run at specific points during queries done by OrmLite. This allows interception of queries and updates to run your own business logic. This allows a high amount of code reuse and simplicity when dealing with your database queries.

Specifically, `UpdateFilter` and `InsertFilter` are functions that run before the update to the database has been persisted and allow us to manipulate the data before saving it. In this example, we are adding timestamps of `Created` and `Modified` to help us keep track of when specific entries were created and updated.

There's more...

If we had the requirement to make sure that specific names of places should be redacted from unauthenticated web services, we could use `OrmLiteResultsFilter`.

First, we need to create our custom results filter. For the example, we will create a filter that looks for the word `secret` in the name and removes it from the data returned to our application:

```
public class PlacesAuditFilter : OrmLiteResultsFilter
{
    public PlacesAuditFilter()
    {
        ResultsFn = PlacesFilter;
    }

    private IEnumerable<Place> PlacesFilter(IDbCommand dbCmd,
    Type place)
    {
        var results = dbCmd.ExecuteReader();
        var typedResults = results.ConvertToList<Place>();
        var secretResults = typedResults.Where(x =>
        x.Name.Contains("secret"));
        foreach (var item in secretResults)
        {
            item.Name = "[REDACTED]";
        }
        return typedResults;
    }
}
```

These filters are applied at the point your application queries your database with OrmLite, so they are strictly opt-in, allowing you to control when they should be used, and when they shouldn't, depending on your requirements. To use the filter, wrap the specific OrmLite query in a `using` statement of the filter, as follows:

```
if (!GetSession().IsAuthenticated)
    {
        using (var filter = new PlacesAuditFilter())
        {
            allPlaces = Db.Select<Place>().ToList();
        }
    }
    else
    {
        allPlaces = Db.Select<Place>().ToList();
    }
```

The previous code shows that only authenticated users will get unaltered results from the database, whereas unauthenticated users results will pass through `ResultsFilter` of `PlacesAuditFilter` before being returned.

`ResultsFilters` are performed before the normal database query return. This can make it ideal for mocking your database returns to isolate other functionality. For example, you could create OrmLite results to simulate a large number of results; these results would be added using the `ResultsFn` filter, which could generate these results. This could be used in a unit test by simply wrapping a database query in the filters using statement.

The filters themselves are also easily tested. In the upcoming text and code, we will test perform an insert query. Later we'll perform a select query with the filter. When used with the "`:memory:`" connection string, testing the functionality of the filter becomes quite simple, as follows:

```
[Test]
public void Places_filter_hide_names_with_secret()
{
    var dbConnectionFactory =
    appHost.Resolve<IDbConnectionFactory>();
    string placeNameResult = "";
    using (var db = dbConnectionFactory.OpenDbConnection())
    {
        db.Insert(new Place { Name = "secret - Test" });
    }
    using (var filter = new PlacesAuditFilter())
```

```
    {
        using (var db = dbConnectionFactory.OpenDbConnection())
        {
            var place = db.Select<Place>().First();
            placeNameResult = place.Name;
        }
    }
    Assert.That(placeNameResult, Is.EqualTo("[REDACTED]"));
}
```

In our example, we are altering sensitive information before it is returned from our web services. The filtered place coming from our services returns the following result from the /places URL:

```
{
    "Id": 4,
    "Name": "[REDACTED]",
    "Description": "Talk about tech",
    "Created": "/Date(1403092183318-0000)/",
    "Modified": "/Date(1403092183318-0000)/"
}
```

Whereas the same data from /places/4 returns the unfiltered results, as follows:

```
{
    "Place": {
        "Id": 4,
        "Name": "secret - Developer Meetup at Bob's Cafe",
        "Description": "Talk about tech",
        "Created": "/Date(1403092627143-0000)/",
        "Modified": "/Date(1403092627143-0000)/"
    }
}
```

The filter is only applied if the OrmLite database queries are made inside the using statement of PlaceAuditFilter.

CRUD and other common operations

When working with a database, CRUD often refers to Create, Read, Update, and Delete. With a relational database, this often maps to the Insert, Select, Update, and Delete operations. You can also loosely associate the concepts with the HTTP verbs GET, DELETE, POST, and PUT, even though it's not a perfect one-to-one mapping.

Getting ready

In this recipe, we will create a simple `Hello World` service that stores a formatted response of a simple greeting in a SQLite database that we can perform our CRUD operations on. To get started, you'll need a new project either created using a template from the ServiceStackVS extension or by following the section *Creating a ServiceStack solution with Visual Studio and NuGet* in *Appendix A, Getting Started*.

How to do it...

1. Create a model for the `UserGreeting` table, as follows. This will be the class we persist using OrmLite:

```
public class UserGreeting
{
    [PrimaryKey]
    [AutoIncrement]
    public int Id { get; set; }
    public string Greeting { get; set; }
}
```

2. Create a service model that will handle our requests and responses for our web service, as follows:

```
[Route("/greetings", Verbs = "POST")]
public class CreateGreeting
{
    public string Greeting { get; set; }
}


public class CreateGreetingResponse
{
    public WebGreeting Greeting { get; set; }
}


[Route("/greetings", "GET")]
public class GetGreetings { }


public class GetGreetingsResponse
{
    public List<WebGreeting> Greetings { get; set; }
}


[Route("/greetings/{Id}/sayto/{Name}")]
```

```
        public class GetUserGreeting
        {
            public int Id { get; set; }
            public string Name { get; set; }
        }

        public class GetUserGreetingResponse
        {
            public string Result { get; set; }
        }
```

3. Create a service to handle these requests:

```
        public class GreetingsService : Service
        {
            public object Any(GetUserGreeting request)
            {
                var userGreeting = Db.SingleById<UserGreeting>(request.Id);
                if (userGreeting == null)
                {
                    throw HttpError.NotFound("Greeting not found");
                }

                return new GetUserGreetingResponse
                {
                    Result = userGreeting.Greeting.Fmt(request.Name)
                };
            }

            public object Get(GetGreetings request)
            {
                var greetings = Db.Select<UserGreeting>();
                return new GetGreetingsResponse
                {
                    Greetings = greetings.ConvertAll((greeting) =>
                    greeting.ConvertTo<WebGreeting>())
                };
            }

            public object Post(CreateGreeting request)
            {
                var item = request.ConvertTo<UserGreeting>();
                Db.Save(item);
                var lastInsertedId = Db.LastInsertId();
```

```
        var userGreeting = Db.Single<UserGreeting>(x =>
        x.Id == lastInsertedId);
        return new CreateGreetingResponse
        {
            Greeting = userGreeting.ConvertTo<WebGreeting>()
        };
    }


}
```

4. Add SQLite support to the main project by installing `ServiceStack.OrmLite.Sqlite.Windows` from NuGet, as follows:

    `Install-Package ServiceStack.OrmLite.Sqlite.Windows`

5. Configure AppHost in the main project to use the SQLite provider and seed some data, as follows:

```
public override void Configure(Funq.Container container)
{
    var dbFactory =
        new OrmLiteConnectionFactory(
            "~/App_Data/db.sqlite".MapHostAbsolutePath(),
            SqliteDialect.Provider);
    container.Register<IDbConnectionFactory>(dbFactory);

    using(var dbConnection = dbFactory.OpenDbConnection())
    {
        dbConnection.DropAndCreateTable<UserGreeting>();
    }

    using (var dbConnection = dbFactory.OpenDbConnection())
    {
        dbConnection.Insert(new UserGreeting
        {
            Greeting = "Hello, {0}"
        });
        dbConnection.Insert(new UserGreeting
        {
            Greeting = "G'day, {0}"
        });
        dbConnection.Insert(new UserGreeting
```

```
            {
                Greeting = "Howdy, {0}"
            });
        }
    }
```

How it works...

OrmLite has a lot of features to make short work of common operations performed on the underlying database. These are mainly exposed as extension methods on the IDbConnection interface.

Reading records, for example, was done in multiple ways in this example to show how it could be used. Here's the code for this operation:

```
Db.SingleById<UserGreeting>(request.Id);
```

What's going on here is that by passing in the type UserGreeting to SingleById, it knows to look for UserGreeting objects matching the integer passed in via request.Id. It uses this information to generate the appropriate SQL for the specific provider, which in this case is SQLite.

The previous line of code generates the following SQL:

```
SELECT "Id", "Greeting"
FROM "UserGreeting"
WHERE "Id" = @Id
```

Other examples of the Db.Single method produces very similar SQL. For example, the following two lines produce the same SQL:

```
Db.Single<UserGreeting>(x => x.Id == request.Id);
Db.Single(Db.From<UserGreeting>().Where(x => x.Id == request.Id));

SELECT "Id", "Greeting"
FROM "UserGreeting"
WHERE ("Id" = 1)
LIMIT 1
```

The addition of LIMIT 1 is due to the fact that Single can act on any property, whereas SingleById must act on the primary key of the table that will be enforced as unique in the database. This shows that how the OrmLite query is constructed affects what query is generated. If performance is becoming a problem, it is a good idea to make sure the SQL being generated is what you expect using Db.GetLastSql().

It is worth noting that at the time of writing this, OrmLite does not support multiple properties with the `[PrimaryKey]` attribute. The suggested workaround for this is to create a read-only property that is constructed from the other primary keys. For example:

```
public class UserGreeting
{
    public string Id
  {
get
{
return this.PrimaryKey1 + "/" + this.PrimaryKey2; }
  }
    public string PrimaryKey1 { get; set; }
    public string PrimaryKey2 { get; set; }
    public string Greeting { get; set; }
}
```

We can also pull out all records using `Db.Select<T>`:

```
public object Get(GetGreetings request)
{
    var greetings = Db.Select<UserGreeting>();
    return new GetGreetingsResponse
    {
        Greetings = greetings.ConvertAll(
        greeting => greeting.ConvertTo<WebGreeting>())
    };
}
```

We could also pass a predicate into `Db.Select` to filter the results, as follows:

```
var greetings = Db.Select<UserGreeting>(ug =>
ug.Greeting.Contains("hello"));
```

This will filter results only to return greetings that contain the string passed in, which is `Hello` in this case.

Creating records

OrmLite exposes the `Db.Insert` method to create new records. We'll accept a DTO and map it to a domain object with the `ConvertTo` method, as follows:

```
public class UserGreeting
{
   [PrimaryKey]
   [AutoIncrement]
```

```
    public int Id { get; set; }
    public string Greeting { get; set; }
}


[Route("/greetings", Verbs = "POST")]
public class CreateGreeting
{
    public string Greeting { get; set; }
}


public object Post(CreateGreeting request)
{
    var item = request.ConvertTo<UserGreeting>();
    Db.Save(item);
    var lastInsertedId = Db.LastInsertId();
    var userGreeting = Db.Single<UserGreeting>(
        x => x.Id == lastInsertedId
        );
    return new CreateGreetingResponse
    {
        Greeting = userGreeting.ConvertTo<WebGreeting>()
    };
}
```

ConvertTo is part of the ServiceStack AutoMapptingUtils class. It notes that the CreateGreeting class contains properties that are also found in UserGreeting, and so it automatically maps those properties over and returns a new UserGreeting object that includes what was passed in the request object.

From there, the Db.Save method inspects the type of the object being passed in and inserts the object it finds there into the right table. Db.Save method makes sure to get the ID that was created from this insert and puts this on the item.Id property. Db.Insert is also available, but it doesn't update the domain object with the inserted Id value. You can retrieve it later using Db.LastInsertId, which retrieves the last ID created by an INSERT statement on your database connection. That's not quite safe in high-volume-write situations, so you might want to stick to Db.Save instead.

Updating records

As you might imagine, the Db.Save method can also help with updating existing records, as follows:

```
public class UpdateGreeting
{
    public int Id { get; set; }
```

```
    public string Greeting { get; set; }
}
public object Put(UpdateGreeting request)
{
    if (!Db.Exists<UserGreeting>(request.Id))
    {
        throw HttpError.NotFound("Greeting not found");
    }
    var userGreeting =
        Db.Single<UserGreeting>(
            Db.From<UserGreeting>().Where(x => x.Id == request.Id)
        );
    userGreeting.PopulateWith(request);
    Db.Save(userGreeting);
    return new UpdateGreetingResponse
    {
        Greeting = userGreeting.ConvertTo<WebGreeting>()
    };
}
```

Since our endpoint advertises that it updates existing records, we want to throw a **404** error message if we are provided with a record that doesn't already exist. If we didn't, the Db.Save method would simply create a new record and return true. This isn't the desired behavior in this case, so we throw the NotFound exception early.

Deleting records

OrmLite provides a DeleteById method that will delete a specified record, as follows:

```
public object Delete(DeleteGreeting request)
{
    if (!Db.Exists<UserGreeting>(request.Id))
    {
        throw HttpError.NotFound("Greeting not found");
    }

    Db.DeleteById<UserGreeting>(request.Id);
    return new DeleteGreetingResponse();
}
```

Since our service assumes that it's being provided with a record that does exist, we'll throw a NotFound exception if the Id doesn't exist. Otherwise, we'll delete the record.

There's more...

It can be tempting to simply reuse your domain model as a DTO given how similar the objects can be, but it's important not to do this. Among other problems, this can lead to serious security issues. Here's what `UserGreeting` and one of the request objects look like:

```
[Route("/greetings/{Id}/sayto/{Name}")]
public class GetUserGreeting
{
    public int Id { get; set; }
    public string Name { get; set; }
}

public class UserGreeting
{
    [PrimaryKey]
    [AutoIncrement]
    public int Id { get; set; }
    public string Greeting { get; set; }
}
```

An obvious difference is the annotations, but it's also important to note that they are two different types. Separating your request/response objects from the classes that represent your database model is an important step to handling change over time in your system. Having separate classes from the start means that this can happen without a change to one affecting the other.

For example, if audit information, such as the creation or modification date, was added to `UserGreeting` in the database, there would be a good chance we wouldn't want to expose that to the clients of our API. If we used `UserGreeting` as both our database model and request object or in our response, code would have to be added to our services to handle this. What is worse is if `UserGreeting` was used as our request object, we could accidently let the user update the audit information of the system.

Keeping them separate and using ServiceStacks auto-mapping extension methods such as `ConvertTo<T>`, `PopulateWith<T>`, and others, can make handling these differences simple while ensuring exactly what the user can and can't update.

If you're modeling a user, another example would be that the DTO might include things like `FirstName`, `LastName`, and `Email` address. The domain model might also include properties like a Boolean for `IsAdministrator`—you wouldn't want to create a situation where users can provide this value over HTTP as you might end up sending that to the database. While you're building your DTO, keep in mind that you want to expose as *little* as possible.

Utilizing stored procedures using OrmLite

When using **object-relation mapping** (**ORM**) frameworks, the queries are constructed using the language of the host application. However, some situations might require the use of a database-specific query using a stored procedure. In this recipe, we will go through an example of this using OrmLite to access your custom-stored procedures and mapping the return value to strongly typed objects.

Getting ready

In this example, we will use Microsoft SQL Server 2012 Express and the AdventureWorks product sample database to illustrate how to access stored procedures. To get started, you'll need a new project created either using a template from the ServiceStackVS extension or by following the section *Creating a ServiceStack solution with Visual Studio and NuGet* in *Appendix A, Getting Started* to help get your project up and running. You will also require SQL Server installed with the AdventureWorks database attached to follow along with the example. At the time of writing this, the database sample is available from CodePlex at `https://msftdbprodsamples.codeplex.com/` along with instructions on how to attach the database product sample.

How to do it...

1. Install MS SQL Server support for OrmLite via NuGet, as follows:

   ```
   Install-Package ServiceStack.OrmLite.SqlServer
   ```

2. Create a POCO that represents the data structure returned by the stored procedure `uspGetEmployeeManagers`, as follows:

   ```
   public class EmployeeWithManagers
   {
       [Alias("BusinessEntityId")]
       public int Id { get; set; }
       public int RecursionLevel { get; set; }
       public string FirstName { get; set; }
       public string LastName { get; set; }
       public string OrganizationNode { get; set; }
       public string ManagerFirstName { get; set; }
       public string ManagerLastName { get; set; }
   }
   ```

3. Create a request-and-response object to allow us to query an AdventureWorks employees' managers, as follows:

```
[Route("/employees/{Id}/managers")]
public class EmployeeManagers
{
    public int Id { get; set; }
}


public class EmployeeManagersResponse
{
    public List<EmployeeWithManagers> EmployeeWithManagers
    { get; set; }
}
```

4. Create a POCO that represents the parameters of the stored procedures:

```
[Alias("uspGetEmployeeManagers")]
[Schema("dbo")]
public class UspGetEmployeeManagers
{
    public int BusinessEntityId { get; set; }
}
```

5. Write a service that will retrieve the employee's managers using the stored procedure, as follows:

```
public class EmployeeServices : Service
{
    public object Get(EmployeeManagers request)
    {
        return new EmployeeManagersResponse
        {
            EmployeeWithManagers =
            Db.SqlList<EmployeeWithManagers>(
            "EXEC dbo.uspGetEmployeeManagers
            @BusinessEntityId",
            new { BusinessEntityId = request.Id })
        };
    }
}
```

How it works...

OrmLite, like a lot of ServiceStack, leans on declared types heavily to produce a convention over configuration approach to many areas of the framework. Though stored procedures aren't common to all SQL implementations, SQLite for example, their use case is almost always around performance optimization or separation of responsibilities within a team. For example, a database administrator might be required to write stored procedures as a way for a development team to access data in a standardized way.

OrmLite provides a method to execute arbitrary SQL commands and return a list of strongly typed results, as follows:

```
Db.SqlList<EmployeeWithManagers>(
"EXEC dbo.uspGetEmployeeManagers @BusinessEntityId",
new { BusinessEntityId = request.Id });
```

Here, we are using an anonymous object to represent the stored command parameters and values.

There are multiple ways of executing stored procedures; to get a better idea what this query is doing, we could create our own method specific to getting employee with managers.

OrmLiteSPStatement

Using this pattern, we construct `DbCommand` and return an `OrmLiteSPStatement` object, which help us convert the return values into a list of our `EmployeeWithManagers` class. First, we will write an extension method for `IDbConnection` so that we can call the method in a similar way. Here's how we write the code for this purpose:

```
public static class StoredProcedureMethods
{
    public static OrmLiteSPStatement UspGetEmployeeManagers
        (this IDbConnection dbConnection, int? businessEntityID =
        null)
    {
        DbCommand dbCommand =
        (DbCommand)dbConnection.CreateCommand();
        dbCommand.CommandText = "uspGetEmployeeManagers";
        dbCommand.CommandType = CommandType.StoredProcedure;
        dbCommand.Parameters.Add(
            CreateNewParameter(dbCommand,
            "BusinessEntityID",
            businessEntityID,
            ParameterDirection.Input,
            DbType.Int32));
        return new OrmLiteSPStatement(dbCommand);
```

```
        }
        private static DbParameter CreateNewParameter
            (DbCommand dbCommand,
            string paramName,
            object paramValue,
            ParameterDirection
            paramDirection, DbType paramType)
        {
            DbParameter param = dbCommand.CreateParameter();
            param.Direction = paramDirection;
            param.DbType = paramType;
            param.ParameterName = paramName;
            param.Value = paramValue;
            return param;
        }
    }
```

In our service, we can now call the following to perform the same function:

```
    public object Put(EmployeeManagers request)
    {
        return new EmployeeManagersResponse
        {
            EmployeeWithManagers =
            Db.UspGetEmployeeManagers(request.Id)
                .ConvertToList<EmployeeWithManagers>()
        };
    }
```

Now, we have a less *stringy* call site, but this pattern is quite verbose. We are going to get tired of writing out a custom function if our database is constantly adding new stored procedures.

Writing our own wrapper

Another technique that lets us treat stored procedures more like service requests is to take advantage of the existing attributes that ServiceStack already uses, such as [Alias] and [Schema]. With the help of some extension methods, we can declare a type that will represent the stored procedure we want to use. First, we will need a method to help use/ generate the SQL used in the Db.SqlList<T> example, as follows:

```
    public static class OrmLiteSPExtensions
    {
        public static List<T> ExecuteStoredProcedure<T>(
        this IDbConnection dbConn, object objWithProperties)
        {
```

```
    var spType = objWithProperties.GetType();
    var aliasAttribute = spType.FirstAttribute<AliasAttribute>();
    var schemaAttribute =
    spType.FirstAttribute<SchemaAttribute>();
    string spName = aliasAttribute != null ?
        aliasAttribute.Name :
        spType.Name;
    spName = schemaAttribute != null ?
        schemaAttribute.Name + "." + spName :
        spName;
    return dbConn.SqlList<T>(
    CreateSPSql(spName, objWithProperties),
        objWithProperties);
}

public static string CreateSPSql(string spName, object
objWithProperties)
{
    var objType = objWithProperties.GetType();
    var properties = objType.GetProperties(
    BindingFlags.Public | BindingFlags.Instance)
        .ToList();

    StringBuilder sql = new StringBuilder();
    sql.Append("EXEC {0} ".Fmt(spName));
    sql.Append(properties.Select(x =>
    "@{0}".Fmt(x.Name)).Join(","));

    return sql.ToString();
}
}
```

This example uses the existing attributes [Alias] and [Schema],
and as we aren't querying tables directly this is unlikely to cause
confusion. In a larger project when both direct table queries and stored
procedures are used, it would be worth creating new attributes for
[Alias] and [Schema] for use solely with stored procedures so as
to avoid confusion.

This method looks for the use of the `Alias` and `Schema` attributes to generate the right name of the stored procedure. This will allow us to create an object type with these attributes that contain the SQL parameters as public properties. For example:

```
[Alias("uspGetEmployeeManagers")]
[Schema("dbo")]
public class GetEmployeeManagers
{
    public int BusinessEntityId { get; set; }
}
```

This pattern allows us to follow a very similar-looking code structure to what ServiceStack services and OrmLite use for requests and table queries respectively. Here's how the code looks:

```
public object Post(EmployeeManagers request)
{
    return new EmployeeManagersResponse
    {
        EmployeeWithManagers =
        Db.ExecuteStoredProcedure<EmployeeWithManagers>(
        new GetEmployeeManagers
        { BusinessEntityId = request.Id })
    };
}
```

The ability to execute stored procedures using OrmLite extension methods list `SqlList<T>` gives us strongly typed results with minimal SQL-specific syntax. Also, as seen in this recipe, with a small helper method and the use of attributes, these queries become easy to manage while still having the option of more control when needed.

The patterns mentioned in the preceding paragraph focused on getting results out of SQL-stored procedures, not on non-query based procedures. If we were to use the stored procedure `HumanResources.uspUpdateEmployeePersonalInfo`, we would use the more generic method of `ExecuteNonQuery`:

```
Db.ExecuteNonQuery("EXEC
HumanResources.uspUpdateEmployeePersonalInfo
@BusinessEntityID,@NationalIDNumber,@BirthDate,@MaritalStatus,@Gen
der",
    new
    {
        BusinessEntityID = 8, //Example value
        NationalIDNumber = "555123123", //Example value
        BirthDate = new DateTime(1980, 1, 30), //Example value
        MaritalStatus = "M", //Example value
        Gender = "M" //Example value
    });
```

There's more...

In this recipe, we looked at using Microsoft SQL Server to execute stored procedures from OrmLite. As SQL implementations differ from implementation to implementation, so do some of the more specific uses of OrmLite between different database types, such as Oracle, SQL Server, and SQLite. At the time of writing this, `ServiceStack.OrmLite.Oracle` has the ability to use an `ExecuteProcedure<T>(T instance)` extension method instead of using `ExecuteNonQuery`. OrmLite has been growing in functionality very quickly, and these functions might converge to be more consistent across database implementations, but it is good to be aware that there might be differences in available functionality between database technologies.

Mapping custom queries to POCOs

One of the big advantages of relational databases is the normalization of data or the ability to avoid data duplication and have the confidence that this is enforced by the database itself. However, as data is not duplicated across tables, we need to perform joins on various tables to group all this non-duplicated data together for our queries. As of version 4.0.22, ServiceStack OrmLite provides API methods capable of creating complex custom queries, including join statements that can be returned mapped to a Plain Old CLR Object of your choosing.

Getting ready

In this recipe, we will create a simple `Hello World` service that stores a formatted response in a SQLite database on which we can perform our OrmLite queries. To get started, you'll need a new project created either using a template from the ServiceStackVS extension or by following the section *Creating a ServiceStack solution with Visual Studio and NuGet* in *Appendix A, Getting Started*.

How to do it...

1. Install SQLite from NuGet using the following command:

   ```
   Install-Package ServiceStack.OrmLite.Sqlite.Windows
   ```

2. We'll need domain objects. We'll use OrmLite to map these back to a SQL database, as follows:

   ```
   public class UserGreeting
   {
       [PrimaryKey]
       [AutoIncrement]
       public int Id { get; set; }
       public string Greeting { get; set; }
   ```

```
        public int? LanguageId { get; set; }
    }

    public class UserLanguage
    {
        [PrimaryKey]
        [AutoIncrement]
        public int Id { get; set; }
        public string Language { get; set; }
    }
```

3. We'll also need an object to which we'll expect OrmLite to map our result set. In this case, we'll ask our query to return a class that we intend to use as a DTO, as follows:

```
    public class GreetingWithLanguage
    {
        public int Id { get; set; }
        public string Greeting { get; set; }
        public int LanguageId { get; set; }
        public string Language { get; set; }
    }
```

4. Once we have the domain set up, we'll create an object that returns our DTO and queries the domain objects, which we'll modify with a join statement built by OrmLite's `SqlExpression` object:

```
    var englishGreetings = db.Select<GreetingResponse>(
    db.From<UserGreeting>()
        .LeftJoin<UserGreeting, UserLanguage>((g, l) =>
        g.LanguageId == l.Id)
        .Where<UserLanguage>(l => l.Language == "English"));
```

How it works...

The basic concept is that `db.From<T>` creates `ServiceStack.OrmLite.SqlExpression`. This object represents a query that allows us to specify the tables that we'd want included and specify how they are related. `LeftJoin` modifies the expression, adding information on another table we'd like to join against and optionally a predicate indicating how to join.

The `Where()` method allows us to add a predicate filter to specify which records we'd like to see. By default, the predicate operates on the type specified in the `From<T>` statement, which would have been `UserGreeting` in this case. Since we wanted to apply a predicate to `UserLanguage`, which we pulled in via the `JOIN`, we needed to specify the type.

The `Select<T>` method executes the resulting `SqlExpression` syntax, returning a list of objects of the type `T`.

If we unpack the `SqlExpression` syntax, it would look like this:

```
var query = db.From<UserGreeting>();
query.LeftJoin<UserGreeting, UserLanguage>(
(g, l) => g.LanguageId == l.Id);
query.Where<UserLanguage>(l => l.Language == "English");
var queryResult = db.Select<GreetingResponse>(query);
Assert.AreEqual(1, queryResult.Count());
```

In some ways, it's a bit simpler, but this syntax is more declarative. It's also easier to think in set-based terms, as in the case of a SQL SELECT statement, which is nice. If you know SQL, you might find the `SqlExpression` syntax more expressive.

Starting with an existing database with OrmLite and T4 templates

Starting with a new technology on a new project makes things much more straightforward. However, more often than not, you might find yourself trying to leverage the advantages of new technologies and frameworks for an existing system that has to be maintained well into the future. In this recipe, we will work through the process of starting with an existing database and exposing that data through services using ServiceStack. We will be working with the constraint that the existing data structure cannot be altered by the application to simulate a real-world situation of using an existing production database.

Getting ready

To get started, you'll need a new project either created using a template from the ServiceStackVS extension or by following the *Creating a ServiceStack solution with Visual Studio and NuGet* section in *Appendix A, Getting Started*. This recipe will also require that an installation of MS SQL Server is installed to be up and running. If you want to also use the AdventureWorks database to explore how this technique is used; at the time of writing this, it can be downloaded from CodePlex at `https://msftdbprodsamples.codeplex.com/`.

First, we are going to need an existing database to use as our example. A simple and commonly known one is the AdventureWorks database product sample from Microsoft for Microsoft SQL Server 2012. The steps in the following recipe are compatible with existing MS SQL databases; however, they will also work with other databases, such as PostgreSQL, with additional steps, which will be covered in the *There's more...* section of this recipe.

How to do it...

1. First, we will need to make sure we have the required NuGet packages installed, including the templates themselves. Run the following commands from **Package Manager Console** targeting your main web project to install the templates. In this example, these are installed to the **ServiceModel** project:

```
Install-Package ServiceStack.OrmLite.T4
```

2. Once these packages are installed, the templates are going to look for a valid connection string from which to query the database structure to generate all the POCOs that we can use to query with using OrmLite. The convention used by T4 templates is to look in web.config or app.config for registered connection strings. As we are generating these classes within a separate class library, we are going to need to add app.config file separately for the T4 template file to use. In this example, we add an app.config file with the following connectionstring tag:

```xml
<?xml version="1.0" encoding="utf-8"?>
<configuration>
  <connectionStrings>
    <add name="AdventureWorks"
        connectionString="Data Source=localhost\
        SQLEXPRESS;Initial Catalog=AdventureWorks2012;Integrated
        Security=True"
        providerName="System.Data.SqlClient" />
  </connectionStrings>
</configuration>
```

Once this is set up, you can run the **T4Template** file from Visual Studio by right-clicking on OrmLite.Poco.tt and selecting **Run Custom Tool**:

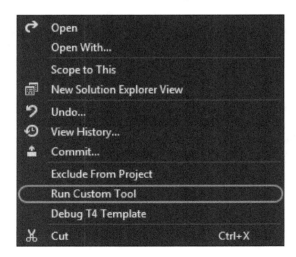

3. You might see a **Security Warning** about running the template. Click on **OK** to continue and generate the model classes, as shown in the following screenshot:

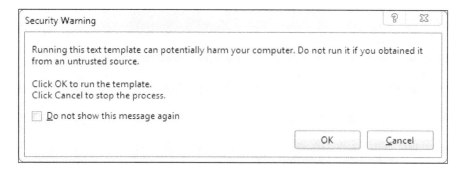

4. One extra package we are going to need in the case of AdventureWorks is the `Microsoft.SqlServer.Types` package due to the use of special types containing geospatial-related data stored in the database:

    `Install-Package Microsoft.SqlServer.Types`

5. Now that we can successfully build the service model project, we are going to need some request objects and services, as shown in the following code:

    ```
    [Route("/person/{PersonId}")]
    public class GetPerson
    {
        public int PersonId { get; set; }
    }

    public class GetPersonResponse
    {
        public Person Person { get; set; }
    }
    ```

6. Install the SQL Server OrmLite provider to your main project, as follows:

    `Install-Package ServiceStack.OrmLite.SqlServer`

7. Create a service to get a person by `PersonId`, as follows:

    ```
    public class PersonService : Service
    {
        public object Get(GetPerson request)
        {
          return new GetPersonResponse
          {
    ```

```
        Person =
        Db.SingleById<Person>(request.PersonId)
    };
}
}
```

8. Now, we can update the `AppHost` class to reference our new service and initialize our database connection factory, specifying `SqlServerDialect.Provider`, as follows:

```
public class AppHost : AppHostBase
{
    public AppHost()
    : base("Starting with an existing database with
    OrmLite and T4 templates", typeof(PersonService).Assembly)
    {

    }

    public override void Configure(Funq.Container
    container)
    {
        var appSettings = new AdventureWorksAppSettings();
        container.Register<AdventureWorksAppSettings>(appSettings);
        container.Register<IDbConnectionFactory>(new
        OrmLiteConnectionFactory(appSettings.ConnectionString,SqlSe
        rverDialect.Provider));
    }
}
```

How it works...

Using tools like `T4 templates` can be a timesaver when first starting off, as it generates and attributes some simple classes that represent what is in our database that you would write by hand without it. ServiceStack uses DTOs for a lot of its core functionality, and this makes it really easy to work with other tools and technologies as they are just objects with no baggage, that is, no inherent behavior.

Now, if we test our new service with a `GET` request to `/person/1`, we get the following result:

 Postman is a free extension for the Chrome browser that can be easily used with ServiceStack thanks to the `PostmanFeature()` Plugin. Postman allows developers to easily create HTTP requests to test web services. The ServiceStack Plugin exposes an endpoint for Postman to automatically import all the types of valid requests that can be used with your services.

Postman is available from Chrome Web Store.

The OrmLite `T4 template` file also generate extension methods to access any stored procedures in your existing database from `IDbConnection`. These might be a bit different than how you might access and execute stored procedures if you had written the methods by hand, but the `OrmLiteSPStatement` class provides an easy to use `IDbCommand` decorator to access the results of the stored procedure in a type-safe way. Let's write a web service and requests that expose the use of the `GetEmployeeManagers` stored procedure:

```
[Route("/employees/{Id}/managers")]
public class GetEmployeeManagers
{
    public int Id { get; set; }
}

public class GetEmployeeManagersResponse
```

```
    {
        public List<EmployeeWithManagers> EmployeeWithManagers
        { get; set; }
    }
```

We need to create the stored procedure POCOs ourselves as the template doesn't know the structure of the return type. In the case of employees with managers, we will look at the structure being returned through either SQL Management Studio or another tool and write the following manually:

```
    public class EmployeeWithManagers
    {
        [Alias("BusinessEntityId")]
        public int Id { get; set; }
        public int RecursionLevel { get; set; }
        public string FirstName { get; set; }
        public string LastName { get; set; }
        public string OrganizationNode { get; set; }
        public string ManagerFirstName { get;set;}
        public string ManagerLastName { get;set;}
    }
```

Now we call the stored procedure from our new service and return GetEmployeeManagersResponse:

```
    public class EmployeeServices : Service
    {
        public object Get(GetEmployeeManagers request)
        {
          return new GetEmployeeManagersResponse
          {
            EmployeeWithManagers =
            Db.uspGetEmployeeManagers(request.Id)
            .ConvertToList<EmployeeWithManagers>()
          };
        }
    }
```

If we query our new endpoint with an ID of 8 using Chrome's Postman extension, we get the following result:

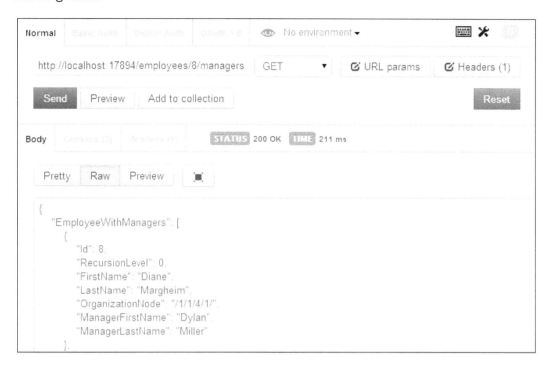

Methods for stored procedures are also added to make it easy to access data returned in a strongly typed way. The use of the stored procedures generated does require the knowledge of what the structure of the result will be; the code generated does not create types that represent the structure of the result with a type, but rather `helper` methods to access that data. For example, you have to know whether you are getting a set or a single result back from the stored procedure and use the appropriate methods, as follows:

```
public List<T> ConvertFirstColumnToList<T>();
public HashSet<T> ConvertFirstColumnToListDistinct<T>();
public T ConvertTo<T>();
public List<T> ConvertToList<T>();
public T ConvertToScalar<T>();
public List<T> ConvertToScalarList<T>();
public int ExecuteNonQuery();
public bool HasResult();
```

A method is a list of operations you can make on the result of a stored procedure. The type you pass to these methods is one you create to represent the known data structure coming back from the store procedure, as follows:

```
public class EmployeeWithManagers
{
    [Alias("BusinessEntityId")]
    public int Id { get; set; }
    public int RecursionLevel { get; set; }
    public string FirstName { get; set; }
    public string LastName { get; set; }
    public string OrganizationNode { get; set; }
    public string ManagerFirstName { get;set;}
    public string ManagerLastName { get;set;}
}
```

Unlike the code generated from `OrmLite.Poco.tt`, the one generated from `OrmLite.SP.tt` does not include the type information that represents the data returning.

There's something else to note; the stored procedure isn't actually fired until one of the `helper` methods is actually used on the `OrmLiteSPStatement` object that is returned from the extension methods (`uspGetEmployeeManagers`, for example) generated from `OrmLite.SP.tt`.

In the situation introduced in this example of an established production database, the structure of which you have little or no control over, OrmLite `T4 templates` and ServiceStack services offer a really nice and efficient way of exposing that data.

There's more...

If you are using a database provider other than MS SQL, such as SQLite or PostgreSQL, there are some additional steps you have to take to get `T4 templates` working. Due to the way these templates work, the database provider assembly has to be registered in the **global assembly cache** (**GAC**) and also registered as a database provider within your .NET installation's `machine.config` file.

These processes will be different depending on which database provider you want to use. If you have installed MS SQL, these settings are already in place, which is why additional steps are not required.

Working with Entity Framework and ServiceStack

While ServiceStack is bundled with OrmLite, you could make it work with any number of ORM tools. In many situations, developers might need to make use of domain models already built against other systems, for instance Microsoft's Entity Framework. We'll cover a little bit about how to use Entity Framework with ServiceStack in this recipe.

 It's important to remember that the code in this recipe is not production tested. It should work fine, but your mileage might vary.

Getting ready

In this example, we'll build a custom domain model with Entity Framework and then use it with ServiceStack. We'll use the code-first paradigm to build up an `EfContext` model that extends `DbContext`, and which we'll use when we need to access data in our services.

Before you can use Entity Framework with your solution, you might need to install the NuGet package, as shown in the following section.

How to do it...

1. Install `EntityFramework` from NuGet, as follows:

   ```
   Install-Package EntityFramework
   ```

2. Once we have `EntityFramework` installed, we can start to build up our data model. In this recipe, we'll attempt a simple greeting service. We'll store several greetings in our `UserGreeting` table, as shown in the following code; in Entity Framework, it's simple to represent by building a POCO to represent our object:

   ```
   public class UserGreeting
   {
     public int Id { get; set; }
     public string Greeting { get; set; }
   }
   ```

3. We'll build an Entity Framework context object and use `DbSet<T>` to indicate to that we want a collection of this entity type in our database:

```
public class EfContext : DbContext
{
    public DbSet<UserGreeting> UserGreetings { get; set; }
}
```

4. In our `AppHost` class, we'll seed our database in the `Configure` method by creating `UserGreeting` objects, adding them to the collection, and then saving them to the database, as follows:

```
public override void Configure(Funq.Container container)
{
    using (var ctx = new EfContext())
    {
        ctx.UserGreetings.Add(
            new UserGreeting
            {
                Greeting = "Hi there, {0}."
            });
        ctx.UserGreetings.Add(
            new UserGreeting
            {
                Greeting = "Howdy {0}!"
            });
        ctx.UserGreetings.Add(
            new UserGreeting
            {
                Greeting = "Hey, {0}..."
            });

        ctx.SaveChanges();
    }
}
```

5. Once we have the seed data, we can query it using the `EfContext` object in our service, as follows:

```
public object Any(GetUserGreeting request)
{
    using (var ctx = new EfContext())
    {
        var greeting = (from g in ctx.UserGreetings
```

```
            where
            g.Id.Equals(request.Id)
            select g).FirstOrDefault();

            if (greeting==null)
            {
              throw HttpError.NotFound("Greeting not
              found.");
            }
            return new GetUserGreetingResponse
            {
                Result = greeting.Greeting.Fmt(request.Name)
            };
        }
    }
```

How it works...

The block that begins `using (var ctx = new EfContext())` creates a new context and allows us to query using the `ctx` variable created. Our service is meant to return a specific greeting object specified in the request. If it doesn't exist, we'll want to throw a `NotFound` exception as expected. Otherwise, we'll go ahead and convert our entity to a POCO DTO and return it.

Something to watch out for when using Entity Framework with ServiceStack services is to make sure all the data to be serialized by ServiceStack for the response of the service needs to have already been loaded into the object. Entity Framework tends to use lazy loading of property values, which becomes a problem as ServiceStack will try to serialize the object, which will cause Entity Framework to try and fetch the results needed after the context has been disposed of.

If you are using Entity Framework, a good habit is to avoid returning any complex object outside of the context using statement and finish select statements with `ToList<T>`, which will ensure the values that should be resolved are resolved and put in memory before the service returns.

5
HTML and Form Data

In this chapter, we are going to look at the functionality ServiceStack brings to building web applications through the following recipes:

- Getting started with the ServiceStack and Razor templates
- Using Markdown for website content
- Handling file uploads and streaming data from services
- Overriding Razor views or templates using attributes
- Creating and displaying a login and registration page based on authentication
- Submitting a form to a service and handling server-side validation on an HTML client

Introduction

Although ServiceStack is focused on enabling developers to write clean, maintainable web services, it also has a full server-side HTML-rendering solution using Razor templates. For application developers who want to write both backend services and their web application code in one single stack, ServiceStack's support for Razor makes this possible. The recipes in this section will cover scenarios where ServiceStack will be the framework for not only the service, but also the application development framework.

If you have had experience with Microsoft's MVC framework, chances are you've been writing views using the Razor syntax—ServiceStack offers the same functionality and adds a Markdown syntax as well. ServiceStack also has some tools to make it easy to wire up HTML forms and cleanly display error and validation information. We will also look at how we can write services to handle file uploads and streaming from different clients and create a login and registration page by displaying different views to authenticated and unauthenticated users.

Getting started with ServiceStack and Razor templates

Getting ready

Before we can work with Razor in ServiceStack, we need to install the `servicestack.razor` NuGet package, as follows:

```
PM> Install-Package ServiceStack.Razor
```

Package Manager will then copy the relevant plugin components and add references for us.

How to do it...

1. We'll start with the basic `HelloWorldService` and build it up adding the Razor bits. Before we are able to work with Razor in our project, of course, we'll also need to add the Razor plugin in the `Configure` method of `AppHost`:

    ```
    public class ApplicationHost : AppHostBase
    {
      public ApplicationHost() : base("Greeting Service",
      typeof (GreetingService).Assembly)
      { }

      public override void Configure(Funq.Container container)
      {
        Plugins.Add(new RazorFormat());
      }
    }
    ```

2. Then, we'll decorate our service with an annotation saying that we'd like ServiceStack to render a specific method for the view that will be created shortly, as follows:

    ```
    public class GreetingService : Service
    {
      [DefaultView("Greeting")]
      public object Get(GetGreeting request)
      {
        return new GetGreetingResponse
        {
          Greeting = "Hello, " + request.Name + "!"
        };
      }
    }
    ```

3. We'll also add a new folder, `Views`, to our project. In that folder, we'll create a new file, `Greeting.cshtml`:

4. Let's start with some very basic Razor syntax in our view:

```
<!doctype html>
<html lang="en-us">
<head>
    <title>@Model.Greeting</title>
    <meta http-equiv="Content-Type" content="text/html;
    charset=utf-8">
</head>
<body>
<div id="body">
    <div id="content">
        <h1>@Model.Greeting</h1>
    </div>
</div>
</body>
</html>
```

5. The `@Model` prefix refers to the response object returned, which is a strongly typed `GetGreetingResponse` in this case, as specified by `GreetingService`.

    There's nothing special in the request DTO; it's just a custom route to indicate where ServiceStack should expect requests, as follows:

    ```
    [Route("/hello/{Name}")]
    public class GetGreeting
    {
        public string Name { get; set; }
    }
    ```

6. The response is equally simple; it's just a DTO to contain a string for our response:

    ```
    public class GetGreetingResponse
    {
        public string Greeting { get; set; }
    }
    ```

7. Now, when a web browser connects to `/hello/World`, instead of seeing a JSON object or a ServiceStack page, we'll see our view handling the request, as shown in the following screenshot:

8. If instead we specified that we wanted a JSON response, for instance, using the `?format=JSON` query parameter, we'll see the JSON output just as we would have in the past, as shown in the following screenshot:

How it works...

When ServiceStack sees the `[DefaultView("Greeting")]` annotation on our `Get` method, it goes looking for a view with the name `Greeting.cshtml`. Having found our view, after rendering the response DTO, it processes that DTO using the Razor syntax found in our view. Anytime it sees the `@` symbol, it knows that the rest of the line is code until it sees something that's obviously HTML again—in this case, the closing `</h1>` tag. The `@Model` prefix refers to the response DTO model object that has been processed with Razor.

The `RazorFormat` plugin can do much more than this, but this simple example neatly gets you going with minimum code. We'll explore other Razor features as we go through the rest of the chapter.

There's more...

In this project, we have explicitly attributed the service with the `DefaultView` attribute, giving it the name `Greeting` so that it uses the view of the same name. Like a lot of things in ServiceStack, there is a convention that can be used if you prefer not to be explicit. If we renamed the request from `GetGreeting` to just `Greeting`, which matches the name of our view, the `DefaultView` attribute is not needed. ServiceStack will infer, by matching the name of the view and the type name of the request object, that they are related and that the `Greeting.cshtml` view should be used.

Using Markdown for website content

Markdown is a very popular plain text formatting syntax. It aims to be human readable at all times, while striking a balance between complexity and powerful features. Popular apps like GitHub and StackOverflow make extensive use of Markdown. GitHub has extended Markdown to make it easy to show source code as well.

For instance, the following Markdown helps us lay out a simple document, including some source code that we want to display, as follows:

```
# This will be an H1

Markdown is very useful stuff!

## This will be an H2
You can easily format text and organize documents with it. Using
the GitHub extensions, you can easily display source code like
this:

```javascript
```
```

```
var a = "Hello World!";
console.log(a);

` ` `
```

GitHub's gist application would render the previous Markdown like this, adding formatting and even color coding for the JavaScript syntax:

ServiceStack allows us to store web content in Markdown, as GitHub and StackOverflow do, and render it as HTML, PDF, or other formats when the time is required. One benefit to storing content in Markdown instead of HTML is that it reinforces the concept of semantic markup.

Semantic markup is the use of markup to reinforce the semantics, or meaning, of the information in web pages rather than to define its presentation or look.

For instance, if you store an article in Markdown, it can easily be repurposed as a lead view—if you want to emphasize this article, or in a mobile app, or in a print view, or a variety of other ways, as required. If you allow non-semantic formatting to leak into your content, then it becomes much harder to repurpose the content. Just like Semantic HTML, Markdown helps you keep that from happening.

Getting ready

To make use of this feature, you'll need to make sure the `ServiceStack.Razor` package is installed if you haven't already. It includes the Markdown components we'll need:

```
PM> Install-Package ServiceStack.Razor
```

In our example, we'll use Markdown to add some Markdown content documentation for our Greeting service.

How to do it...

First, we'll need a directory in which we can place our documentation content. In this example, we'll create a folder called `Content` for that purpose. The directory name will be part of the URL for our content later.

In that folder, we'll create `_Layout.cshtml`. This Razor syntax template will drive the look and feel of all of the content pages in this folder, as follows:

```
@inherits ViewPage
@{
    ViewBag.Title="Service Documentation";
}
<!doctype html>
<html lang="en-us">
<head>
    <title>@ViewBag.Title</title>
</head>
    <body>
        <h1>@ViewBag.Title</h1>
        <div>
            @RenderBody()
        </div>
    </body>
</html>
```

Next, we'll create a view for our documentation. We'll name it `Documentation.cshtml`:

```
@inherits ViewPage
@Html.Partial("greeting-documentation")
```

The `Html.Partial` function accepts an argument of the name of the content file to render. We could also place other variables here to pick up variables that the service returned in the response DTO.

Next, we'll create our Markdown content file. We'll name it `greeting-documentation.md`. Here's how we create the file:

```
Reidson Industries Greeting Service
-----------------------------------


Reidson Industries is pleased to announce version 1.0 of its
greeting service.

Introduction
------------
```

```
* Using the Reidson Industries Greeting service is simple. First,
you must decide who you
would like to greet.  We'll call this the greeting recipient.
* Next, create a URL that first contains the route to the service,
`/hello`, followed by the name of the recipient:
`/hello/{recipient}`
* By default the greeting service renders the greeting using the
greeting viewer. If you'd prefer JSON, simply add the appropriate
request header or `?format=json` to the URL.

An [example JSON URL][1] is below.

~~~~

http://servername/hello/example-recipient?format=json
~~~~


The result of calling such a service would be the JSON including
the Greeting.

~~~~

{"Greeting":"Hello, example-recipient!"}
~~~~


   [1]: /hello/example-recipient?format=json
```

The end result will look like this in Solution Explorer:

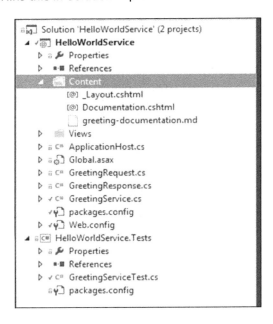

How it works...

With all of this done, we can visit `/Content/Documentation` for our service, and we should be greeted with the resulting output, which is as follows:

As you can see, we pick up the title from the `_Layout.cshtml` template. ServiceStack will look for the closest `_Layout.cshtml` file, looking in the content root in the directory that the content is located in and in any parent directories as well. As we requested the URL documentation, ServiceStack will look for files named `Documentation.cshtml` and also for folders named `Documentation` with a `Default.cshtml` file present. Once `Documentation.cshtml` is located, ServiceStack processes the `Html.Partial` command and the Markdown content is rendered as HTML as you would expect.

At development time, when you press *F5* in VisualStudio, IIS Express is started and given the project folder as the content root. This means that you can request any filename located in your solution. By default, IIS will refuse to serve the contents of your `.cs` files, of course, but you can traverse the directories that contain your code. When you deploy your solution to a web server, your code files shouldn't be published; only the compiled assemblies should be published.

Our Markdown source content is marked with **Build Action** set as **Content**, which ensures that it will be copied to the web server.

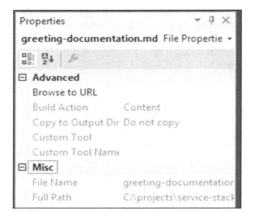

Handling file uploads and streaming data from services

A common requirement for web applications is to enable users to upload files to a server. In this recipe, we will build a service to handle file uploads and give an example of it working with both a web client and a .NET client.

Getting ready

If you are starting with a new project, please go to section *Creating a ServiceStack solution with Visual Studio and NuGet, Appendix A, Getting Started*, to help you get set up.

How to do it...

1. Create the request object for the file upload service, as follows:

```
[Route("/fileupload/simple")]
public class SimpleFileUploadRequest
{
    public string FileName { get; set; }
    public string UploadedByUserName { get; set; }
}
```

2. Create the service to handle the file upload, as follows:

```
public object Post(SimpleFileUploadRequest request)
{
  if (Request.Files.Length == 0)
  {
    throw new HttpError(HttpStatusCode.BadRequest,
    "NoFile");
  }
  string resultFile = @"../../" +
  Request.Files[0].FileName;
  Request.Files[0].SaveTo(resultFile);
  Response.StatusCode = 200;
  return HttpStatusCode.OK;
}
```

3. Ensure IIS settings regarding the maximum request size are increased to handle larger file uploads by adding the `maxRequestLength` XML attribute to the `httpRuntime` element within the `system.web` section of the `web.config` file by providing a value in *kilobytes*:

```
<httpRuntime targetFramework="4.5"
maxRequestLength="1073741824" />
```

4. Also ensure the `maxAllowedContentLength` attribute is set in the security section of `system.webServer` shown as follows. This attribute expects a value in *bytes*:

```
<requestLimits maxAllowedContentLength="1073741824" />
```

How it works...

In the example stated earlier, we are utilizing a couple of helpers that ServiceStack provides to make it easy to handle an uploaded file. The `Request` object within a service has a number of properties about the request, including an array of `IHttpFile` objects. The `SaveTo` method of the `IHttpFile` object helps us save the file to disk by providing the full path to the method. We are also using some simple metadata about the file contained within the `IHttpFile` object, such as `FileName`.

There is a common error at this point related to permissions of the account running the web application. Ensure that the Windows account running the AppPool of the web application has sufficient permissions to write files to the location you've specified. Also, be warned that duplicate filenames will be overwritten.

There are various ways you can get the file itself uploaded to this web service to be saved. If you were going to save this file from a website, straight from a file upload control, you would have to specify the correct path to the web service in the form element, as follows:

```
<form action="/fileupload/simple"
      method="post"
      enctype="multipart/form-data">
  <label for="file">Upload</label>
  <input type="file" name="file" id="file">
  <input type="submit" name="submit" value="Submit">
</form>
```

There's more...

If you are dealing with very large files, a simple web client as shown earlier might run into problems related to OutOfMemory exceptions and other issues around memory constraints as these large files will be copied to memory prior to being written to disk. In .NET, you can stream the data to a service with a few changes to the service provided earlier. The Request object needs to be told that the request has to be handled differently, as follows:

```
[Route("/fileupload/stream")]
public class StreamFileUpload : IRequiresRequestStream
{
    public Stream RequestStream { get; set; }
}
```

The service should also handle the request differently to ensure the file is not being pulled into memory during the upload:

```
public object Post(StreamFileUploadRequest request)
{
    string resultFile = @" ../../teststream.dat";
    using (FileStream file = File.Create(resultFile))
    {
        request.RequestStream.WriteTo(file);
    }
    Response.StatusCode = 200;
    return HttpStatusCode.OK;
}
```

 Note that the file path is fixed to simplify the example; additional metadata can be provided with the request through parameters or query strings that ServiceStack will bind to the request object.

Testing file uploads

Creating integration tests for our file upload endpoints is a simple task but requires a slightly different technique than tests shown previously. As the utilities we've used until now don't allow fine-grained control over file uploads, one approach would be to create `WebRequest`, upload the file, and verify that we receive the response we expect. We'll connect to a container hosted in `TestAppHost`, which extends `AppSelfHostBase`:

```
class TestAppHost : AppSelfHostBase
{
  public TestAppHost()
    : base("Tests",typeof(FileUploadService).Assembly)
  { }

  public override void Configure(Funq.Container container)
  { }
}
```

We'll initialize `apphost` in a method decorated with the `[TestFixtureSetUp]` annotation, as follows:

```
[TestFixture]
public class FileUploadContractTests
{
  private const string URLBase = "http://localhost:32399";
  ServiceStackHost appHost;

  [TestFixtureSetUp]
  public void Init()
  {
    appHost = new TestAppHost();
    appHost.Init().Start(URLBase + "/");
  }

  [TestFixtureTearDown]
  public void Cleanup()
  {
    appHost.Dispose();
  }
```

The code for testing the simple file upload is as follows:

```
[Test]
public void ShouldAcceptSimpleUploads()
{
  string filePath = @"..\..\Assets\UploadTestFile.txt";
```

```
        var client = (HttpWebRequest)WebRequest
            .Create(URLBase + "/fileupload/simple");
        client.Method = WebRequestMethods.Http.Post;

        client.AllowWriteStreamBuffering = false;
        client.SendChunked = true;
        client.Accept = "application/json";
        client.ContentType = "multipart/form-data;";
        client.Timeout = int.MaxValue;

        client.UploadFile(new FileInfo(filePath),"");

        Stream responseStream =
          client.GetResponse()
            .GetResponseStream();

        Assert.IsNotNull(
          responseStream,
          "responseStream should not be null");

        var response = new StreamReader(responseStream)
            .ReadToEnd();

        Assert.AreEqual("OK".ToJson(), response);
    }
```

The code for testing the stream uploader follows a similar pattern, but instead of the `client.UploadFile` method, we'll stream the file, as follows:

```
    [Test]
    public void ShouldAcceptStreamUploads()
    {
      string filePath = @"..\..\Assets\UploadTestFile.txt";

      var client = (HttpWebRequest)WebRequest
          .Create(URLBase + "/fileupload/stream");
      client.Method = WebRequestMethods.Http.Post;
      client.AllowWriteStreamBuffering = false;
      client.SendChunked = true;
      client.Accept = "application/json";
      client.ContentType = "multipart/form-data;";
      client.Timeout = int.MaxValue;

      using (FileStream fileStream = File.OpenRead(filePath))
```

```
    {
        fileStream.CopyTo(client.GetRequestStream());
    }

    Stream responseStream =
        client.GetResponse()
            .GetResponseStream();

    Assert.IsNotNull(
        responseStream,
        "responseStream should not be null");

    var response = new StreamReader(responseStream)
        .ReadToEnd();

    Assert.AreEqual("OK".ToJson(), response);
}
```

One thing that becomes evident when working with raw `WebClient` is just how much code we get to skip when using ServiceStack's built-in `JsonServiceClient` and HTTP utilities! With these tests in place, we can have confidence that our uploaders continue to work as expected.

Overriding Razor views or templates using attributes

One easy way to specify a view is to place a `DefaultView` attribute on either a service method or on an entire service class, or both. The attribute placed on the service class can apply as a default, while an attribute placed on a service method can override this default.

Getting ready

`DefaultView` takes two different arguments, a view and optionally a template. This allows you to specify each separately to control the rendering of the page.

The template parameter allows you to specify one of multiple templates. In a small application, you might only have one `_Layout.cshtml`, which would get picked up by default, and so you would not need to specify it. In a larger application, you might have a template for a microsite, another template for the home page, and another template for a content page. This allows you to group together pages that have a similar look and feel into separate templates.

The view parameter allows you as a developer to specify a piece of Razor code that is more specific to a given page, or view. For instance, on a page where a user is trying to register, we might use the default template but want to leverage a view created specifically to render our registration form and handle validation logic.

How to do it...

The `DefaultView` attribute overrides the convention that ServiceStack normally employs that automatically searches for a view that corresponds with the request or response object. To override this behavior, simply create your view, annotate your method with the `DefaultView` attribute, and specify the view, as follows:

```
@{
    ViewBag.Title = "Razor Greeting Viewer";
}

<div>
    <h1>Your greeting: @Model.Greeting</h1>
</div>
```

A view is simply a file with a `.cshtml` extension that contains a bit of Razor syntax that specifies the view we want to render. The preceding view is stored in a file named `Greeting.cshtml`.

We can specify that this view should handle a specific response by setting the `DefaultView` parameter to `Greeting`, as follows:

```
public class GreetingService : Service
{
  [DefaultView("Greeting")]
  public object Get(GetGreeting request)
  {
    return new GetGreetingResponse
    {
      Greeting = "Hello, " + request.Name + "!"
    };
  }
}
```

In some scenarios, you'll want custom Razor files to handle different methods on a service—for instance, a GET request, which provides a list of records, might want one view model, while a GET for a specific record might want another view model that handles that specific case. However, if every method on our service should return the same view, we can do that by placing the annotation at the class level instead. Here's how the code for this purpose looks:

```
[DefaultView("Greeting")]
public class GreetingService : Service
{
  public object Get(GetGreeting request)
  {
    return new GetGreetingResponse
    {
      Greeting = "Hello, " + request.Name + "!"
    };
  }
}
```

How it works...

ServiceStack has a priority system when attempting to locate the correct view to render a response, as follows:

1. HttpResult can specify a view that will trump all other directives.

2. The second-highest priority is applying the DefaultView annotation on the service method.

3. After that, ServiceStack will look at a DefaultView annotation on our service class.

4. The ClientCanSwapTemplates directive allows a developer to specify that users can select a view, for instance, to request a special print view.

5. ServiceStack will look for views with the same name as the Request object provided to the service method.

6. Finally, ServiceStack will look for a view with the same name as the response object that our service method returns.

 Note that at the time of writing, the following reference is available for more information on the priority sequence at https://github.com/ServiceStack/ServiceStack/wiki/View-and-template-selection.

There's more...

The `ClientCanSwapTemplates` attribute allows more flexibility when doing frontend development. Just by passing an additional query string parameter to the URL of a service or view, we can get a custom HTML template for a service. For example, if we created a view called `Excited.cshtml` and placed it within another subdirectory of views, for example, `Custom`, we can call this view simply by adding `View=Excited` to our URL.

This functionality makes it easy to try out new changes in the UI and compare them to existing templates just by changing a query string value.

Creating and displaying a login and registration page based on authentication

In this recipe, we will create a `HelloWorld` page that requires authentication to be rendered by the server. We will also go over binding a simple form, with validation, to register new users and store information about them using ServiceStack's `IUserAuthRepository`.

Getting ready

If you are starting from a new project, please see the section *Creating a ServiceStack solution with Visual Studio and NuGet* in *Appendix A, Getting Started*. We also recommend installing the ServiceStackVS-Visual Studio extension if you are using Visual Studio 2013 Community Edition or later. If you have this extension, create a new project using the **ServiceStack ASP. NET with Bootstrap** template.

Note that the ServiceStackVS extension can be found at `https://visualstudiogallery.msdn.microsoft.com/5bd40817-0986-444d-a77d-482e43a48da7`.

How to do it...

1. Create a new **ServiceStack ASP.NET with Bootstrap** project, as follows:

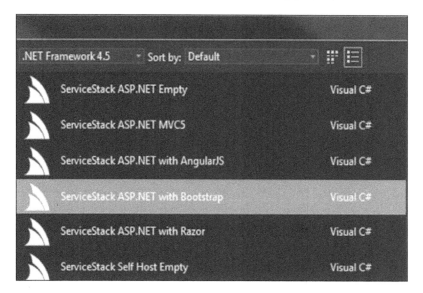

2. Add the `ServiceStack.Ormlite.Sqlite.Windows` package using NuGet to the main host project. This is the project that contains `AppHost`:

   Install-Package ServiceStack.OrmLite.Sqlite.Windows

3. Create an application setting in `web.config` for your connection string, as follows:

   `<add key="ConnectionString" value="~/App_Data/db.sqlite" />`

4. Inside the `Configure` method of `AppHost`, register a Sqlite connection factory to the IoC container, as follows:

```
var appSettings = new AppSettings();
container.Register(appSettings);
container.Register<IDbConnectionFactory>(
new OrmLiteConnectionFactory(
  appSettings.GetString("ConnectionString")
    .MapHostAbsolutePath(), SqliteDialect.Provider));
```

5. Also, inside the `Configure` method, register a new `AuthFeature` plugin configured for `CredentialsAuthProvider`, as follows:

```
Plugins.Add(new AuthFeature(() => new AuthUserSession(),
  new IAuthProvider[]
  {
    new CredentialsAuthProvider()
  })
{
  HtmlRedirect = "~/foo",
  IncludeRegistrationService = true
});
```

6. Also, register `IUserAuthRepository` using the Sqlite `IDbConnectionFactory` method, as follows:

```
container.Register<IUserAuthRepository>(c =>
  new OrmLiteAuthRepository(c.Resolve<IDbConnectionFactory>())
  {
    MaxLoginAttempts = appSettings.Get("MaxLoginAttempts", 5)
  });
```

Now that your application is configured for credential-based authentication, we can now work on the Razor UI and registration form. We'll make use of the `Url.Content` function provided by Razor to resolve the correct location for our URL paths.

7. Add the `ss-utils.js` library to your application by adding the script included on the `Views/_Layout.cshtml` page:

```
<!-- jQuery (necessary for Bootstrap's JavaScript plugins)
-->
<script src="@Url.Content(
"~/scripts/jquery-1.9.0.min.js")"></script>
<!-- Include all compiled plugins (below), or include
individual files as needed -->
<script src="@Url.Content(
"~/scripts/bootstrap.min.js")"></script>
<script src="@Url.Content(
"~/js/ss-utils.js")"></script>
```

8. We want to restrict the current `HelloWorld` page from being used by anyone but authenticated users. Wrap the controls in an `if` statement using the @ Razor syntax, as follows:

```
@if (IsAuthenticated)
{
  <div>
```

```
            <input class="form-control input-lg"
                   ng-model="name"
                   id="Name"
                   type="text"
                   placeholder="Type your name">
        <p id="helloResult"
           style="font-size: large; margin-top: 15px;"></p>
    </div>
```

9. If they are not authenticated, show the registration form in place of the `HelloWorld` input box:

```
} else {
  <form id="form-register" method="POST"
        action="@(new Register().ToPostUrl())">
    <input type="hidden" name="AutoLogin" value="true"/>
    <div class="form-group">
      <input class="form-control input-lg"
             type="text" id="FirstName" name="FirstName"
             value="" placeholder="First Name">
      <span class="help-block"></span>
    </div>
    <div class="form-group">
      <input class="form-control input-lg"
             type="text" id="LastName" name="LastName"
             value="" placeholder="Last Name">
        <span class="help-block"></span>
    </div>
    <div class="form-group">
      <input class="form-control input-lg"
             type="text" id="Email" name="Email"
             value="" placeholder="Email">
      <span class="help-block"></span>
    </div>
    <div class="form-group">
      <input class="form-control input-lg"
            type="password" id="Password" name="Password"
            value="" placeholder="Password">
      <span class="help-block"></span>
    </div>
    <div class="form-group">
      <button class="btn btn-lg btn-default"
      type="submit">Register</button>
```

```
        </div>
        <div class="clearfix"></div>
    </form>
```

10. Bind the form using the `ss-utils.js` method `bindForm`:

```
<script>
  $("#form-register").bindForm({
    success: function(r) {
    location.href = '/';
    }
  });
</script>
```

How it works...

When you now initially load the page, you are greeted with the registration form and login, as shown in the following screenshot:

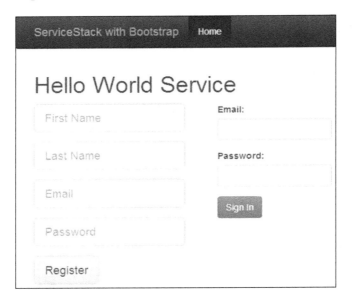

This is because the only HTML being rendered is that in the `else` statement in the `default.cshtml` file. If you're dealing with sensitive information where it would be inappropriate to just hide/show elements on the client, this can be good practice even for **Single-Page Applications (SPA)** using AngularJS or another SPA JavaScript framework.

If the user is authenticated, they are greeted with the original `HelloWorld` demo. The authentication and registration is being handled by the plugins and services that were configured in the `AppHost` class of the application, as follows:

```
Plugins.Add(new AuthFeature(() => new AuthUserSession(),
  new IAuthProvider[] {
    new CredentialsAuthProvider()
  })
{
  HtmlRedirect = "~/",
  IncludeRegistrationService = true
});
```

The `AuthFeature` plugin being registered here is the standard `AuthFeature` plugin that is bundled with the `ServiceStack.Server` package. For more details on `AuthUserSession` and all manner of `IAuthProvider` and their role and how to customize them, see *Chapter 7, Security and Authentication*.

One line to note about enabling registration is the line `IncludeRegistrationService = true` inside `AuthFeature`. This property ensures that another plugin is being registered. If you didn't include this line or `Plugins.Add(new RegistrationFeature())`, the registration of new users wouldn't work.

Now that the registration of new users is enabled and configured, we still need somewhere this data can be stored. ServiceStack provides the `IUserAuthRepository` interface to handle user authorization and storing them alongside user details, as follows:

```
container.Register<IUserAuthRepository>(c =>
new OrmLiteAuthRepository(c.Resolve<IDbConnectionFactory>())
{
  MaxLoginAttempts = 5
});
```

`OrmLiteAuthRepostiory` requires the use of `IDbConnectionFactory`, which in this example's case, is a Sqlite connection factory as specified by `SqliteDialect.Provider` when we registered `OrmLiteConnectionFactory`. We have configured `OrmLiteAuthRepository` to accept the maximum number of login attempts as 5, as shown in the preceding code snippet.

When we try to log in to a valid account using a registered email but attempt more than 5 times, the account becomes locked. Here's how the screen would look when an incorrect username or password is used:

On the client side, we are utilizing the built-in `ss-utils.js` library to bind our forms. For more information on this, see the recipe Using ServiceStack JS library to handle form submission, validation and error messages in this chapter.

This enables our forms to cleanly display error and validation messages provided the correct HTML is used. The HTML class of `error-summary` is used for any errors coming back from the server, which includes authentication errors or server exceptions but not validation messages. Validation messages look for the HTML class of `help-block` as a sibling of the previous input element. Here's how the code for this purpose looks:

```
<div class="form-group">
    <input class="form-control input-lg" type="text" id="Email"
    name="Email" value="" placeholder="Email">
    <span class="help-block"></span>
</div>
```

Hello World Se

Test

McTest

test@test

'Email' is not a valid email address

·········

Register

Once we successfully log in or register, the user will be presented with the original demo and they successfully authenticate. If the user returns with a valid session token, the registration/login will not be displayed, as shown in the following screenshot:

Hello World Service

world

Hello, world!

There's more...

In this example, we showed you how to switch between rendering HTML intended for authenticated and unauthenticated users. However, the `Hello` web services are *not secured*. In this example, we are simply changing the renderer HTML depending on whether a user is authenticated; an anonymous user could still utilize the `/hello` service. To require authentication on the service as well, a single attribute can be used on the service method. Here's how the example code looks:

```
[Authenticate]
public object Any(Hello request)
{
    return new HelloResponse { Result = "Hello,
    {0}!".Fmt(request.Name) };
}
```

Now, if we try to manually navigate to `/hello/test`, we end up back on the default page, but with the following URL:

```
http://localhost:4930/?redirect=http%3a%2f%2flocalhost%3a4930%2fhello
%2ftest
```

We end up back on the home page due to the `HtmlRedirect` property set on `AuthFeature`, `HtmlRedirect = "~/"`. If we log in on the home page, the demonstration works as normal, and we can successfully navigate to the `/hello/test` path.

Submitting a form to a service and handling server-side validation on an HTML client

In this recipe, we will look at an example of submitting an HTML form to an existing ServiceStack service. We will utilize some JavaScript that the ServiceStack server hosts, which helps us bind data from a form.

Getting ready

If you are starting with a new project, please go to the section *Creating a ServiceStack solution with Visual Studio and NuGet* in *Appendix A*, *Getting Started*, to help you get set up.

We will be using some existing services from the `PlacesToVisit` examples with some modification to show the use of validation.

How to do it...

1. Within the `Configure` method of your application host, register dependencies for the use of Sqlite and the repository interface from the `PlacesToVisit` domain, as follows:

```
container.RegisterAutoWired<PlacesToVisitAppSettings>();
var appSettings =
  container.Resolve<PlacesToVisitAppSettings>();
var dbFactory = new OrmLiteConnectionFactory(
appSettings.Get("sqlLiteConnectionString", "")
    .MapHostAbsolutePath(),
  SqliteDialect.Provider);
container.Register<IDbConnectionFactory>(dbFactory);
container.RegisterAutoWiredAs<PlacesToVisitRepository,
  IPlacesToVisitRepository>();
container.RegisterAutoWiredAs<MemoryCacheClient,
  ICacheClient>();
container.Resolve<IPlacesToVisitRepository>()
    .InitializeSchema();
```

2. Register plugins to enable Razor templates and validate using `FluentValidation`:

```
Plugins.Add(new ValidationFeature());
container.RegisterValidators(typeof(PlaceService).Assembly);
Plugins.Add(new RazorFormat());
```

3. Create a validator for the `CreatePlaceToVisit` request object:

```
public class PlaceValidator :
  AbstractValidator<CreatePlaceToVisit>
{
  public PlaceValidator()
  {
    RuleFor(x => x.Name).NotEmpty();
  }
}
```

4. Create a fluent rule for the `CreatePlaceToVisit` request, which ensures an empty `Name` cannot be provided, as follows:

```
RuleFor(x => x.Name).NotEmpty();
```

5. Create an HTML form inside a Razor template, which in this case is the `default.cshtml` file, as follows:

```
<form id="form-addplace" action="@(
    new PlacesToVisit.ServiceModel
        .CreatePlaceToVisit().ToPostUrl())"
    method="POST">
  <div class="row">
    <div class="col-sm-3 form-group">
      <label for="Name">Name</label>
      <input class="form-control input-sm"
             type="text" id="Name" name="Name"
             value="" placeholder="">
      <span class="help-block"></span>
    </div>
    <div class="col-sm-3 form-group">
      <label for="Description">Description</label>
      <input class="form-control input-sm"
             type="text" id="Description"
             name="Description"
             value="" placeholder="">
      <span class="help-block"></span>
    </div>
    <div class="col-sm-1 form-group">
      <label> </label><br />
      <button class="btn btn-sm btn-default"
              type="submit">Create place</button>
    </div>
  </div>
  <div class="clearfix"></div>
</form>
```

6. Include the required JavaScript/CSS dependencies, jQuery, Bootstrap, and ServiceStack's `ss-util.js` in the `_Layout.cshtml` page so they are included in all child views, as follows:

```
<head>
  <title>ServiceStack with Razor</title>
  <script type="text/javascript"
  src="//cdnjs.cloudflare.com/ajax/libs/jquery/2.1.1/jquery.m
  in.js"></script>
  <script type="text/javascript"
  src="//maxcdn.bootstrapcdn.com/bootstrap/3.2.0/js/bootstrap
  .min.js"></script>
```

```
<script type="text/javascript"
src="@Url.Content("~/js/ss-utils.js")"></script>
<link
href="//maxcdn.bootstrapcdn.com/bootstrap/3.2.0/css/bootstr
ap.min.css" rel="stylesheet" />
</head>
```

7. Bind the form using jQuery and `ss-utils.js`:

```
$("#form-addplace").bindForm({
  success: function (response) {
    addPlace(response.Place);
    $("#form-addplace input").val('')
      .first().focus();
  }
});
```

How it works...

In this example, we are using the features of Razor and `ss-utils.js` to help find a form, post data, view the results, and handle validation errors on the client.

For persistence, we are using Sqlite with `ServiceStack.OrmLite` for access. For more information on using OrmLite, see *Chapter 4, Object Relational Mapping (OrmLite)*.

To enable validation, we need to register the `ValidationFeature` plugin:

```
Plugins.Add(new ValidationFeature());
```

Once added, the IoC container needs to know which assembly, or assemblies, to look in to add any custom validation classes we might have. For this example, we have created a custom validator that checks to make sure a `Name` was provided when creating a new place via the `CreatePlaceToVisit` POST request, as follows:

```
public class PlaceValidator :
AbstractValidator<CreatePlaceToVisit>
{
    public PlaceValidator()
    {
    RuleFor(x => x.Name).NotEmpty();
    }
}
```

As can be seen in the preceding code, the validator is registering a rule for the `Name` property of the request. For more information on writing custom validators and rules, see *Chapter 6, Filters and Validators*.

Now that the services have been set up, we move to the client to use the `ss-utils.js` library to help us handle these requests and responses from our server. The `ss-utils.js` library is actually in the ServiceStack framework, so no additional files have to be downloaded and the version of the `ss-utils.js` library always matches that of the server you are running. This file is accessible at the path of your services with `/js/ss-utils.js` appended. So, for example, if you were hosting your web services at `http://localhost:8080/services/api`, the full address to the `ss-utils.js` library would be `http://localhost:8080/services/api/js/ss-utils.js`. In the example, we are hosting the web services at the root path of the server, as follows:

```
<script type="text/javascript" src="@Url.Content(
"~/js/ss-utils.js")"></script>
```

This library does have a dependency on jQuery, so you will have to include jQuery before the script tag mentioned in the preceding code is included on your page.

The form on the page we are using is written into a Razor template. One of the advantages of using Razor with client-side frameworks, such as AngularJS and/or jQuery, is to let the server handle logic around paths for web services. In the example, the form action attribute gets the URL from the server at the time of rendering the HTML, as follows:

```
<form id="form-addplace"
action="@(new
PlacesToVisit.ServiceModel.CreatePlaceToVisit().ToPostUrl())"
method="POST">
```

Using the preceding code, the HTML doesn't have to change even if the path for the `CreatePlaceToVisit` service changes. The URL is resolved at runtime using the Razor syntax above. This information is available via an extension method that looks for the related route of the request object. This will only work with a class that has been registered with the server as a route.

The form element and its related input fields need to follow a naming convention that matches the request object they will be populating. This is for two reasons, which are as follows:

► To populate the request object upon the action of the form

► To map the client with the help of `ss-utils.js`

```
<input class="form-control input-sm" type="text"
id="Name" name="Name"
value="" placeholder="">
```

Either the `Name` attribute or the `id` attribute can be used to match with the request object. Both are not needed for `ss-utils.js` to bind to the correct property of the request object. Both are illustrated to show the valid choices of HTML attributes that can be used to map.

Another client-side library to reference is the Bootstrap library. Validation and error styling bind together with the use of `ss-utils.js`. If we add an element next to an input field that is in a form bound with the `ss-utils.js` library, we can display user-friendly validation messages associated with that field, as follows:

```
<label for="Name">Name</label>
    <input class="form-control input-sm" type="text"
    id="Name" name="Name" value="" placeholder="">
    <span class="help-block"></span>
```

This `<span>` element will be displayed and populated by `ss-utils.js` if the server returns any validation errors after a POST request. If you want to display error messages to the user, we can add an element at the bottom of our form with the class `error-summary`, as follows:

```
<span class="error-summary"></span>
```

Last of all is the script that binds all this together. Form elements must be initially bound so that the aforementioned functionality is enabled. Custom logic on a successful action can also be registered here, as follows:

```
$("#form-addplace").bindForm({
    success: function (response) {
        addPlace(response.Place);
        $("#form-addplace input").val('')
            .first().focus();
    }
});
```

As shown in the previous code, a JavaScript object with a `success` property can be added to handle logic after a successful request. If you are familiar with jQuery AJAX functionality, this should look familiar. The preceding code is handling the additional client side and then focusing on the first input field ready for the next place to be added.

To take full advantage of the `ss-utils.js` library, Bootstrap, CSS, and JS should be used. This combination makes short work of the simple CRUD web form where it might take a lot longer to get the same functionality with more sophisticated client-side frameworks, such as AngularJS or Ember.

6

Filters and Validators

In this chapter, we will go through the following recipes:

- ▶ Creating static validation rules using fluent syntax
- ▶ Returning meaningful HTTP error messages
- ▶ Adding custom headers via response filter
- ▶ Restricting file uploads by type using filters
- ▶ Creating a user-configurable HTTP callback service using a response filter
- ▶ Applying a rate limit to a web service endpoint using a request filter
- ▶ Restrict user actions with session details using a validator

Introduction

In this chapter, we are looking at filtering and validating requests and responses. Filters can help keep the logic in your service simple and easy to maintain, while validators can help with form presentation of errors as well as isolating the validation logic from your services. Filters and validators in ServiceStack provide a huge amount of functionality to simplify your web services. Request-and-response filters allow you to control what happens before a request is processed as well as providing a nice way to do any postprocessing to the response if required. Server-side validation with human-readable messages is always something a web application requires, and ServiceStack validators, along with fluent syntax creates an encapsulated and easy-to-read way of building that functionality into your web application.

The fluent syntax style often leads to code that is more expressive and, thereby, more easily understood. This style is often thought to be richer and more concise than other techniques, and its addition to ServiceStack certainly improved matters in that it has made validation much easier to implement.

ServiceStack includes the popular open source FluentValidation library in order to enable this feature. You can read more about FluentValidation at its CodePlex site at `http://fluentvalidation.codeplex.com/`.

Validations and request filters run before your main service code runs, while response filters run after your main service code runs. You can visualize the flow of requests and responses through this pipeline in the following way:

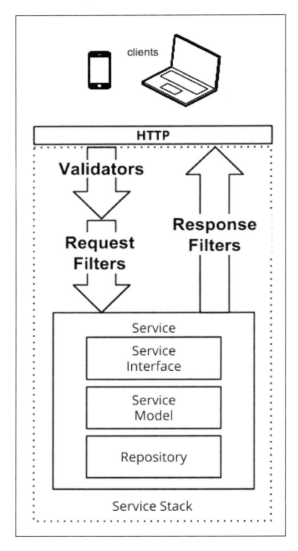

We will have a look at returning meaningful errors from your API as well, as this aids the developers in building clients against your services with debugging.

Filters can be used for restriction as well as extension, and we will cover filtering uploads, enabling webhooks, rate limiting your web services, and some advanced extension by enabling session validation.

Creating static validation rules using fluent syntax

ServiceStack offers a number of ways to do validation of client requests. One of the easiest and the most powerful is the **Fluent Validation syntax**—we can use **Language-Integrated Query** (**LINQ**) to create expressions that describe the rules we want ServiceStack to follow when validating request DTOs. ServiceStack includes the type `IRuleBuilder` that has built-in things such as `NotEmpty`, `NotEqual`, `LessThan`, and so on, along with more advanced features, such as validating credit cards and e-mail addresses.

How to do it...

What we're going to do is add a validation for `Greeting` in order to show how validation works:

1. The first thing we're going to need to do is add the `ValidationFeature` plugin, as follows:

    ```
    Plugins.Add(new ValidationFeature());
    ```

2. Next, we'll create a `GreetingRequestValidator` class that extends the `AbstractValidator<T>` class. In the constructor, we'll create rules for the `Greeting` objects that our service processes, as follows:

    ```
    public class GreetingRequestValidator :
    AbstractValidator<Greeting>
    {
      public GreetingRequestValidator()
      {
        RuleFor(request => request.Name).NotEqual("name");
      }
    }
    ```

    This rule specifies that `Greetingrequest` should not have a `Name` property that is equal to the `name` string.

3. Once we've created our validator, we'll tell ServiceStack where to find the validation rules in our `Configuration` object, as follows:

```
public override void Configure(Funq.Container container)
{
  Plugins.Add(new ValidationFeature());
  container.RegisterValidators(
typeof(GreetingRequestValidator).Assembly);
}
```

How it works...

When ServiceStack sees the incoming `HTTPRequest` class and maps it to the `Greeting` type, it knows that the `GreetingRequestValidator` class has been registered to handle validation of this request. ServiceStack then runs the logic we put into the constructor, which, in this case, simply insists that the `Name` property of `Greeting` isn't the string name. As our request object failed this validation, ServiceStack will return a **400 status message** indicating that a bad HTTP request was received. It will also include a `ResponseStatus` object in the JSON format that will include some details as to why the request failed. Here's how the status message including the `ResponseStatus` object looks:

```
ResponseStatus: {
  ErrorCode: "NotEqual",
  Message: "'Name' should not be equal to 'name'.",
  Errors: [
      {
        ErrorCode: "NotEqual",
        FieldName: "Name",
        Message: "'Name' should not be equal to 'name'."
      }
    ]
}
```

There's more...

This example covers the simplest scenario. We can do much more complex validations if required using `.Must()`. For instance, we could pass in a function that does a complex validation:

```
public class GreetingRequestValidator :
AbstractValidator<Greeting>
{
    public GreetingRequestValidator()
```

```
  {
    RuleFor(gr => gr.Name)
      .Must(notBeBadWord);
  }

  bool notBeBadWord(string word)
  {
    var badWords = new List<string> {"abc", "def"};
    return ! badWords.Contains(word);
  }
}
```

In this case, `GreetingRequestValidator` will execute the `notBeBadWord` method on the `Name` property of `Greeting`, which performs a series of operations. In some cases, this is an easier way to run validation logic that exists in other places, instead of maintaining the validation logic in the validator itself, which can increase maintainability.

Returning meaningful HTTP error messages

The HTTP specification has several standard HTTP error messages. The 1.0 draft of the Hypertext Transfer Protocol from 1996 established the notion of standardized response status codes. The **404 Not Found** status code is perhaps the most famous, as web users have generally seen this at least once in their travels, even when websites return a friendly page when a 404 error is encountered.

The status codes have withstood the test of time and were included in the HTTP 1.1 draft that came out three years later in 1999, which continues to be the standard HTTP protocol today. HTTP 2.0, which will most likely replace it, is in only in draft form today.

One reason that it can be important to return status codes that are standardized and meaningful is that HTTP-aware networking equipment and web browsers can then make intelligent decisions about what to do when a response is encountered.

For instance, a network proxy might cache the content of a `GET` request that results in a **200 series response** as `GET` requests are meant to be idempotent. A search engine might see a **404 Not Found** status code and decide not to return that URL in search results as it appears not to exist anymore. It's also common practice when building web applications to use status codes between client logic and the web server to make decisions about what the client should do.

 A list of some useful HTTP status codes can be found at the end of this chapter. Consider using one of these instead of throwing a general exception.

When you're building a service that other developers (or even you) will need to use, it can make it easier to consume when the status codes themselves make sense. For instance, a server might return a **400 Bad Request** status code when a malformed request object arrives or a request object contains data that isn't valid according to the server. However, **409 Conflict** might be a better code to return when a user tries to save and create a new record with an ID of an existing record. If the server returns human-readable text along with this status code, the web app can decide to display that human-readable text to the user along with some visualization of how the user can correct the issue; for instance, turning on a red x symbol next to the form field when the user might have entered invalid data.

Getting ready

In this example, we'll develop a barebone web app that posts data to a ServiceStack endpoint. In the case of a failed validation, the server will return an HTTP status code that's useful to the client, and then the client will render the results based on the HTTP status code that the server returns. We'll build upon the Greeting service from the previous recipe's basic HelloWorldService, as follows:

```
[Route("/hello","POST")]
[Route("/hello/{Name}")]
public class Greeting:IReturn<GreetingResponse>
{
    public string Name { get; set; }
}

public class GreetingResponse
{
    public string Greeting { get; set; }
    public string GreetingName { get; set; }
}

public class GreetingService : Service
{
    [DefaultView("Greeting")]
    public object Any(Greeting request)
    {
        return new GreetingResponse
                {
                    Greeting = "Hello, " + request.Name + "!",
                    GreetingName = request.Name
                };
    }
}
```

How to do it...

One way to set the HTTP status code is to have the service throw a specific exception that ServiceStack will recognize. For instance, we could add the following logic to our `Any` method:

```
[DefaultView("Greeting")]
public object Any(Greeting request)
{
  if (isExistingName(request.Name))
  {
    throw new HttpError(
    HttpStatusCode.Conflict, "That name already exists.");
  }

  return new GreetingResponse
            {
                Greeting = "Hello, " + request.Name + "!",
                GreetingName = request.Name
            };
  bool isExistingName(string word)
  {
    var existingNames = new List<string> { "Kyle", "Darren" };
    return existingNames.Contains(word);
  }
}
```

Next, we'll develop a simple web app that can post data to this service and handle service errors when they are received. To keep things simple, we won't use any specific JavaScript frameworks in this example besides a little bit of jQuery:

```
'<script type="text/javascript">
    var sendGreeting = function (name) {
        $.ajax({
            url: '/hello',
            data: { "Name": name },
            dataType: "json",
            type: "POST",
            statusCode: {
                409: function (error) {
                    $('#greeting_display')
                            .text("Sorry, name already in use.");
                }
            },
```

```
                    success: setGreeting
          });
     };
     var setGreeting = function (greeting) {
          $('#greeting_display').text(greeting.Greeting);
          $('#name').val(greeting.GreetingName);
     };
</script>

<div>
     <form action="/hello" method="POST"
          onsubmit="sendGreeting($('#name').val()); return false">
          Name for greeting:
          <input id="name" type="text" name="Name" />
          <input type="submit" />
     </form>
     <h1>Your greeting:
     <div id="greeting_display">@Model.Greeting</div></h1>
</div>
```

 Most modern JavaScript frameworks have ways to handle HTTP status codes from AJAX requests. For instance, take a look at Angular's `$http` service that could easily be used.

As the service returns the correct status code, it's simple for us to add a handler in our JavaScript that does the right thing when we encounter this error.

How it works...

When we throw `HttpError` with the first argument of `HttpStatusCode.Conflict`, ServiceStack understands that we want to return an HTTP `409` status code in this case. We can make use of this in our web app with some simple JavaScript.

In the web app, our `$.ajax()` call has a `409` property in the `statusCode` configuration object that contains a function that we want to run whenever we throw this specific exception. We could easily add more handlers for other status codes too, both in our ServiceStack code and in our JavaScript.

There's more...

While the preceding example showed an example handled purely in the service, we can also make use of FluentValidators, discussed in previous recipes. FluentValidators are a concise way to keep logic about our domain models in one place instead of spreading it out over all of our services.

When we make use of FluentValidators, generally ServiceStack returns a **400 Bad Request** status code, with status text that's specific to the kind of validation that fails. For instance, FluentValidators allow you to provide a predicate that will validate certain properties of the request DTO by saying that a property must fulfill the predicate. If you pass a Must() predicate into a rule, ServiceStack returns a **400 Predicate** status if that predicate doesn't return true. Likewise, if you use the .NotEmpty() validator on a specific property, ServiceStack returns a **400 NotEmpty** status. This could allow us to further develop this application to handle those cases in JavaScript as well. This is how the code for this purpose looks:

```
public class GreetingRequestValidator :
AbstractValidator<Greeting>
    {
        public GreetingRequestValidator()
        {
            RuleFor(gr => gr.Name)
                .NotEmpty()
                .Must(notBeReservedWord);
        }

        bool notBeReservedWord(string word)
        {
            var reservedWords = new List<string> {"abc", "def"};
            return ! reservedWords.Contains(word);
        }
    }
```

In this case, we don't need to specify that we want to return a 400 error message because ServiceStack defaults to this behavior. For instance, if we tried to submit the name abc, our .Must() predicate would return false. In that case, ServiceStack would return the following status code:

```
HTTP/1.1 400 Predicate
```

We could handle both of these cases easily in our JavaScript by adding a 400 property to the statusCode object of our $.ajax call, as follows:

```
var sendGreeting = function (name) {
    $.ajax({
        url: '/hello',
        data: { "Name": name },
        dataType: "json",
        type: "POST",
        statusCode: {
            409: function (error)
            {
                $('#greeting_display')
                    .text("Sorry, that name is already in use.");
            },
            400: badRequest
        },
        success: setGreeting
    });
};
var badRequest = function (error) {
    if (error.statusText == "Predicate") {
    $('#greeting_display')
    .text("We're not accepting names like that right now.");
    } else if (error.statusText == "NotEmpty") {
        $('#greeting_display').text("You must provide a name.");
    }

};
```

Adding custom headers via the response filter

In some situations, developers might need to attach custom headers to requests and responses from your web service APIs. An example of this might be additional information about a resource in the response, such as an expiry date. In this example, we will have a look at adding a custom header to the response via an attribute filter.

Getting ready

If you are using a non-express version of Visual Studio, you can start this recipe using ServiceStackVS and creating a project based on the **ServiceStack ASP.NET Empty** template. In this example, we are going to use Postman as the client to test and view the custom headers in the response. If you are using an express version of Visual Studio, please follow *Creating a ServiceStack solution with Visual Studio and NuGet* in *Appendix A, Getting Started* and start from the third instruction in the following *How to do it...* section.

How to do it...

1. Create a new project using a template from the ServiceStackVS extension. For this example, we will be using the **ServiceStack ASP.NET Empty** template:

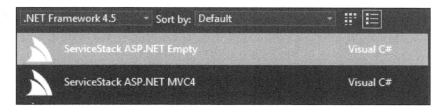

2. Create a new class for the custom attribute filter inherited from `ResponseFilterAttribute`, as follows:

```
public class CustomHeaderFilterAttribute :
ResponseFilterAttribute
{
  public IAppSettings Settings { get; set; }

  public override void Execute(
  IRequest req, IResponse res, object responseDto)
  {
    var originalResponse =
    res.OriginalResponse as HttpResponseWrapper;
    string customHeader =
    "X-Hello-Request-Processed-DateTime";
    if (originalResponse != null &&
     originalResponse.Headers.HasKeys() &&
     !originalResponse.Headers.AllKeys.Contains(customHeader))
    {
```

```
        res.AddHeader(customHeader,
        DateTime.Now.ToString("HH:m:s tt
        zzz"));
      }
    }
  }
```

3. Apply the filter to the method of the request, as follows:

```
public class MyService : Service
{
  [CustomHeaderFilter]
  public object Any(Hello request)
  {
    return new HelloResponse
    {
      Result = "Hello, {0}!".Fmt(request.Name)
    };
  }
}
```

How it works...

Filter attribute base classes are provided in the ServiceStack framework to make it easy to write your own custom filter attribute. This applies to both request and response filters.

This response filter is processed after the service method has successfully returned. Once the request has been processed, our filter's Execute method is processed, as follows:

```
if (originalResponse != null &&
    originalResponse.Headers.HasKeys() &&
    !originalResponse.Headers.AllKeys.Contains(customHeader))
{
  res.AddHeader(customHeader,
  DateTime.Now.ToString("HH:m:s tt zzz"));
}
```

After safety checking to add our custom HTTP header, we add the current DateTime object.

An advantage of using the ResponseFilterAttrbiute base class over IHasResponseFilter is that auto-wiring dependencies to properties on your custom attribute class. Register your custom application settings from your filter and write the following property:

```
public IAppSettings Settings { get; set; }
```

For more information on dependency injection using ServiceStack's Funq container, see *Managing dependencies with Funq and Inversion of Control (IoC)* recipe in *Chapter 1, Configuration and Routing.*

The following is a screenshot of the response to the preceding property:

```
Hello-Request-Processed-DateTime — 17:2:52 PM +10:00

Server — Microsoft-IIS/8.0

Vary — Accept

X-AspNet-Version — 4.0.30319
```

Although this example is simple, custom response headers are a very useful addition that can be added per service method using an easy-to-understand custom attribute.

There's more...

Filter attributes offer a clean way of injecting a method call before or after the request is processed. However, if we want to interact with the actual request or response DTO, we need to cast the object. One way around this is to use `RegisterTypedRequestFilter<T>` or `RegisterTypedResponseFilter<T>` to register the same method used in the attribute, but this time with a type-safe request or response DTO. These can be registered from the configuration step of the application. For example, if you wanted to add the `Name` property of the `Hello request` argument to a header, you could write the following method:

```
RegisterTypedResponseFilter<HelloResponse>(
(request, response, helloResponse) =>
{
    var originalResponse =
    response.OriginalResponse as HttpResponseWrapper;
    if (originalResponse != null &&
        originalResponse.Headers.HasKeys() &&
        !originalResponse.Headers.AllKeys.Contains(
        "Hello-Request-Message-Processed"))
    {
        response.AddHeader("Hello-Request-Message-Processed",
        helloResponse.Result);
    }
});
```

The preceding code results in the following response viewed in the Postman Chrome plugin:

```
Hello-Request-Message-Processed → Hello, test!
Hello-Request-Processed-DateTime → 17:2:52 PM +10:00
Server → Microsoft-IIS/8.0
Vary → Accept
```

It's worth noting some of the benefits and drawbacks of using `TypedRequestFilter<T>` or `TypedResponseFilter<T>`. Typed filters are quite broadly applied to the DTO as opposed to the service method that processes the request. This might be beneficial depending on your requirements, so it's something to keep in mind when choosing which pattern you are going to use for filters. Also, although the addition of a strongly typed request or response DTO is a benefit, they can only be registered in `AppHost` of the application. This also might not be a problem, but it can break the encapsulation of application and service logic, which is encouraged to be separated by the project pattern of `Application`, `Application.ServiceInterface`, `Application.ServiceModel`, and `Application.Test`. If filter behavior is dictated by the application and not by the service interface, testing can become more problematic.

Restricting file uploads by type using filters

In this recipe, we will create a file upload service that restricts allowed media types to a predefined whitelist. This will be done by using a request filter attribute and applying it to a service that handles file uploading.

Getting ready

If you are using a non-express version of Visual Studio, you can start this recipe using ServiceStackVS and create a project based on ServiceStack ASP.NET with the Bootstrap template or one of the others that supports Razor by default. If you are using an express version of Visual Studio, please follow *Creating a ServiceStack solution with Visual Studio and NuGet* in *Appendix A, Getting Started* and start from the second instruction in the *How to do it...* section that is follows.

How to do it...

1. Create a new project using the ServiceStackVS template and based on **ServiceStack ASP.NET with Bootstrap**, as follows:

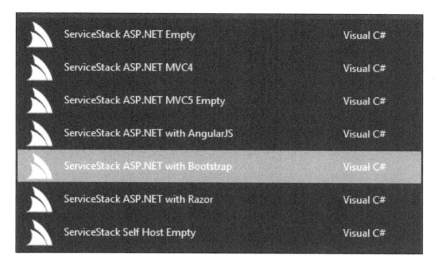

2. Create the file upload request and response objects with the configured `Route` of `/upload` within the `ServiceModel` project, as follows:

```
[Route("/upload")]
public class FileUpload : IReturn<FileUploadResponse>
{

}

public class FileUploadResponse
{
    public string FileName { get; set; }
}
```

3. Create a service to handle the file upload request and save to a temporary location. The service should be in the `ServiceInterface` project:

```
public class FileUploadService : Service
{
    public object Post(FileUpload request)
    {
        Request.Files[0].SaveTo("C:\\Temp\\" +
        Request.Files[0].FileName);

        return new FileUploadResponse
        {
            FileName = Request.Files[0].FileName
        };
    }
}
```

4. Create a request filter with a configurable `whitelist` string of file types, as follows:

```
public class FileUploadFilterAttribute :
RequestFilterAttribute
{
  private static string[] whiteList =
  {
    "application/vnd.openxmlformats-officedocument" +
    ".wordprocessingml.document",
    "application/vnd.openxmlformats-officedocument" +
    ".spreadsheetml.sheet",
    "application/vnd.openxmlformats-officedocument" +
    ".presentationml.presentation"
  };

  public override void Execute(
    IRequest req, IResponse res, object requestDto)
  {
    var appSettings = req.TryResolve<IAppSettings>();
    var fileTypeList = appSettings == null
                          ? whiteList
                          : appSettings.Get(
                            "FileUploadWhiteList",
                            whiteList);
    if (req.Files.Length == 0)
    {
      throw new HttpError(
        HttpStatusCode.BadRequest,
        "400",
        "No file upload provided");
    }

    if (!req.Files.All(
      file => fileTypeList.Any(
        type => type == file.ContentType))))
    {
      throw new HttpError(HttpStatusCode.UnsupportedMediaType,
        "Unsupported file type");
    }
  }
}
```

5. Apply the filter to the service:

```
public class FileUploadService : Service
{
  [FileUploadFilter]
  public object Post(FileUpload request)
  {
    Request.Files[0].SaveTo("../../" +
    Request.Files[0].FileName);
    return new FileUploadResponse
    {
      FileName = Request.Files[0].FileName
    };
  }
}
```

How it works...

Request filter attributes are executed *before* the service has had the chance to process the request. If the filter throws no exception and returns a response, the originally intended request will continue. In the filter itself, we have access to the original request, response and request DTO object, which allows us to resolve any required dependencies that the filter might need to use during the request.

In this example, we are using optional IAppSettings attribute to resolve a configured whitelist of accepted MIME types. If IAppSettings was not registered or the FileUploadWhiteList setting was not set, we have a list of accepted types to fall back on:

```
var appSettings = req.TryResolve<IAppSettings>();
var fileTypeList = appSettings == null ? whiteList :
appSettings.Get("FileUploadWhiteList", whiteList);
```

ServiceStack is already providing ContentType property of the file via the Files array of IHttpFile, so the filter uses the content type to compare with our configurable list.

When the filter encounters a request without a file or with a file that is not present on the whitelist string, we throw an appropriate HttpError.

There's more...

Ensuring that the service or filter throws the appropriate HttpError makes integration by other clients simpler and more consistent as the client can simply look at the returned status code to gauge how to handle the error on the client.

Due to the content type of file uploads, the server will respond with the content type of text/HTML. If there is no Razor view present, this will be ServiceStack's default Snapshot preview of the response. To make the response more useful, we can create a Razor view for file uploads. This will allow us, in a simple situation, to show the user some information about the success or failure of the file upload.

1. In the default view, create a basic form to use to upload the specific file:

```
@inherits ViewPage
@{
    ViewBag.Title = "File upload service";
}
<div>
    <div>
        <form action="/upload"
                method="POST"
                enctype="multipart/form-data">
            <div class="form-group">
                <input type="file"
                        name="fileUpload"
                        value=" "
                        class="form-control" />
            </div>
            <div class="form-group">
                <input type="submit"
                        value="Upload"
                        class="form-control"/>
            </div>
        </form>
    </div>
</div>
```

2. Create a new view inside the `Views` folder called `FileUpload.cshtml`:

```
@inherits ViewPage<FileUploadResponse>
@{
    ViewBag.Title = "File upload service";
}

@if (Response.StatusCode == 200)
{
    <div>File upload success - @Model.FileName</div>
}
else
```

```
{
  <div>Failed to upload file -
  @Response.StatusDescription</div>
}
```

Creating a user-configurable HTTP callback service using a response filter

In this recipe, we will look at adding callbacks or webhooks into your API. Webhooks are a method of using custom callbacks to alter the behavior of a web application often in order to provide a capability to integrate two separate web applications. For instance, GitHub provides a webhook that will call a service you define anytime someone forks your code—you might take advantage of them by creating an API that receives notifications when someone forks your code. You provide the service that GitHub calls, and GitHub makes sure to call your service any time that happens.

 You can read more about this and the many other webhooks GitHub provides at `https://developer.github.com/webhooks/`.

We will be focusing how to get this going using filter attributes so that you are also able to control which of your web services allows these callbacks. This technique can be useful for developers writing APIs for longer-running tasks for system-to-system integration, such as document generation, or perhaps a JavaScript client that wants to be notified when data changes in the backend processes.

 We will focus on the integration point within the ServiceStack framework, which doesn't include fault tolerance or logging. For a more robust solution, the incorporation of a message-queuing system will handle possible issues with the outgoing HTTP request.

Getting ready

First, we will create a new project from the ServiceStack Visual Studio extension, ServiceStackVS.

If you are using a Visual Studio Express edition, you can follow *Creating a ServiceStack solution with Visual Studio and NuGet* in *Appendix A, Getting Started*.

For this recipe, we are going to build an example client as well as the server. The client will be in place of another developer who is using the API and who wants to incorporate their own hosted services with the webhooks provided by the server solution.

In normal use, web users will call a service **HelloWorldService**. However, should it be requested, **HelloWorldService** can also register new requests for webhooks and even list what webhooks have been previously requested. The result of requesting a new webhook is that **HelloWorldService** will inspect incoming requests and call to any listeners when events arrive that match the requests for webhooks that we've seen until now:

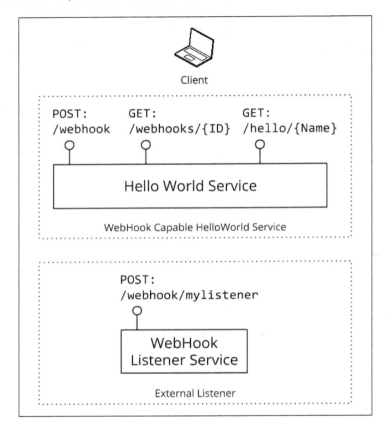

In this example, **HelloWorldService** is analogous to GitHub—a service that will provide callbacks if requested.

How to do it...

1. Create a new project using the **ServiceStack Self Host Empty** template from the `ServiceStackVS` extension:

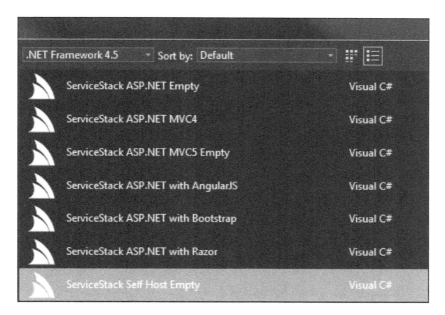

2. Create the `WebHook` and `WebHookResponse` classes to handle the request that will be sent from the server with the registered `webhook` listener. We will be hooking into another `Hello` request, so we can reuse the `Hello` and `HelloResponse` objects within the `WebHook` request:

```
[Route("/webhook/mylistener")]
public class WebHook
{
    public Hello Request { get; set; }
    public HelloResponse Response { get; set; }
}

[Route("/hello/{Name}")]
public class Hello : IReturn<HelloResponse>
{
    public string Name { get; set; }
}

public class HelloResponse
```

```
    {
        public string Result { get; set; }
    }
```

3. Create a service that writes out to the console window so that we can verify that the webhook listener is being handled by our service, as follows:

```
public class WebHookService : Service
{
    public object Post(WebHook request)
    {
        Console.WriteLine(
        "Hello, {0}, via webhook!".Fmt(request.Request.Name));
        return new {};
    }

    public object Any(Hello request)
    {
        return new HelloResponse {
           Result = "Hello, {0}!".Fmt(request.Name)
        };
    }
}
```

4. Run the self-hosted application to listen for requests, as follows:

Now that we have an example client listening to hooked requests, we can implement the server. In this example, we are only going to allow authenticated users to register and initiate webhook events, so we will need to enable user registration and authentication. More information about how this works can be found in *Chapter 7, Security and Authentication*. We will also use SQLite for persistence with OrmLite; for more information on using OrmLite, refer to *Chapter 4, Object Relational Mapping (OrmLite)*.

5. Create a new project from **ServiceStack ASP.NET with AngularJS**, as shown in the following screenshot:

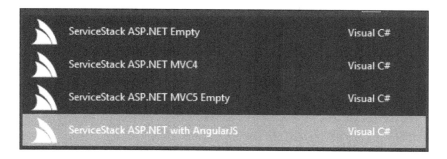

6. Install the `ServiceStack.OrmLite.Sqlite.Windows` NuGet package from the **Package Manager Console**:

```
Install-Package ServiceStack.OrmLite.Sqlite.Windows
```

7. Register `OrmLiteConnectionFactory` with a Sqlite dialect provider from within the `Configure` method of `AppHost`, as follows:

```
container.Register<IDbConnectionFactory>(
    new OrmLiteConnectionFactory(
      "~/App_Data/db.sqlite".MapHostAbsolutePath(),
      SqliteDialect.Provider));
```

8. Register `AuthFeature` with `CredentialAuthProvider` and the `RegistrationFeature` method from within the `Configure` method of `AppHost`:

```
Plugins.Add(
    new AuthFeature(
        () => new AuthUserSession(), new IAuthProvider[]
            {
                new CredentialsAuthProvider()
            }
        ));
Plugins.Add(new RegistrationFeature());
```

9. Register and Initialize `OrmLiteAuthRepository` from within the `Configure` method of `AppHost`, as follows:

```
container.Register<IUserAuthRepository>(new
OrmLiteAuthRepository(Resolve<IDbConnectionFactory>()));
container.Resolve<IUserAuthRepository>().InitSchema();
```

10. Create a class to represent `WebHookInstance` within a SQL table using OrmLite attributes, as follows:

```
public class WebHookInstance
{
    [AutoIncrement]
    public int Id { get; set; }
    public string UserName { get; set; }

    public string Url { get; set; }
    public string Name { get; set; }
    public string IncomingVerb { get; set; }
    public string IncomingRequestType { get; set; }
}
```

11. Ensure that the `WebHookInstance` database table is created on startup from within the `Configure` method of `AppHost`, as follows:

```
var dbConnectionFactory =
container.Resolve<IDbConnectionFactory>();
using (IDbConnection db =
dbConnectionFactory.OpenDbConnection())
{
    db.CreateTableIfNotExists<WebHookInstance>();
}
```

Now that our user authentication and database has been set up, we can create the web service to handle the registration of new webhooks.

12. Create request and response objects with `Route` to handle the incoming registration, as follows:

```
[Route("/webhook",Verbs = "POST")]
public class CreateWebHook : IReturn<WebHookResponse>
{
    public string Url { get; set; }
    public string Name { get; set; }
    public string IncomingVerb { get; set; }
    public string IncomingRequestType { get; set; }
}

public class WebHookResponse
{
    public List<WebHookInstance> WebHooks { get; set; }
    public WebHookInstance WebHook { get; set; }
}
```

13. Create a service to create and persist `WebHookInstance`:

```
[Authenticate]
public object Post(CreateWebHook request)
{
    WebHookInstance webHookInstance =
    request.ConvertTo<WebHookInstance>();
    webHookInstance.UserName =
    SessionAs<AuthUserSession>().UserName;
    Db.Insert(webHookInstance);

    return new WebHookResponse
    {
        WebHook = webHookInstance
    };
}
```

14. Create a response filter attribute to apply functionality to specific services, as follows:

```
public class WebHookFilterAttribute :
ResponseFilterAttribute
{
    public override void Execute(
      IRequest req, IResponse res, object responseDto)
    {
        var dbConnectionFactory =
        req.TryResolve<IDbConnectionFactory>();
        var session = req.GetSession();
        if (session == null || session.IsAuthenticated ==
        false)
        {
            return;
        }

        string verb = req.Verb;
        string typeName = req.Dto.GetType().Name;

        using (var db =
        dbConnectionFactory.OpenDbConnection())
        {
            var webHooks =
            db.Select<WebHookInstance>(
            x => x.UserName ==
            session.UserName).ToList();

            if (webHooks.Count == 0)
```

```
        {
            return;
        }

        if (webHooks.Any(
        x => x.IncomingVerb == verb &&
        x.IncomingRequestType == typeName) == false)
        {
            return;
        }
        foreach (var webHookInstance in webHooks)
        {
            var request = new WebHookData
            {
                Request = req.Dto,
                Response = res.Dto
            };
            WebHookInstance webHook = webHookInstance;
            new Task(
                () => NotifyExternalListener(
                    webHook.Url, request)).Start();
        }
    }
}

private static void NotifyExternalListener(
    string url, WebHookData request)
{
    JsonServiceClient client = new JsonServiceClient();
    client.Post<WebHookDataResponse>(url, request);
}
}
```

15. Attribute the existing `Hello` service with the new filter, as follows:

```
[WebHookFilter]
public object Any(Hello request)
{
    return new HelloResponse
    {
        Result = "Hello, {0}!".Fmt(request.Name)
    };
}
```

How it works...

With the example created, we are going to need to do the following four actions to the server to test the new functionality:

1. Register a new user
2. Log in
3. Create a new `WebHook` service using the `CreateWebHook` service request
4. Send a request to the `Hello` service with the client self-hosted service running

An easy way to illustrate this is using the `PostmanFeature` plugin so that we can use the Postman Chrome extension to make the following requests.

1. Register a new **Test** user by posting to the registration service:

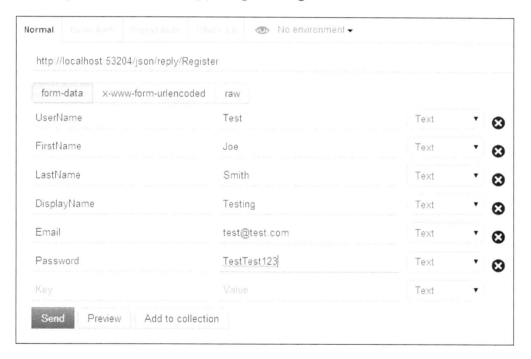

2. Log in as that new user, as follows:

3. Create `WebHookInstance` using the new service:

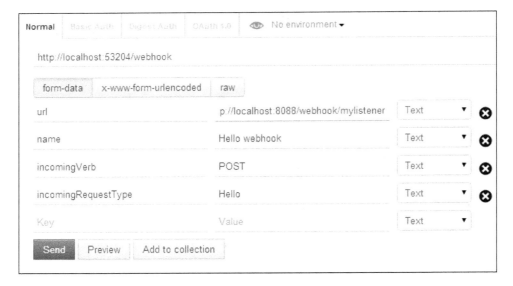

If you are using the Chrome Postman extension and have used it to log in to the application, you will have a valid authenticated session within Chrome. While the self-hosted web services are running, if you use Postman to make a request to the `Hello` service, the `WebHookFilterAttribute` class will be picked up and fired as a response filter. These filters run after the request has been processed but before the result has returned to the client.

In this example, we use a simple `Task.Start` command to run the additional HTTP requests asynchronously; otherwise, the client would be waiting for the webhooks to be processed before getting the response to their service request. A more robust solution would be using Redis or another message queue provider to queue the webhook requests to be processed by another process listening to the queue. To keep things simple for the sake of the example, we're omitting logging and exception handling as well.

Applying a rate limit to a web service endpoint using request filter

When creating a live API for developers to consume, it's a good idea to protect your API from abuse or misuse by limiting how many times developers can make requests within a specific timeframe. How much this is restricted will depend on a number of factors, including server resources, load generated by a request, and others. In this recipe, we will write a request filter attribute that can be applied to a web-service method to restrict the number of requests in a timeframe a single session can make. This recipe describes a technique that works well for a single server—if your web application has more than one web app server, you'll need to use a distributed cache of some kind, possibly a Redis instance instead of `MemoryCache`, which has been used in this recipe.

Getting ready

If you are using a non-express version of Visual Studio, you can start this recipe using ServiceStackVS and create a new project based on any of the ServiceStack templates available. If you are using an express version of Visual Studio, please follow *Creating a ServiceStack solution with Visual Studio and NuGet* in *Appendix A, Getting Started* and start from the second instruction in the following section.

How to do it...

1. Create a new project based on a template from ServiceStackVS.

2. Register `ICacheClient` in `AppHost` of the new project, as follows:

```
public override void Configure(Container container)
{
    //Config examples
    //this.Plugins.Add(new PostmanFeature());
    //this.Plugins.Add(new CorsFeature());
    container.Register<ICacheClient>(new
    MemoryCacheClient());
    this.Plugins.Add(new RazorFormat());
}
```

3. Create a new class that will represent the state of a rate limited service, as follows:

```
public class RateLimit
{
    public int Limit { get; set; }
    public int Remaining { get; set; }
    public DateTime Reset { get; set; }
}
```

4. Create a new filter attribute inheriting from `RequestFilterAttribute`, which is where all the logic for the rate filter is contained, as follows:

```
public class RateLimitedAttribute : RequestFilterAttribute
{
    public ICacheClient Cache { get; set; }

    public int RequestLimit { get; set; }
    public int RequestTimeInSeconds { get; set; }

    public override void Execute(
        IRequest req, IResponse res, object requestDto)
    {
        var session = req.GetSession();
        var rateLimit = Cache.Get<RateLimit>(session.Id);
        if (rateLimit != null && rateLimit.Remaining == 0)
        {
          throw new HttpError(429,
            "Too Many Requests",
            "You have exceeded your rate limit, it will be" +
            "reset in " +
            (rateLimit.Reset - DateTime.Now).TotalSeconds +
            " seconds");
        }
        if (rateLimit == null)
        {
            //First request since reset
            rateLimit = new RateLimit
            {
                Limit = RequestLimit,
                Remaining = RequestLimit,
                Reset = DateTime.Now.AddSeconds(
                            RequestTimeInSeconds)
            };
        }
```

```
                    //Update existing record
                    rateLimit.Remaining--;
                    Cache.Set<RateLimit>(session.Id,
                    rateLimit,
                    rateLimit.Reset -
                    DateTime.Now);
                    res.AddHeader("RateLimit",
                        RequestLimit.ToString());
                    res.AddHeader("Remaining",
                        rateLimit.Remaining.ToString());
                    res.AddHeader("Reset",
                    rateLimit.Reset
                    .ToUnixTime()
                    .ToString());
                }
            }
```

5. Apply the new filter to an existing web service using the attribute, as follows:

```
public class MyServices : Service
{
    [RateLimited(RequestLimit = 5,RequestTimeInSeconds =
    10)]
    public object Any(Hello request)
    {
      return new HelloResponse { Result = "Hello,
      {0}!".Fmt(request.Name) };
    }
}
```

How it works...

The new request filter uses the ServiceStack `session Id` as an identifier for the client. This is done by getting the current session from the `IRequest` object and retrieving any records stored in `ICacheClient` for that ID, as follows:

```
var session = req.GetSession();
var rateLimit = Cache.Get<RateLimit>(session.Id);
```

Once the current rate limit value has been retrieved from the cache, we can check whether the limit has been exceeded and if it has, thrown an appropriate HTTP error, which in this case is a **429** error code with its message, as follows:

```
if (rateLimit != null && rateLimit.Remaining == 0)
{
    throw new HttpError(429,
```

```
                "Too Many Requests",
                "You have exceeded your rate limit, it will be " +
                "reset in " +
                (rateLimit.Reset - DateTime.Now).TotalSeconds +
                " seconds");
    }
```

The rate limit value will be null if it hasn't been set before or if it has expired. In this case, we need to instantiate a new `RateLimit` which configures from the attribute:

```
    if (rateLimit == null)
    {
        //First request since reset
        rateLimit = new RateLimit
        {
            Limit = RequestLimit,
            Remaining = RequestLimit,
            Reset = DateTime.Now.AddSeconds(RequestTimeInSeconds)
        };
    }
```

This information will be used for future requests as well as to populate response headers to inform the client about their rate limit. The client can then use this information to programmatically regulate their requests.

The new or existing rate limit is then updated and assigned to the response headers, as follows:

```
    //Update existing record
    rateLimit.Remaining--;
    Cache.Set<RateLimit>(
        session.Id, rateLimit, rateLimit.Reset - DateTime.Now);
    res.AddHeader("RateLimit", RequestLimit.ToString());
    res.AddHeader("Remaining", rateLimit.Remaining.ToString());
    res.AddHeader("Reset", rateLimit.Reset.ToUnixTime().ToString());
```

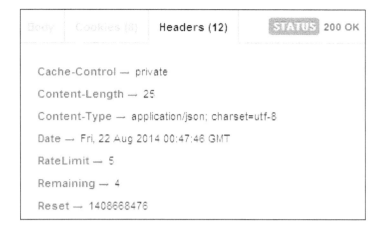

When the client exceeds the rate specified, they receive the **429** status code, as follows:

There's more...

Using `RequestFilterAttribute`, we are applying the same rate limitation to all web services using the preceding attribute. This could cause problems if we wanted different rates for different web service endpoints and/or methods. It also makes it difficult to group rates between web services. One way around this would be to use `RegisterTypeRequestFilter<T>` from the application's `AppHost` class. To rate limit, this might make more sense as it can be controlled on a host-by-host basis. You might want a more restrictive rate limit on one server in a particular datacenter than another due to costs. Here's how the code for rate limiting looks:

```
public override void Configure(Container container)
{
    //Config examples
    //this.Plugins.Add(new PostmanFeature());
    //this.Plugins.Add(new CorsFeature());
    container.Register<ICacheClient>(new MemoryCacheClient());
    container.Register<AppSettings>(new AppSettings());
    this.RegisterTypedRequestFilter<Hello>(this.LimitHello);
    this.Plugins.Add(new RazorFormat());
}

private void LimitHello(IRequest req, IResponse res, Hello
requestDto)
```

```
{
    var appSettings = req.TryResolve<AppSettings>();
    var limit = appSettings.Get<int>("Hello-Rate-Limit", 5);
    var timeLimit = appSettings.Get<int>("Hello-Rate-Time", 10);
    RateLimitFilter(limit, timeLimit, req, res);
}

private void RateLimitFilter(int limit, int timeLimit, IRequest
req, IResponse res)
{
    var session = req.GetSession();
    var cache = req.TryResolve<ICacheClient>();
    var rateLimit = cache.Get<RateLimit>(session.Id);
    if (rateLimit != null && rateLimit.Remaining == 0)
    {
        throw new HttpError(429,
            "Too Many Requests",
            "You have exceeded your rate limit, it will be " +
            "reset in " +
            (rateLimit.Reset - DateTime.Now).TotalSeconds +
            " seconds");
    }
    if (rateLimit == null)
    {
        //First request since reset
        rateLimit = new RateLimit
        {
            Limit = limit,
            Remaining = limit,
            Reset = DateTime.Now.AddSeconds(timeLimit)
        };
    }
    rateLimit.Remaining--;
    cache.Set<RateLimit>(session.Id, rateLimit, rateLimit.Reset -
    DateTime.Now);
    res.AddHeader("RateLimit",
    limit.ToString(CultureInfo.InvariantCulture));
    res.AddHeader("Remaining",
    rateLimit.Remaining.ToString(CultureInfo.InvariantCulture));
    res.AddHeader("Reset",
    rateLimit.Reset.ToUnixTime().ToString(CultureInfo.InvariantCulture
    ));
}
```

If you wanted to group web-service methods together, a pattern could be added to how the cache is stored, as follows:

```
private void RateLimitFilterWithGroup(int limit, int timeLimit,
string groupName, IRequest req, IResponse res)
{
    var session = req.GetSession();
    var cache = req.TryResolve<ICacheClient>();
    var rateLimit = cache.Get<RateLimit>(session.Id + "-" +
    groupName);
    if (rateLimit != null && rateLimit.Remaining == 0)
    {
        throw new HttpError(429,
            "Too Many Requests",
            "You have exceeded your rate limit, it will be " +
            "reset in " +
            (rateLimit.Reset - DateTime.Now).TotalSeconds +
            " seconds");
    }
    if (rateLimit == null)
    {
        //First request since reset
        rateLimit = new RateLimit
        {
            Limit = limit,
            Remaining = limit,
            Reset = DateTime.Now.AddSeconds(timeLimit)
        };
    }
    rateLimit.Remaining--;
    cache.Set<RateLimit>(session.Id + "-" + groupName,
                        rateLimit,
                        rateLimit.Reset - DateTime.Now);
    res.AddHeader("RateLimit", limit.ToString());
    res.AddHeader("Remaining", rateLimit.Remaining.ToString());
    res.AddHeader("Reset",
                rateLimit.Reset.ToUnixTime().ToString());
}
```

If you are using an authenticated service, it makes more sense to use a user-identifying property for the cache as the user could get around the method shown by spawning new sessions.

Restrict user actions by session details using a validator

One common pattern for web applications today is to encourage or require new users to register for an account before they can use certain features. One way to simplify authentication for application users is to integrate with a social media platform. Certain areas of your application might be available to anonymous and registered users, while other areas might require authentication. In this situation, you would want to restrict actions that require this external service. In this recipe, we will look at creating a validator that checks certain session properties of the user and returns a validation response if a predefined rule is not met.

Getting ready

If you are using a non-express version of Visual Studio, you can start this recipe using ServiceStackVS and create a new project based on any of the ServiceStack templates available. If you are using an express version of Visual Studio, please follow *Creating a ServiceStack solution with Visual Studio and NuGet* in *Appendix A, Getting Started* and start from the second instruction in the following section.

How to do it...

1. Create a new project based on a template from ServiceStackVS.

2. Install the `ServiceStack.OrmLite.Sqlite.Windows` NuGet package from Visual Studio, as follows:

    ```
    Install-Package ServiceStack.OrmLite.Sqlite.Windows
    ```

3. Register `IDBConnectionFactory` using `SqliteDialect.Provider`, as follows:

    ```
    container.Register<IDbConnectionFactory>(
        new OrmLiteConnectionFactory(
          "~/App_Data/db.sqlite".MapHostAbsolutePath(),
          SqliteDialect.Provider));
    ```

4. For this example, we are going to use the standard `AuthUserSession` method and verify that `DisplayName` is not null in our validator. Create and add the `AuthFeature` plugin with the default `AuthUserSession` and `CredentialsAuthProvider` method, as follows:

    ```
    this.Plugins.Add(new AuthFeature(() => new
    AuthUserSession(),
        new IAuthProvider[] {
            new CredentialsAuthProvider()
        })
    ```

```
    {
        HtmlRedirect = "~/",
        IncludeRegistrationService = true
    });
```

5. Register `OrmLiteAuthRepository` as `IUserAuthRepository` used for the persistence of our user information, and initialize the schema, as shown in the following code:

```
container.Register<IUserAuthRepository>(
    new OrmLiteAuthRepository(
        container.Resolve<IDbConnectionFactory>()));
container.Resolve<IUserAuthRepository>().InitSchema();
```

6. Create a `RequestDtoWithSession` class to act as a container for our session and request information, as follows:

```
public class RequestDtoWithSession<T>
{
    public AuthUserSession Session { get; set; }
    public T RequestDto { get; set; }
}
```

7. Create `DisplayNameValidator` inheriting from `AbstractValidator<T>`. The type provided must match the object being validated, so we will need to pass `T` as `RequestDtoWithSession<Hello>`, as follows:

```
public class DisplayNameValidator :
    AbstractValidator<RequestDtoWithSession<Hello>>
{
    public DisplayNameValidator()
    {
        RuleFor(x => x.Session.DisplayName)
          .NotNull()
          .WithName("Session.DisplayName")
          .WithMessage(
          "Display name is empty, please update your details");
    }
}
```

8. Create an `AppHostBase` extension method to handle session validations and request types in a generic way, as follows:

```
public static class SessionValidationExtensions
{
    public static void
    RegisterSessionValidationWithRequest<
```

```
              T, TK>(this AppHostBase appHost)
              where T :
              AbstractValidator<RequestDtoWithSession<TK>>
          {
              Container container = appHost.GetContainer();
              var validator = Activator.CreateInstance<T>();
              container.Register(validator);
              appHost.RegisterTypedRequestFilter<TK>(
                RequiresValidDisplayName<T,TK>);
          }

          private static void RequiresValidDisplayName<T, TK>(
              IRequest request, IResponse response, TK dto)
              where T :
              AbstractValidator<RequestDtoWithSession<TK>>
          {
              var validator = request.TryResolve<T>();
              var requestWithSession = new
              RequestDtoWithSession<TK>
              {
                  RequestDto = dto,
                  Session = request.GetSession() as AuthUserSession
              };
              ValidationResult result =
              validator.Validate(requestWithSession);
              if (!result.IsValid)
              {
                  response.StatusCode = 400;
                  response.Write(result.ToErrorResult().ToJson());
                  response.EndRequest();
              }
          }
      }
  }
```

9. Use the extension to register `DisplayNameValidator` with the `Hello` request in the `AppHost` `Configure` method, as follows:

```
this.RegisterSessionValidationWithRequest<
    DisplayNameValidator<Hello>,
    Hello>();
```

How it works...

Session information is not injected into validators, so we have to do a little bit of work to get access to them. Also, due to filters not returning a body by default, we have to write the response with our validation information and set an appropriate status code.

The extension method in the eighth step of the preceding set of steps enables the registration of both a validator and `TypedRequestFilter` to enable any custom session validation with any request object, provided that the validator does not require a parameterized constructor, as follows:

```
public static void RegisterSessionValidationWithRequest<
    T, TK>(this AppHostBase appHost)
    where T : AbstractValidator<RequestDtoWithSession<TK>>
{
    Container container = appHost.GetContainer();
    var validator = Activator.CreateInstance<T>();
    container.Register(validator);
    appHost.RegisterTypedRequestFilter<TK>(
        RequiresSessionValidation<T,TK>);
}
```

`AppHost` then registers the validator, which in this case is `DisplayNameValidator<Hello>`, and then registers `TypedRequestFilter<Hello>` using the `RequiresSessionValidation` method that processes the request as a filter.

The filter itself resolves the registered validator, constructs the newly created `RequestDtoWithSession` object that the validator needs to attempt to validate the request, as follows:

```
private static void RequiresSessionValidation<T, TK>(
    IRequest request, IResponse response, TK dto)
    where T : AbstractValidator<RequestDtoWithSession<TK>>
{
    var validator = request.TryResolve<T>();
    var requestWithSession = new RequestDtoWithSession<TK>
    {
        RequestDto = dto,
        Session = request.GetSession() as AuthUserSession
    };
    ValidationResult result =
      validator.Validate(requestWithSession);
    if (!result.IsValid)
    {
        response.StatusCode = 400;
```

```
        response.Write(result.ToErrorResult().ToJson());
        response.EndRequest();
    }
}
```

If the result is not valid, we have to update the response manually as filters so as not to return a serialized body. The validation result is converted to an error result, which matches the structure of a standard validation and serializes it to JSON. The last statement, if the result is invalid, ends the request. This is important as without this step, the service call will continue and the response of the error will be ignored.

There's more...

When creating other validators that are to be used with the `RequestDtoWithSession` object, it is important to keep it generic. For example, `DisplayNameValidator<T>` is only instantiated within the custom registration extension method, when the concrete version is not declared.

Common HTTP status codes

The following table consists of Common HTTP status codes:

Code	Status text	Description	
Informational responses			
100	Continue	This interim response indicates that everything until now is OK, and that the client should continue with the request or ignore it if it is already finished.	
101	Switching protocol	This code is sent in response to an upgrade: request header by the client and indicates the protocol, the server is switching to. It was introduced to allow migration to an incompatible protocol version and is not in common use.	
Successful responses			
200	OK	The request has succeeded.	
201	Created	The request has succeeded, and a new resource has been created as a result of it. This is typically the response sent after a PUT request.	
202	Accepted	The request has been received, but not yet acted upon. It is non-committal, which means that there is no way in HTTP to later send an asynchronous response indicating the outcome of processing the request. It is intended for cases where another process or server handles the request or for batch processing.	

203	Non-Authoritative Information	This response code means that the returned meta-information set is not the exact set as available from the origin server, but collected from a local or a third-party copy. Except this condition, 200 OK response should be preferred instead of this response.
204	No Content	There is no content to send for this request, but the headers might be useful. The user-agent might update its cached headers for this resource with the new ones.
205	Reset Content	This response code is sent after accomplishing the request to tell the user-agent to reset the document view, which sent this request.
206	Partial Content	This response code is used because of the Range Header sent by the client to separate a download into multiple streams.
Redirection messages		
301	Moved Permanently	This response code means that the URI of the requested resource has been changed. The new URI would probably be given in the response.
302	Found	This response code means that the URI of the requested resource has been changed temporarily. New changes in the URI might be made in the future. Therefore, this same URI should be used by the client in future requests.
303	See Other	The server sent this response directing the client to get the requested resource to another URI with a GET request.
304	Not Modified	This is used for caching purposes. It is telling the client that the response has not been modified. So, the client can continue to use the same cached version of the response.
307	Temporary Redirect	The server sent this response directing the client to get the requested resource to another URI with the same method that used the previous request. This has the same semantic as the 302 Found HTTP response code, with the exception that the user-agent must not change the HTTP method used: if a POST was used in the first request, a POST must be used in the second request.
Client error responses		
400	Bad Request	This response means that the server was unable to understand the request due to invalid syntax.
401	Unauthorized	Authentication is needed to get the requested response. This is similar to 403, but in this case, authentication is possible.
402	Payment Required	This response code is reserved for future use. The initial aim of creating this code was using it for digital payment systems; however, this is not used currently.
403	Forbidden	The client does not have access rights to the content, so the server refuses to give a proper response.

404	Not Found	The server cannot find the requested resource. This response code probably is the most famous one due to the frequency of its occurrence on the Web.
405	Method not allowed	The request method is known by the server but has been disabled and cannot be used. The two mandatory methods, `GET` and `HEAD`, must never be disabled and should not return this error code.
407	Proxy authentication required	This is similar to 401, but authentication is needed to be done by a proxy.
408	Request Timeout	This response is sent on an idle connection by some servers even without any previous request by the client. It means that the server would like to shut down this unused connection. This response is used much more as some browsers, such as Chrome and Internet Explorer 9, use HTTP pre-connection mechanisms to speed up surfing (see bug 634278, which tracks the future implementation of such a mechanism in Firefox). Also, note that some servers merely shut down the connection without sending this message.
409	Conflict	This response is sent when a request conflicts with the current state of the server.
412	Precondition failed	The client has indicated preconditions in its headers, which the server does not meet.
415	Unsupported media type	The media format of the requested data is not supported by the server, so the server rejects the request.
Server error responses		
500	Internal Server Error	The server has encountered a situation that it doesn't know how to handle.
501	Not implemented	The request method is not supported by the server and cannot be handled. The only methods that servers are required to support (and therefore must not return this code) are `GET` and `HEAD`.
502	Bad Gateway	This error response means that the server, while working as a gateway to get a response, needed to handle the request and got an invalid response.

503	Service Unavailable	The server is not ready to handle the request. Common causes include a server that is down for maintenance or that is overloaded. Note that, together with this response, a user-friendly page explaining the problem should be sent. This response should be used for temporary conditions, and the Retry-After: HTTP header should, if possible, contain the estimated time before the recovery of the service. The webmaster must also take care about the caching-related headers that are sent along with this response, as these temporary condition responses should usually not be cached.
504	Gateway Timeout	This error response is given when the server is acting as a gateway and cannot get a response in time.

7
Security and Authentication

In this chapter, we will cover the following topics:

- ▶ Getting started with authentication, sessions, registration, and user repositories
- ▶ Getting started with Twitter authentication
- ▶ Getting started with Google authentication
- ▶ Getting started with Facebook authentication
- ▶ Using multiple authentication providers and persisting a user's preferred profile image
- ▶ Handling password resets for credential-based authentication
- ▶ Accessing Windows identity information from ServiceStack for an intranet application
- ▶ Validating password complexity with a custom registration validator
- ▶ Migrating users from another system by overriding ServiceStack's credential-based authentication
- ▶ Writing your own OpenID authentication provider

Introduction

In this chapter, we are going to look at what ServiceStack has to offer when it comes to security and different forms of authentication. ServiceStack has a built-in authentication model that is highly configurable by just a few common interfaces and comes with a large number of implementations already built-in. A lot of the supported methods of authentication are focused around the OAuth and OpenID of popular online applications, such as Facebook, Twitter, Google, and others. Both OAuth and OpenID allow web services and applications to reliably confirm the identity of a user in a familiar and convenient way for your clients. This is also good for developers as it removes the burden and potential risk of storing the user's credentials. Once the user has their identity successfully verified (authenticated), ServiceStack also helps you in controlling what access a user has in your system (authorization), by providing attributes for your web services and their methods.

Authentication in ServiceStack and related libraries has a large number of implementations that we can use to get up and running faster. It also is built on a very extensible set of interfaces and conventions, allowing us to build custom authentication providers while still leveraging common persistence, caching, and session management if required. In this chapter, we will go step by step to integrate your application with some of the most common social media vendors of OAuth implementations as well how to write our own integration with existing OpenID vendors. Also, we will look at starting an intranet site that requires Windows authentication and a possible migration technique to minimize user impact and password reset functionality.

Getting started with authentication, sessions, registration, and user repositories

ServiceStack has a wide range of options when it comes to authentication. These options have a common structure that makes them pluggable into a set of common services, models, and interfaces. In this recipe, we will cover the main components of authentication with ServiceStack and work with the credential-authentication example.

Getting ready

If you are using a non-express version of Visual Studio, including the free Visual Studio 2013 Community Edition, you can start this recipe using ServiceStackVS and create a new project based on any of the C# ServiceStack templates available. If you are using an express version of Visual Studio or one that does not support extensions, please follow the *Creating a ServiceStack solution with Visual Studio and NuGet* section in *Appendix A, Getting Started*, and start from the second instruction in the *How to do it...* section.

How to do it...

1. Create a new project based on a C# template in ServiceStackVS.

2. Install the `ServiceStack.OrmLite.Sqlite.Windows` package from NuGet, as follows:

   ```
   Install-Package ServiceStack.OrmLite.Sqlite.Windows
   ```

3. Create a list of `IAuthProviders`, adding just `CredentialsAuthProvider`:

   ```
   var authProviders = new List<IAuthProvider>();
   authProviders.Add(new CredentialsAuthProvider());
   ```

4. Create a factory method that will return `IAuthUserSession`:

   ```
   private IAuthSession SessionFactory()
   {
       return new AuthUserSession();
   }
   ```

5. Create an instance of an `AuthFeature` plugin, and register it to the IoC container, as follows:

   ```
   var authFeature = new AuthFeature(SessionFactory,
   authProviders.ToArray());
   this.Plugins.Add(authFeature);
   ```

6. Register `IDbConnectionFactory` using Sqlite, as follows:

   ```
   var dbFactory = new OrmLiteConnectionFactory(
     "~/App_Data/db.sqlite".MapHostAbsolutePath(),
     SqliteDialect.Provider);
   container.Register<IDbConnectionFactory>(dbFactory);
   ```

7. Register and initialize `IUserAuthRepository` using `OrmLiteAuthUserRepository`, as shown in the following code:

   ```
   var authRepo = new OrmLiteAuthRepository(dbFactory);
   container.Register<IUserAuthRepository>(authRepo);
   ```

8. Register `ICacheClient` using `MemoryCacheClient`, as follows:

   ```
   container.Register<ICacheClient>(new MemoryCacheClient());
   ```

9. Enable user registration using the `RegistrationFeature` plugin, as follows:

   ```
   this.Plugins.Add(new RegistrationFeature());
   ```

10. Apply the `Authenticate` attribute to the `MyServices` class and the `Any` method to secure `Hello` request:

```
[Authenticate]
public object Any(Hello request)
{
    return new HelloResponse { Result = "Hello, {0}!".Fmt(request.
Name) };
}
```

How it works...

In this example, there are a few different moving parts that all work together within ServiceStack's security model. `AuthFeature` is one of the more central components and it takes two parameters to construct it. The first is a factory method that returns `IAuthSession`. This method will be invoked whenever a client requires a session to interact with a service that requires authentication. The other parameter is an `IAuthProvider` array. This can be an array as we can support multiple providers of authentication at once, but the same session factory method is used. In this example, we are only using the `CredentialsAuthProvider` method to illustrate its use in ServiceStack authentication, as follows:

```
var authProviders = new List<IAuthProvider>();
authProviders.Add(new CredentialsAuthProvider());
var authFeature = new AuthFeature(SessionFactory,
authProviders.ToArray());
this.Plugins.Add(authFeature);
```

After we have the provider and the session factory, we will also need somewhere to persist the user's information. ServiceStack provides another interface, `IUserAuthRepository`, that already has quite a few implementations in the framework, including the `OrmLiteAuthRepository`. We are going to use this implementation as it's flexible with the different database providers OrmLite supports:

```
var dbFactory = new OrmLiteConnectionFactory(
  "~/App_Data/db.sqlite".MapHostAbsolutePath(),
  SqliteDialect.Provider);
container.Register<IDbConnectionFactory>(dbFactory);
var authRepo = new OrmLiteAuthRepository(dbFactory);
container.Register<IUserAuthRepository>(authRepo);
authRepo.InitSchema();
```

The last piece is the caching of sessions. This uses the `ICacheClient` interface to store sessions based on a cookie ID that is provided to the client. Once another request has been made, and if the cookie of the existing session is provided, the cached session can be retrieved using the `GetSession` method from any of your services.

Now that we have an overview of how authentication is handled within ServiceStack, let's see how we can interact with our example now that the `Hello` service requires authentication:

```
Handler for Request not found:


Request.HttpMethod: GET
Request.PathInfo: /login
Request.QueryString: redirect=http%3a%2f%2flocalhost%3a52690%2fhello%2ftest
Request.RawUrl: /login?redirect=http%3a%2f%2flocalhost%3a52690%2fhello%2ftest
```

`AuthFeature` has a default `HtmlRedirect` property that points to the `/login` URL with the original address URL encoded to the redirect property. This can be used to handle default behavior for your web application's user authentication.

Next, we can use Postman to register a new user as we enabled user registration by adding the `RegistrationFeature` plugin to our application. An easy way to use Postman with any ServiceStack application is to register `PostmanFeature` in your AppHost's configure method, as follows:

```
this.Plugins.Add(new PostmanFeature());
```

This is how the resultant screenshot looks:

We can **POST** to the `/register` URL with the previous parameters to register a new user. For a successful response, we'll be returned the following JSON:

```
{
    "UserId": "1",
    "ResponseStatus": {}
}
```

With our new user, we can now authenticate to the URL `/auth/:provider`. The `:provider` part of the URL is a placeholder showing that we have to specify the provider we are authenticating with in that part of the URL. For this example, we have registered `CredentialsAuthProvider`, which has the provider name `credentials`. The following screenshot shows how your screen will look:

Now that we have a valid authenticated session, we can use the same browser to navigate directly to a `Hello` service URL like `/hello/test`. If you do this with another browser, you will get denied and redirected to the `/login` route, as you do not have a valid cookie present. After authenticating, the session cookie is stored by your browser and then used to look up a valid session in the server's cache.

Getting started with Twitter authentication

ServiceStack has great support for integration with OAuth providers like Twitter. In this recipe, we will have a look at setting up an application so that Twitter users can easily sign in to your application.

Getting ready

First, we are going to need an application to integrate. We will start with a template from the ServiceStackVS Visual Studio extension. If you are using Visual Studio Express or a version prior to 2012, please see the *Creating your ServiceStack solution with Visual Studio and NuGet* section in *Appendix A, Getting Started*, and continue from the second instruction in the *How to do it...* section.

We will also need to register an application with Twitter. This will give us unique application keys so that users can be told which application they are registering their Twitter account with.

 Please note that these instructions are valid at the time of writing; however, changes to how Twitter allows the registration of applications might have occurred since the writing of this recipe.

The following steps should be followed to create a new Twitter application:

1. Log in to Twitter with an account from which you want to manage your application authentication.

2. Navigate to `https://apps.twitter.com/`. The resultant screen will look like this:

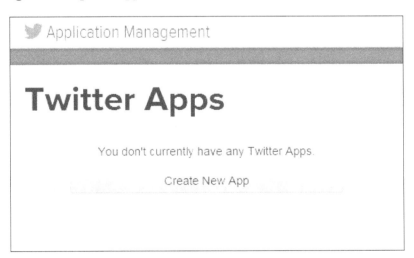

3. Fill in a name and description for your application. If you are using your application to tweet on behalf of another user, your name will be used as an attribution.

4. For the callback URL, we want to provide an endpoint of our local application that will authenticate the user's Twitter account. ServiceStack authentication is usually located at `/auth/:provider`, where the provider identifies the type of authentication being used. In this case, the URL will be `http://localdev.reidsonindustries.net/auth/twitter` as a placeholder. Once you enter these URLs, click on **create**. These can be updated in the future. The following screenshot shows how your resultant screen will look:

Website *

http://localdev.reidsonindustries.net:54511/

Your application's publicly accessible home page, where users can go to download, make source attribution for tweets created by your application and will be shown in user-facing a (If you don't have a URL yet, just put a placeholder here but remember to change it later.)

Callback URL

http://localdev.reidsonindustries.net:54511/auth/twitter

Where should we return after successfully authenticating? OAuth 1.0a applications should here. To restrict your application from using callbacks, leave this field blank.

5. By default, ServiceStack's OAuth providers will include a callback URL as a query string to the vendor, which in this case is Twitter. At the time of writing, Twitter returned to the URL provided by our application, which makes localhost testing very straightforward; however, not all providers will act in this way. If this is causing a problem, see the *Testing external service callbacks locally using Fiddler2 and IIS Express* section in *Appendix B, Testing Locally*, for a possible workaround.

Now that we have our application, Twitter can give us API keys specific to our new application. To access your application API keys, click on **New Application** and locate the tab called *API keys*, as shown in the following screenshot:

Reidson Industries

Details   Settings   API Keys   Permissions

Once you are on this screen, you will have access to **API key** and **API secret**. You will need both these pieces of information to configure your application to authenticate with Twitter users, as shown in the following screenshot:

Application settings

Keep the "API secret" a secret. This key should never be human-readable in your application.

API key   89ACol4UtKgzgmfFwFXOyXOlb

API secret

Access level   Read-only (modify app permissions)

How to do it...

1. Create a new application using a template from the ServiceStackVS Visual Studio extension. For this example, we will use the **AngularJS** template.

2. Install the `ServiceStack.OrmLite.Sqlite.Windows` package from NuGet, as follows:

```
Install-Package ServiceStack.OrmLite.Sqlite.Windows
```

3. Add the `AuthFeature` plugin with a `TwitterAuthProvider` using the default `AuthUserSession` method, as follows:

```
var authProviders = new List<IAuthProvider>();
var appSettings = new AppSettings();
authProviders.Add(new TwitterAuthProvider(appSettings));
Func<IAuthSession> sessionFactory = () => new AuthUserSession();
var authFeature = new AuthFeature(
    sessionFactory,
    authProviders.ToArray());
this.Plugins.Add(authFeature);
```

4. Use `OrmLiteAuthRepository` backed by the Sqlite provider, as follows:

```
var dbFactory = new OrmLiteConnectionFactory(
    "~/App_Data/db.sqlite".MapHostAbsolutePath(),
    SqliteDialect.Provider);
container.Register<IDbConnectionFactory>(dbFactory);
var authRepo = new OrmLiteAuthRepository(dbFactory);
container.Register<IUserAuthRepository>(authRepo);
authRepo.InitSchema();
```

5. Update `appSettings` to include Twitter OAuth settings to provide to `TwitterAuthProvider`, as shown in the following code:

```xml
<appSettings>
    <add key="webPages:Enabled"
        value="false" />
    <add key="oauth.twitter.RedirectUrl"
        value="http://localhost:54511/"/>
    <add key="oauth.twitter.CallbackUrl"
        value="http://localhost:54511/auth/twitter"/>
    <add key="oauth.twitter.ConsumerKey"
        value="{YourAPIKeyFromTwitter}"/>
    <add key="oauth.twitter.ConsumerSecret"
        value="{YourAPIKeySecretFromTwitter}"/>
</appSettings>
```

6. Create a login button for Twitter using the **Sign in with Twitter** image from its documentation. For this example, it has been copied locally to the project's `/images` directory:

```html
<ul class="nav navbar-nav">
    <li class="active"><a href="#">Home</a></li>
    @if (!IsAuthenticated)
    {
        <li>
        <a href="/auth/twitter">
         <img src="images/sign-in-with-twitter-gray.png" />
        </a>
    </li>
    }
    else
    {
        var user = (SessionAs<AuthUserSession>());
        <li>
         <a href="http://twitter.com/@user.TwitterScreenName">
          @user.TwitterScreenName
         </a>
        </li>
        <li>
         <a href="/auth/logout">Logout</a>
        </li>
    }
</ul>
```

Here's what the resultant screen looks like:

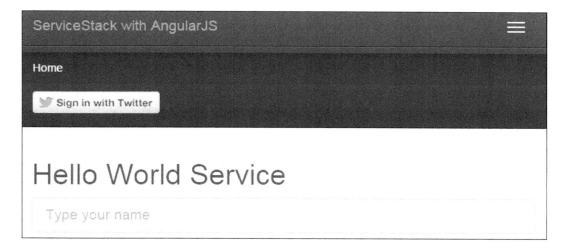

How it works...

ServiceStack provides implementations of various popular OAuth providers, including Twitter. These implementations handle the required OAuth interactions between providers and your application, as shown in this example. If we look at the `TwitterAuthProvider` class, we can see that it inherits from a base `OAuthProvider` class, overriding two specific methods to load specific data from Twitter's response. As shown in other recipes in this chapter, this pattern of detailing with OAuth providers and security allows us to implement support for a large range of OAuth providers that come with ServiceStack. It also gives a good starting point to implement your own OAuth provider if required.

The Twitter provider is available, like all authentication providers, at `/auth/{provider}`, where Twitter is the current provider. A request to this address will start the OAuth process specific to the provider. This is why, to link to the authentication, we simply have to provide a link with the URL `/auth/twitter` to get started. The callback URL provided to Twitter controls what happens after the user has authorized your application.

The settings for our application are coming from our `web.config` file's `appSettings`, which ServiceStack is accessing via its own `AppSettings` class passed in to the constructor of `TwitterAuthProvider`, as shown in the following code:

```
authProviders.Add(new TwitterAuthProvider(new AppSettings()));
```

In the Razor view, we are checking whether the session is authenticated and displaying a Twitter login button if the user isn't authenticated. If the user is authenticated, we are simply displaying their Twitter screen name with a link to their profile and a generic logout button that links to `/auth/logout`.

Once your application has moved from initial development, and authentication with Twitter is working, remember to change the website and callback URL in Twitter's `appsettings` to your production URL.

 For more information on Twitter's OAuth services, see their documentation at `https://dev.twitter.com/oauth`.

Getting started with Google authentication

A popular login option to give users is to allow them to authenticate with your application using their Google account. ServiceStack provides a built-in OAuth provider to make this as easy as possible. In this recipe, we will go through how to get started with Google authentication and ServiceStack.

Getting ready

First, we are going to need an application to integrate, we will start with a template from the ServiceStackVS Visual Studio extension. If you are using Visual Studio Express, please see the *Creating your ServiceStack solution with Visual Studio and NuGet* section in *Appendix A, Getting Started*, and continue from the second instruction in the *How to do it...* section.

At the time of writing, Google provides an OAuth2 endpoint to authenticate. Thankfully, ServiceStack comes with support for Google's OAuth2 provider; however, a separate library does have to be added to support it. The NuGet package, `ServiceStack.Authentication.OAuth2`, will need to be installed to your project to support OAuth2. Google's original OAuth provider that was implemented in ServiceStack, is however now deprecated by Google.

To begin with, you will need a Google account to add support for the Google OAuth2 provider; you will need to obtain the relevant API keys from **Google Developer Console**. Once you have signed up for Google developer access with your Google account, you will need to create a project. If you don't wish to use the default project, create a new project, as follows:

1. Log in to your Google account from which you want to manage your applications, OAuth2 and API keys.

2. Navigate to `https://console.developers.google.com/`. The resultant screen will look like this:

3. Create a new project following the steps outlined in the following screenshot:

4. **Create a new Client ID**. This can be accessed from the **APIs & auth** menu on the left-hand side, as shown in the following screenshot:

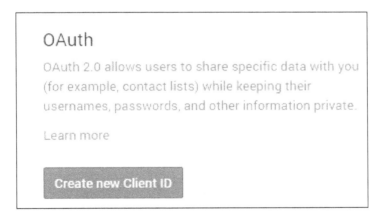

5. To make sure you are able to test locally, callback URLs must be specified in the correct case. At the time of writing, testing locally proved difficult with errors regarding a URL mismatch if the case of the callback URL was not correct. This is an easy mistake to make, and it should be the first thing to be checked if problems arise when testing locally. For the `GoogleOAuthProvider`, the provider's name is **GoogleOAuth**, and the callback URL should end with the same provider name.

Now that we have our Google Client ID setup, we will be given a **Client ID** and **Client Secret** that will be used in `appSettings` to authenticate users, as shown in the following screenshot:

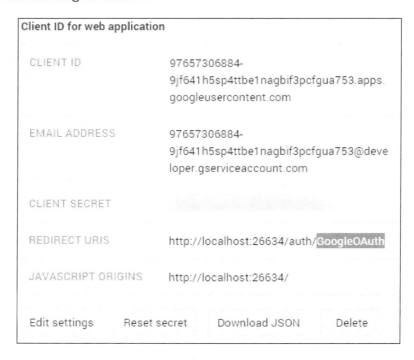

We will also need to update the **Consent Screen** section to ensure the project has **Product Name** and associated **Email Address**, as shown in the following screenshot:

If you don't provide a product name, you might get an **Invalid Client** error when trying to authenticate.

How to do it...

1. Create a new application using a template from the ServiceStackVS Visual Studio extension. For this example, we will use the AngularJS template.

2. Install the `ServiceStack.OrmLite.Sqlite.Windows` package from NuGet, as follows:

```
Install-Package ServiceStack.OrmLite.Sqlite.Windows
```

3. Install the `ServiceStack.Authentication.OAuth2` NuGet package, as follows:

```
Install-Package ServiceStack.Authentication.OAuth2
```

4. Add an `AuthFeature` plugin with a single `GoogleOAuth2Provider` class using the default `AuthUserSession` method, as follows:

```
var authProviders = new List<IAuthProvider>();
authProviders.Add(new GoogleOAuth2Provider(new
AppSettings()));
Func<IAuthSession> sessionFactory = () => new
AuthUserSession();
var authFeature = new AuthFeature(
    sessionFactory,
    authProviders.ToArray());
this.Plugins.Add(authFeature);
```

5. Update `appSettings` in `web.config` to include the Google **Client ID** and **Client Secret** in as `ConsumerKey` and `ConsumerSecret`, respectively:

```
<appSettings>
  <add key="webPages:Enabled"
      value="false" />
  <add key="oauth.googleoauth.ConsumerKey"
      value="{YourClientIDFromGoogle}" />
  <add key="oauth.googleoauth.ConsumerSecret"
      value="{YourClientSecretFromGoogle}" />
  <add key="oauth.googleoauth.RedirectUrl"
      value="http:// localhost:26634/" />
  <add key="oauth.googleoauth.CallbackUrl"
      value="http://localhost:26634/auth/GoogleOAuth" />
</appSettings>
```

6. Create a login button for Google authentication using the recommended image provided in the Google documentation. For this example, this has been copied to the project's `/images` directory, as shown in the following code:

```
<ul class="nav navbar-nav">
    <li class="active"><a href="#">Home</a></li>
    @if (!IsAuthenticated)
    {
```

```
        <li>
          <a href="/auth/googleoauth">
            <img src="images/sign-in-with-google.png"/>
          </a>
        </li>
    }
    else
    {
        var user = (SessionAs<AuthUserSession>());
        <li>
          <img src="@user.GetProfileUrl()" />
            <a href="@user.GetOAuthTokens("googleoauth").
Items["link"]">
              @user.UserName
            </a>
        </li>
        <li><a href="/auth/logout">Logout</a></li>
    }
</ul>
```

The following screenshot shows how your resultant screen will look:

How it works...

Unlike the Twitter example, which comes with the ServiceStack core libraries, we had to include an external dependency to get OAuth2 working with Google. This is due to the use of the OAuth2Provider base class that is in the separate library of ServiceStack. Authentication.OAuth2. This was separated as it has a dependency on another authentication library that is only needed for OAuth2 authentication. At the time of writing, the original OAuth is still very common and easy to use without the need to add another dependency. OAuth2Provider, just like OAuthProvider, is extensible, which makes it very easy to write your own OAuth2 provider if required.

For a developer using an OAuth2 provider, many aspects are the same as using Twitter or other OAuth providers. The required `ConsumerKey` and `ConsumerSecret` still apply, and the convention in the application settings of `oauth.<provider>.ConsumerKey`, for example, still applies.

These settings for our application, coming from `web.config AppSettings`, are used by `OAuth2Provider` when passed in to the constructor of `GoogleOAuth2Provider`, as shown in the following code:

```
authProviders.Add(new GoogleOAuth2Provider (new AppSettings()));
```

In the Razor view, we check whether the session is authenticated and displaying a Google login button if the user isn't authenticated. If the user is authenticated, we simply display their Google account e-mail address and Google Plus profile image and link to their Google Plus profile. Next to it, we also show a generic logout button that links to `/auth/logout`.

Once your application has moved from initial development and the authentication with Google is working, remember to change the website and callback URL in the Google project settings to your production URL.

 For more information on Google's OAuth2 services, see their documentation at `https://developers.google.com/accounts/docs/OAuth2`.

Getting started with Facebook authentication

Similar to Twitter and Google, Facebook offers OAuth integration for developers to allow users to log in to external applications using their Facebook account. The ServiceStack framework provides a prebuilt OAuth provider to make this integration process with your application as smooth as possible.

Getting ready

First, we are going to need an application to integrate. We will start with a template from the ServiceStackVS Visual Studio extension. If you are using Visual Studio Express, please see the *Creating your ServiceStack solution with Visual Studio and NuGet* section in *Appendix A, Getting Started*, and continue from the second instruction in the *How to do it...* section.

We will also have to register an application with Facebook. This will require a verified account with Facebook before we can create this application.

At the time of writing, to create an application, we need to take the following steps:

1. Visit `https://developers.facebook.com/apps` while logged in to Facebook.

2. Click on **Add a New App** in the top-right corner of the screen, as follows:

3. Since we are building integration with our ServiceStack web application, select **Website** in the far-right, as shown in the following screenshot:

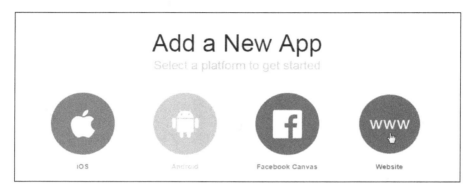

4. As we are not using the default JavaScript SDK for our integration, we can click on **Skip Quickstart** in the top-right corner:

5. Next, we need to provide **Display Name** and **Category** for the application, as shown in the following screenshot:

6. Now that our application has been created, we can get access to **App ID** and **App Secret**, which we will need to configure our ServiceStack application, as shown in the following screenshot.

7. Click on **Select Platform** at the bottom of your application's Dashboard page, as follows:

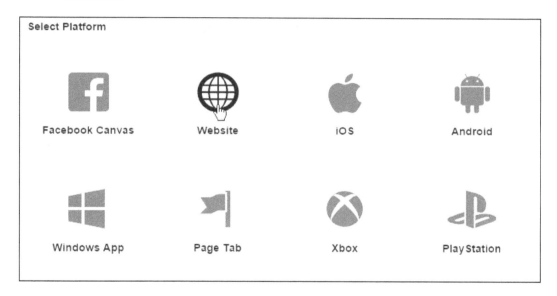

8. Select **Website**, and provide a URL for your application. At the time of writing, Facebook would not accept `localhost` as a valid domain. Testing locally can still work with `localhost`; however, you should add your localhost's callback URI in the **Advanced** settings of the Facebook settings, as shown in the following screenshot:

How to do it...

1. Create a new application using a template from the ServiceStackVS Visual Studio extension. For this example, we will use the AngularJS template.

2. Install the `ServiceStack.OrmLite.Sqlite.Windows` package from NuGet, as follows:

```
Install-Package ServiceStack.OrmLite.Sqlite.Windows
```

3. Add the `AuthFeature` plugin with a single `FacebookAuthProvider` class using the default `AuthUserSession` method, as follows:

```
var appSettings = new AppSettings();
var authProviders = new List<IAuthProvider>();
authProviders.Add(new FacebookAuthProvider(appSettings));
var authFeature = new AuthFeature(
    () => new AuthUserSession(),
    authProviders.ToArray());
this.Plugins.Add(authFeature);
```

4. Use the `OrmLiteAuthRepository` class backed Sqlite provider:

```
var dbFactory = new OrmLiteConnectionFactory(
    "~/App_Data/db.sqlite".MapHostAbsolutePath(),
    SqliteDialect.Provider);
container.Register<IDbConnectionFactory>(dbFactory);
var authRepo = new OrmLiteAuthRepository(dbFactory);
container.Register<IUserAuthRepository>(authRepo);
authRepo.InitSchema();
```

5. Update the `appSettings` section of `web.config` to include `App ID` and `App Secret` listed on the page of your newly created Facebook application:

```
<add key="oauth.facebook.AppID"
    value="{YourAppIDFromFacebook}" />
<add key="oauth.facebook.AppSecret"
    value="{YourAppSecretFromFacebook}" />
<add key="oauth.facebook.RedirectUrl"
    value="http://localhost:24080/" />
<add key="oauth.facebook.CallbackUrl"
    value="http://localhost:24080/auth/facebook" />
```

6. Create a login using an image Facebook provides from its SDKs. To interact with the ServiceStack OAuth provider, simply create a link to `/auth/facebook`, as follows:

```
<ul class="nav navbar-nav">
    <li class="active"><a href="#">Home</a></li>
    @if (!IsAuthenticated)
    {
        <li>
          <a href="/auth/facebook">
           <img src="images/Log_in_with_Facebook.png"
           width="150" height="30" />
          </a>
        </li>
    }
    else
    {
        var user = (SessionAs<AuthUserSession>());
        <li>
          <img src="@user.GetProfileUrl()" />
          <a style="display: inline">@user.UserName</a>
        </li>
        <li><a href="/auth/logout">Logout</a></li>
    }
</ul>
```

The following image shows how the example's front page looks:

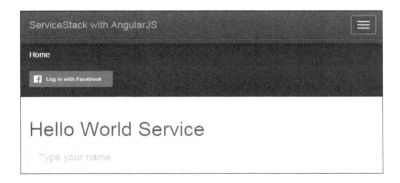

How it works...

The Facebook OAuth provider works like other OAuth providers. ServiceStack provides a consistent way to include OAuth user authentication in your web application. The main difference to note is the naming of the settings in the `web.config` file. What is `ConsumerKey` and `ConsumerSecret` in other OAuth providers should be changed to `AppID` and `AppSecret` respectively.

Once this is working, sending a `GET` request via an anchor on our example's front page to `/auth/facebook` initiates the process of authentication.

Using multiple authentication providers and persisting a user's preferred profile image

Commonly in web application, we want to make it as easy as possible for new or existing users to authenticate and interact with our application, letting users choose their preferred way of identifying themselves. In this recipe, we will use Twitter, Google, and Facebook OAuth providers together and allow users to set a preferred profile image. This will show how ServiceStack's `UserAuth` database tables can be extended as well as how they interact when multiple providers are added.

Getting ready

In this example, you will need to already have API keys for the authentication providers we will use: Twitter, Facebook, and Google. If you are unsure how to obtain these API keys, please see previous recipes in this chapter, which will help you to get started with each provider.

Also, we are going to need an application to integrate. We will start with a template from the ServiceStackVS Visual Studio extension. If you are using Visual Studio Express, please see the *Creating your ServiceStack solution with Visual Studio and NuGet* section in *Appendix A, Getting Started*, and continue second instruction from in the *How to do it...* section.

How to do it...

1. Create a new application using a template from the ServiceStackVS Visual Studio extension. For this example, we will use the AngularJS template.

2. Install `Servicestack.OrmLite.Sqlite.Windows` from NuGet, as follows:

    ```
    Install-Package ServiceStack.OrmLite.Sqlite.Windows
    ```

3. Install `ServiceStack.Authentication.OAuth2` from NuGet, as follows:

    ```
    Install-Package ServiceStack.Authentication.OAuth2
    ```

4. Create a new class that inherits from `UserAuth` and has a property to store the user's default profile URL, as follows:

```
public class CustomUserAuth : UserAuth
{
    public string DefaultProfileUrl { get; set; }
}
```

5. Create a new class that inherits from `AuthUserSession`, which will also store a URL for each provider's profile image URL as well as a default image URL. It will also handle the authentication of a user. The following code shows us how to obtain the required results spelled out in this paragraph:

```
public class CustomUserSession : AuthUserSession
{
    public string DefaultProfileUrl { get; set; }

    public string FacebookProfileUrl { get; set; }
    public string GoogleProfileUrl { get; set; }
    public string TwitterProfileUrl { get; set; }

    public override void OnAuthenticated(IServiceBase
    authService, IAuthSession session, IAuthTokens tokens,
    Dictionary<string, string> authInfo)
    {
        base.OnAuthenticated(authService, session, tokens,
        authInfo);

        foreach (var authTokens in
        session.ProviderOAuthAccess)
        {
            if (authTokens.Provider.ToLower() ==
            "facebook")
            {
                FacebookProfileUrl =
                authTokens.GetProfileUrl();
            }
            if (authTokens.Provider.ToLower() ==
            "googleoauth")
            {
                GoogleProfileUrl =
                authTokens.GetProfileUrl();
            }
            if (authTokens.Provider.ToLower() == "twitter")
            {
                TwitterProfileUrl =
                authTokens.GetProfileUrl();
```

```
                }
            }

            bool setProfile =
            string.IsNullOrEmpty(DefaultProfileUrl);
            if (setProfile)
            {
                DefaultProfileUrl =
                        GoogleProfileUrl ??
                        FacebookProfileUrl ??
                        TwitterProfileUrl;
                var dbFactory =
                authService.TryResolve<IDbConnectionFactory>();
                using (var db = dbFactory.OpenDbConnection())
                {
                  var userAuth =
                    db.SingleById<CustomUserAuth>(session.UserAuthId);
                  userAuth.DefaultProfileUrl =
                  DefaultProfileUrl;
                 db.Save(userAuth);
                }
            }
        }
    }


    public static class AuthUserSessionExtensions
    {
        public static string GetProfileUrl
        (this IAuthTokens tokens)
        {
            string profileUrl = null;
            if (tokens.Items.ContainsKey
            (AuthMetadataProvider.ProfileUrlKey))
            {
                profileUrl =
                tokens.Items[AuthMetadataProvider
                .ProfileUrlKey];
            }
            return profileUrl;
        }
    }
```

6. Configure your application host. We will use Sqlite for persistence and add Twitter, Facebook, and Google support to `AuthFeature`, as follows:

```
public override void Configure(Container container)
{
    this.Plugins.Add(new RazorFormat());
    container.RegisterAs<MemoryCacheClient,
    ICacheClient>();
    container.Resolve<ICacheClient>().InitSchema();

    var dbFactory = new OrmLiteConnectionFactory(
    "~/App_Data/db.sqlite".MapHostAbsolutePath(),
    SqliteDialect.Provider);

    Plugins.Add(new AuthFeature(() => new
    CustomUserSession(),
        new IAuthProvider[] {
            new TwitterAuthProvider(AppSettings),
            new FacebookAuthProvider(AppSettings),
            new GoogleOAuth2Provider(AppSettings)
        })
    {
        HtmlRedirect = "~/",
    });

    var authRepo = new OrmLiteAuthRepository
    <CustomUserAuth, UserAuthDetails>(dbFactory);
    container.Register<IUserAuthRepository>(authRepo);
    authRepo.InitSchema();
}
```

7. Create a new request-and-response class that will handle which URL to use for the user's default profile image, as follows:

```
[Route("/myprofile/image/{ProviderName}", Verbs = "PUT")]
public class ProfileImage : IReturn<ProfileImageResponse>
{
    public string ProviderName { get; set; }
}

public class ProfileImageResponse
{
    public string Url { get; set; }
}
```

8. Create a service method to handle this request. This should go in either an existing or a new `Service` class inside your `ServiceInterface` project, as follows:

```
[Authenticate]
public object Put(ProfileImage request)
{
    var userSession = SessionAs<CustomUserSession>();
    var customUserAuth =
    Db.SingleById<CustomUserAuth>(userSession.UserAuthId);
    var oauthTokens =
    userSession.GetOAuthTokens(request.ProviderName);
    if (oauthTokens == null)
    {
        throw HttpError.NotFound("No image for Provider");
    }

    customUserAuth.DefaultProfileUrl =
    oauthTokens.GetProfileUrl();
    Db.Save(customUserAuth);
    userSession.DefaultProfileUrl =
    oauthTokens.GetProfileUrl();
    return new ProfileImageResponse
    {
        Url = customUserAuth.DefaultProfileUrl
    };
}
```

9. Inside the `_Layout.cshtml` Razor page, show the user's current default profile image, as shown in the following code:

```
<ul class="nav navbar-nav">
    <li class="active"><a href="#">Home</a></li>
    @if (IsAuthenticated)
    {
        var userSession = SessionAs<CustomUserSession>();
        <li>
          <img src="@userSession.DefaultProfileUrl"/>
        </li>
        <li>
          <a href="/auth/logout">Logout</a>
        </li>
    }
</ul>
```

10. Create a default Razor view to allow users to preview and switch profile images. Create an AngularJS module to handle the request to update `http.put`, as shown in the following code:

```
@using Recipe5.ServiceInterface
@inherits ViewPage
@{
    ViewBag.Title = "Profile Image Service";
}
<script>
    var app = angular.module('profileApp', []);

    app.controller('profileCtrl', [
        '$scope', '$http', function ($scope, $http) {
            $scope.updateDefaultProfileImage =
                function (provider) {
                    $http.put(
                        '/myprofile/imageurl',
                        {ProviderName: provider}
                    )
                    .success(
                        function (response) {
                        //Refresh page
                        window.location = '/';
                    });
                }
            }
    ]);
</script>
```

11. Create a Bootstrap panel that will contain the Razor logic to display user profile images, as follows:

```
<div ng-app="profileApp">
    <div style="margin: 10px 0">
        <div class="panel panel-default">
            <div class="panel-heading">
                <h3>Link your Social Media accounts</h3>
            </div>
            <div class="panel-body" ng-
            controller="profileCtrl">

            </div>
        </div>
    </div>
</div>
```

12. Inside the panel, use the user session to work out which images the user can select from or add other social media accounts to link to, as depicted in the following code:

```
@if (!IsAuthenticated)
{
    <div>
        <a class="btn btn-block" href="/auth/twitter">
            <i></i>Sign in with Twitter
        </a>
        <a class="btn btn-block" href="/auth/facebook">
            <i></i>Sign in with Facebook
        </a>

        <a class="btn btn-block" href="/auth/GoogleOAuth">
            <i></i>Sign in with Google
        </a>
    </div>
}
else
{
    <div>
        @{
            var userSession =
            SessionAs<CustomUserSession>();

            if (userSession != null)
            {
              if
              (!string.IsNullOrEmpty
              (userSession.GoogleProfileUrl))
              {
                <div style="margin: 10px">
                  <img src="@userSession.GoogleProfileUrl"
/>
                  @if (userSession.DefaultProfileUrl !=
                  userSession.GoogleProfileUrl)
                  {
                  <a href="#"
                  ng-click="updateDefaultProfileImage
                  ('googleoauth')">
                    Make Default Profile Image
                  </a>
                  }
                </div>
              }
              else
              {
                <div>
```

```
     <a href="/auth/googleoauth">
       Link your Google account
     </a>
</div>
}
if
(!string.IsNullOrEmpty
(userSession.FacebookProfileUrl))
{
  <div style="margin: 10px">
   <img
   src="@userSession.FacebookProfileUrl"/>
   @if (userSession.DefaultProfileUrl !=
   userSession.FacebookProfileUrl)
      {
 <a
href="#"
ng-click="updateDefaultProfileImage
('facebook')">
Make Default Profile Image
</a>
      }
   </div>
}
else
{
 <div>
    <a href="/auth/facebook">
      Link your Facebook account
    </a>
 </div>
}
if
(!string.IsNullOrEmpty
(userSession.TwitterProfileUrl))
{
    <div style="margin: 10px">
<img
src="@userSession.TwitterProfileUrl"/>
 @if (userSession.DefaultProfileUrl
!= userSession.TwitterProfileUrl)
        {
  <a
  href="#"
ng-
click="updateDefaultProfileImage
  ('twitter')">
Make Default Profile Image
```

```
            </a>
                }
              </div>
        }
        else
        {
              <div>
                <a href="/auth/twitter">
                  Link your Twitter account
                </a>
              </div>
        }
      }
    }
  </div>
}
```

13. Add API keys to the `web.config` file's `applicationSettings` section for Twitter, Facebook, and Google OAuth providers, as follows:

```
<add key="oauth.RedirectUrl"
    value=" http://localhost:65220/"/>
<add key="oauth.CallbackUrl"
    value=" http://localhost:65220/auth/{0}"/>
<add key="oauth.twitter.ConsumerKey"
    value="{YourTwitterAPIKey}"/>
<add key="oauth.twitter.ConsumerSecret"
    value="{YourTwitterSecret}"/>
<add key="oauth.googleoauth.ConsumerKey"
    value="{YourGoogleClientID}"/>
<add key="oauth.googleoauth.ConsumerSecret"
    value="{YourGoogleClientSecret}"/>
<add key="oauth.facebook.AppID"
    value="{YourFacebookAppID}"/>
<add key="oauth.facebook.AppSecret"
    value="{YourFacebookAppSecret}"/>
```

How it works...

As we've seen is previous recipes, ServiceStack's `AuthFeature` plugin accepts an array of `IAuthProvider` in its constructor. This is because it is designed to handle multiple forms of authentication working together.

`AuthFeature` requires the use of `IUserAuthRepository` to persist user authentication information. By default, we can use the standard `OrmLiteAuthUserRepository` class, as follows:

```
Var dbFactory = container.Resolve<IDbConnectionFactory>();
Var authRepo = new OrmLiteAuthRepository(dbFactory);
container.Register<IUserAuthRepository>(authRepo);
```

This will create two tables in the form of `UserAuth` and `UserAuthDetails`. The `UserAuth` table has a one-to-many relationship with `UserAuthDetails`, for example, a single `UserAuth` package can have multiple `UserAuthDetails` class.

A simple use case to illustrate how this works would be: User-1 authenticates via Twitter, creating a row in each table. User-2 then authenticates with Facebook; we will again get two new rows in each of these tables. If User-1, while still authenticated via Twitter with a valid ServiceStack session, authenticates with their own Facebook account, only the `UserAuthDetails` table will get a new entry referencing the original row created by User-1 in the `UserAuth` table.

This workflow is handled seamlessly by ServiceStack's authentication system. This allows us to provide a way to users to link their accounts in a very easy way. Another advantage of this system is that we can extend the data `OrmLiteUserAuthRepository` stores.

Instead of registering the default `IUserAuthRepository` interface shown previously, we can specify the types we want to persist, using the following syntax:

```
var authRepo = new OrmLiteAuthRepository
  <CustomUserAuth, UserAuthDetails>(dbFactory);
container.Register<IUserAuthRepository>(authRepo);
```

Now that we are persisting our `CustomUserAuth` class instead of the default `UserAuth` package, in this case, with the extra `DefaultProfileUrl`. We have also added this to `CustomUserSession` with the same name and type. ServiceStack encourages *Convention over configuration*, and this is another example. By having the same name and type values on our user session object and our user authentication object, the population of these values is automatically discovered. So, if we want to persist more information on our authenticated user, the related session object should also include the new values should you want to use them.

`CustomUserSession` is also where we override the `OnAuthenticated` method, allowing us to intercept and, if required, persist data from these services separately. In this example, we check the current session's authenticated provider tokens and persist each profile URL as well as the default value if it is the first time they are authenticating.

To update this URL, we are using AngularJS to call a Profile PUT request to our service that updates our `CustomUserSession` and `CustomUserAuth` tables. To achieve this end, perform the following steps:

1. Create an AngularJS HTTP request, as follows:

```
$scope.updateDefaultProfileImage = function (provider) {
    $http.put(
        '/myprofile/imageurl',
        {ProviderName: provider}
    ).success(function (response)
      {
      //Refresh page
      window.location = '/';
        });
}
```

2. Create a service login to update the session and `CustomUserAuth` tables:

```
var userSession = SessionAs<CustomUserSession>();
var customUserAuth =
Db.SingleById<CustomUserAuth>(userSession.UserAuthId);
var oauthTokens =
userSession.GetOAuthTokens(request.ProviderName);
if (oauthTokens == null)
{
    throw HttpError.NotFound("No image for Provider");
}

customUserAuth.DefaultProfileUrl =
oauthTokens.GetProfileUrl();
Db.Save(customUserAuth);
userSession.DefaultProfileUrl =
oauthTokens.GetProfileUrl();
return new ProfileImageResponse
{
    Url = customUserAuth.DefaultProfileUrl
};
```

The default Razor view is used to give our example a simple interface for users to log in and link other accounts, as shown in the following screenshot:

Once logged in, users can add additional accounts, allowing them to select which profile image they want to use for our application, as shown in the following screenshot:

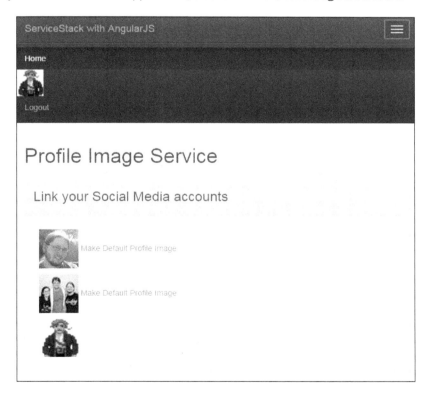

ServiceStack handles authentication between these different accounts by default. So, if User-1 originally signed in with Twitter, and then linked Google and Facebook, the user can use any of the three OAuth providers to authenticate with our application and access their singular profile on our application.

Handling password resets for credential-based authentication

A common piece of functionality that a lot of users expect is a simple password reset, where they provide their e-mail ID, click on a link, and create a new password. In this recipe, we will go through an example of allowing users to register and log in using ServiceStack's built-in plugins and then building two services: forgot password and reset password.

Getting ready

First, we are going to need an application to integrate. We will start with a template from the ServiceStackVS Visual Studio extension. If you are using Visual Studio Express, please see the *Creating your ServiceStack solution with Visual Studio and NuGet* section in *Appendix A, Getting Started*, and continue from the second instruction in the *How to do it...* section.

We are also going to send e-mails that will be saved to our filesystem. By default, the example saves these emails to `C:\Temp`. If this is not a valid location on your system, please update this in the `web.config` file.

How to do it...

1. Create a new application using a template from the ServiceStackVS Visual Studio extension. For this example, we will use the AngularJS template.

2. Install `Servicestack.OrmLite.Sqlite.Windows` from NuGet, as follows:

    ```
    Install-Package ServiceStack.OrmLite.Sqlite.Windows
    ```

3. Create a simple wrapper class to send e-mails in the `ServiceInterface` project:

    ```
    public class EmailFactory
    {
        public IAppSettings Config { get; set; }

        public const string PasswordResetHtml =
        @"<h1>Password Reset Requested</h1>
    <p>
     A password reset for ReidsonIndustries has been requested.
     <a href='{0}/ResetPassword?ResetPasswordToken
    ={1}&Email={2}'>
     Please reset your password
    ```

```
    </a>.
    </p>";


    public void SendEmail(
                string toAddress,
                string subject,
                string body)
        {
            using (var smtpClient = new SmtpClient(
                Config.Get<string>("SmtpHost", ""),
                Config.Get<int>("SmtpPort", 21)))
            {
                smtpClient.Credentials = new NetworkCredential(
                    Config.Get<string>("SmtpUserName",""),
                    Config.Get<string>("SmtpPassword","")
                    );
                //Must be false for SpecifiedPickupDirectory
                smtpClient.EnableSsl = false;
                MailMessage mailMessage = new MailMessage();
                mailMessage.To.Add(toAddress);
                mailMessage.Subject = subject;
                mailMessage.Body = body;
                mailMessage.IsBodyHtml = true;
                mailMessage.From =
                  new MailAddress(
                  Config.Get<string>(
                  "FromAddres",
                  "admin@reidsonindustries.net")
                        );
                smtpClient.Send(mailMessage);
            }
        }
    }
```

4. In your `AppHost` configure method, register `EmailFactory`, `ICacheClient` and `OrmLiteConnectionFactory` using Sqlite, as follows:

```
container.RegisterAs<MemoryCacheClient, ICacheClient>();
container.Resolve<ICacheClient>().InitSchema();
container.Register(AppSettings);
container.RegisterAutoWired<EmailFactory>();
var dbFactory = new OrmLiteConnectionFactory(
  "~/App_Data/db.sqlite".MapHostAbsolutePath(),
  SqliteDialect.Provider));
container.Register<IDbConnectionFactory>(dbFactory);
```

5. Also, register an `AuthFeature` plugin with just the `CredentialsAuthProvider` and `RegistrationFeature` methods, as follows:

```
Plugins.Add(new AuthFeature(() => new AuthUserSession(),
    new IAuthProvider[] {
        new CredentialsAuthProvider(),
    })
{
    HtmlRedirect = "~/",
});
Plugins.Add(new RegistrationFeature());
```

6. Finally, in the `AppHost` configure method, register and initialize `IUserAuthRepository`, as follows:

```
Var authRepo = new OrmLiteAuthRepository(dbFactory);
container.Register<IUserAuthRepository>(authRepo);
authRepo.InitSchema();
```

Now that persistence and e-mail are set up, we will need to expose two services: one to allow users to notify of a forgotten password and another to confirm they have received an e-mail and reset it.

We will use Razor views for these services to make the UI; however, there is nothing that prevents you from using a JSON client to produce the same functionality. Perform the following steps to that end:

1. Create a `ForgetPassword` and `ResetPassword` request-and-response object:

```
[Route("/forgotpassword")]
public class ForgotPassword
{
    public string Email { get; set; }
}


public class ForgotPasswordResponse
{
    public string Email { get; set; }
}


[Route("/resetpassword")]
public class ResetPassword
{
    public string ResetPasswordToken { get; set; }
    public string Email { get; set; }
```

```
        public string NewPassword { get; set; }
        public string ConfirmPassword { get; set; }
    }

    public class ResetPasswordResponse
    {
        public bool ValidToken { get; set; }
        public bool PasswordReset { get; set; }
    }
```

2. Create a POST service method to allow users to register a forgotten password for an account, as follows:

```
public object Post(ForgotPassword request)
{
    if (string.IsNullOrEmpty(request.Email))
    {
        throw new
        HttpError(400,"BadRequest","No email provided");
    }

    var userAuth = Db.Single<UserAuth>(
    x => x.Email == request.Email);
    if (userAuth == null)
    {
        throw HttpError.NotFound(
        "The email address provided is not registered.");
    }

    string resetId = Guid.NewGuid().ToString();
    var passwordResetRequest =
    request.ConvertTo<ResetPassword>();
    passwordResetRequest.ResetPasswordToken = resetId;
    Cache.Add<ResetPassword>(
      resetId,
      passwordResetRequest,
      new TimeSpan.FromHours(3));

    EmailFactory.SendEmail(
        userAuth.Email,
        "Password Reset requested",
        EmailFactory.PasswordResetHtml.Fmt(
            AppSettings.Get("WebHostBaseUrl",""),
            resetId,
            request.Email
```

```
        ));

        return new ForgotPasswordResponse
        {
            Email = request.Email
        };
    }
```

3. Create a GET service method that will handle the click on the link e-mailed to users to reset their password, as follows:

```
public object Get(ResetPassword request)
{
    Guid tokenGuid = new Guid();
    if (!Guid.TryParse(request.ResetPasswordToken, out
    tokenGuid))
    {
        return new ResetPasswordResponse() { ValidToken =
        false };
    }

    var resetrequest =
    Cache.Get<ResetPassword>(request.ResetPasswordToken);

    var response = new ResetPasswordResponse();
    response.ValidToken = resetrequest != null;
    return response;
}
```

4. Create a POST service method that accepts the new password, as follows:

```
public object Post(ResetPassword request)
{
    Guid tokenGuid = new Guid();
    if (!Guid.TryParse(request.ResetPasswordToken, out
    tokenGuid))
    {
        throw new HttpError(
        400,
        "BadRequest",
        "Password reset token is invalid");
    }

    if (string.IsNullOrEmpty(request.Email))
    {
        throw new HttpError(
```

```
            400,
            "BadRequest",
            "No email provided");
    }

    var userAuth =
    Db.Single<UserAuth>(x => x.Email ==
    request.Email);
    if (userAuth == null)
    {
        throw HttpError.NotFound(
          "The email address provided is not
          registered.");
    }

    var resetrequest =
    Cache.Get<ResetPassword>(request.ResetPasswordToken);

    if (resetrequest == null)
    {
        throw new HttpError(
        400,
        "BadRequest",
        "Password reset token is invalid");
    }

    if (request.NewPassword != request.ConfirmPassword)
    {
        throw new HttpError(
        400,
        "BadRequest",
        "New password does not match confirmation");
    }

    UserAuthRepository.UpdateUserAuth(
                        userAuth,
                        userAuth,
                        request.NewPassword);

    Cache.Remove(resetrequest.ResetPasswordToken);
    return new ResetPasswordResponse
    {
        PasswordReset = true
    };
}
```

For this example, `default.cshtml` contains forms for registration, login, and reset password. The form for reset password asks for an e-mail address. Write the following code to achieve this objective:

```
<div class="form-group col-lg-6 col-md-6 col-sm-6">
    <h3>Reset Password</h3>
    <form
    method="POST"
    action="@(new ForgotPassword().ToPostUrl())">
        <div class="form-group">
            <input
            class="form-control
            input-lg" type="text"
            id="Email"
            name="Email"
            value=""
            placeholder="Email">
        </div>
        <div class="form-group">
          <button
          class="btn btn-primary form-control"
          type="submit">
                Submit
          </button>
        </div>
    </form>
</div>
```

This simply makes a POST to our `ForgotPassword` route where a Razor view will display the result `ForgotPassword.cshtml` in the `Views` folder, as follows:

```
<div>
    <div>
        @if (!Request.IsErrorResponse())
        {
            <span>An email has been sent to
            '@Model.Email'.</span>
        }
        else
        {
            <span>@GetErrorMessage()</span>
        }
    </div>
</div>
```

Another Razor view for `ResetPassword` is used to collect the new password from the user, as follows.

```
<div class="form-group col-lg-6 col-md-6 col-sm-6">
    <h3>Reset Password</h3>
    <form
    id="reset-password"
    method="POST"
        action="@(new ResetPassword().ToPostUrl())">
        <input
        type="hidden"
        id="Email"
        name="Email" value="@Request.QueryString["Email"]">
        <input type="hidden" id="ResetPasswordToken"
        name="ResetPasswordToken"
        value="@Request.QueryString["ResetPasswordToken"]" />
        <div class="form-group">
            <input
            class="form-control input-lg"
            type="password"
            id="NewPassword"
            name="NewPassword"
            value="" placeholder="New Password">
            <span class="help-block"></span>
        </div>
        <div class="form-group">
            <input
            class="form-control
            input-lg"
            type="password"
            id="ConfirmPassword"
            name="ConfirmPassword"
            value="" placeholder="Confirm Password">
            <span class="help-block"></span>
        </div>
        <div class="form-group"><button class="btn btn-primary
        form-control" type="submit">Submit</button></div>
    </form>
</div>
```

How it works...

The workflow shown in the two services we built go through the following steps:

1. The user provides e-mail of an account they no longer know the password for:
   1. The account is validated
   2. The reset password token is generated and stored in the cache to expire in 3 hours
   3. An e-mail is sent providing a link that has both e-mail and token as a query string

2. The user receives an e-mail advising them to follow the link to reset:
   1. A GET request is received.
   2. The server validates that the token is present within the cache; the token remains in the cache

3. The user is prompted to provide a new password and to confirm it:
   1. The token is validated once again along with the e-mail
   2. The password is validated to match
   3. The account password is updated via IUserAuthRepository
   4. The token is removed from the cache

These services utilize the built-in functionality of ICacheClient to persist data temporarily while an unauthenticated user is resetting their password. The TimeSpan argument passed to the Add<ResetPassword> function specifies an expiry for the value stored.

The use of ICacheClient in this example is MemoryCacheClient; however in a production environment, the RedisClient or OrmLiteCacheClient would be more appropriate to avoid potential issues caused by the loss of a token.

There's more...

This kind of functionality is a good candidate for a standalone plugin. Creating a plugin is a good way of reusing common functionality and encapsulating it in a way that can be used easily by other ServiceStack hosts and environments.

As an example, to create a simple `PasswordResetFeature` plugin, we would want to let consumers of the plugin control the UI and notification of their user. So, unlike how it is currently used in the example, we would separate the service from the Razor views as well as package request/response objects and services into a separate project. Although not structured in this way, an example of the plugin reusing service models and services is in this project under the `ServiceInterface` project. Write the following code to achieve the aforementioned objective:

```
public class PasswordResetFeature : IPlugin
{
    private readonly Action<IUserAuth, string> notifyUser;
    public string ForgotPasswordAtRestPath { get; set; }
    public string ResetPasswordAtRestPath { get; set; }
    public PasswordResetFeature(
            Action<IUserAuth,string> notifyUserOfToken)
    {
        notifyUser = notifyUserOfToken;
        ForgotPasswordAtRestPath = "/forgotpassword";
        ResetPasswordAtRestPath = "/resetpassword";
    }

    public void Register(IAppHost appHost)
    {
        var userAuthRepository =
                appHost.TryResolve<IUserAuthRepository>();
        if (userAuthRepository == null)
        {
            throw new ArgumentNullException(
    "Missing required IoC registration of IUserAuthRepository");
        }
        appHost.Register(new PasswordResetNotifier(notifyUser));
        appHost.RegisterService<ForgotPasswordService>
        (ForgotPasswordAtRestPath);
        appHost.RegisterService<ResetPasswordService>
        (ResetPasswordAtRestPath);
    }
}

public class PasswordResetNotifier
{
    private readonly Action<IUserAuth,string> notifyUser;
```

```
public PasswordResetNotifier(Action<IUserAuth, string>
notifyUserOfToken)
{
    notifyUser = notifyUserOfToken;
}

public void NotifyUser(IUserAuth userAuth, string token)
{
    if (notifyUser == null)
        throw new ArgumentNullException("Notify user action is
        null");
    notifyUser(userAuth, token);
}
}
```

Accessing Windows identity information from ServiceStack for an intranet application

Within corporate environments, its commonplace to have an intranet that only staff have access to while using the internal network, be it locally or via VPN. Though a lot of authentication providers built into ServiceStack are focused on Internet services, you still have access to Windows authentication information when hosted on IIS.

Getting ready

This recipe requires the use of an IIS host that can enable Windows authentication. If you are on a PC that doesn't enable Windows authentication on IIS and try to turn it on, your options will probably look something like this:

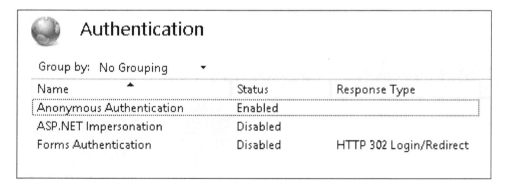

If you are running a version of Windows that supports Windows authentication in IIS, you will be able to add it via **Programs and Features** for Windows 7/8 or through **Server Management** if you are working on Windows Server, as shown in the following screenshot:

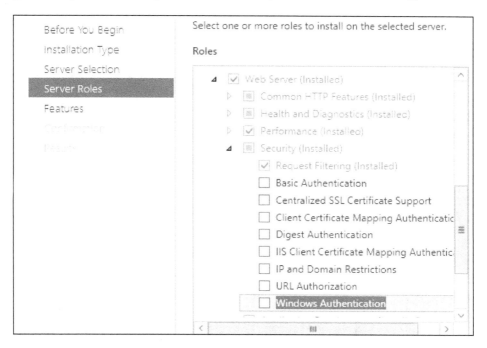

Once the preceding instructions have been followed, we can enable **Windows Authentication**. If only **Windows Authentication** is on, any interaction with the site will be challenged for Windows credentials. In this example, we will look at providing a `Hello` service to Windows-authenticated users only and another service for anonymous users. Due to this, you will need to enable anonymous users in IIS:

First, we are going to need an application to integrate; we will start with a template from the ServiceStackVS Visual Studio extension. If you are using Visual Studio Express, please see the *Creating your ServiceStack solution with Visual Studio and NuGet* section in *Appendix A, Getting Started*, and continue from the second instruction in the *How to do it...* section.

How to do it...

1. Create a new application using a template from the ServiceStackVS Visual Studio extension. For this example, we will use the AngularJS template.

2. Install `Servicestack.OrmLite.Sqlite.Windows` from NuGet, as follows:

   Install-Package ServiceStack.OrmLite.Sqlite.Windows

3. In your `AppHost` configure method, register `ICacheClient` and an `OrmLiteConnectionFactory` using the Sqlite provider, as follows:

   ```
   container.RegisterAs<MemoryCacheClient, ICacheClient>();
   container.Resolve<ICacheClient>().InitSchema();
   container.Register<IDbConnectionFactory>(
           new OrmLiteConnectionFactory
           ("~/App_Data/db.sqlite".MapHostAbso
           lutePath(), SqliteDialect.Provider));
   ```

4. Register `AspNetWindowsAuthProvider` specifying `AllowAllWindowsAuthUsers` to equal `true`, as follows:

   ```
   Plugins.Add(new AuthFeature(() => new AuthUserSession(),
   new IAuthProvider[]
   {
       new AspNetWindowsAuthProvider(this)
       {
           AllowAllWindowsAuthUsers = true
       }
   }));
   ```

5. Register and initialize `OrmLiteAuthRepository`, as follows:

   ```
   container.Register<IUserAuthRepository>(new
   OrmLiteAuthRepository(container.Resolve<IDbConnectionFactor
   y>()));
   container.Resolve<IUserAuthRepository>().InitSchema();
   ```

6. Alter the existing `Hello` service to require authentication and create a new `Greetings` request, response, and service that is an unauthenticated version of the `Hello` service, as follows:

   ```
   public class MyServices : Service
   {
       [Authenticate]
   ```

```
    public object Any(Hello request)
    {
        return new HelloResponse { Result = "Hello,
        {0}!".Fmt(SessionAs<AuthUserSession>().UserName) };
    }

    public object Any(Greetings request)
    {
        return new GreetingsResponse() { Result = "Hello,
        {0}!".Fmt(request.Name) };
    }
}

[Route("/hello/{Name}")]
public class Hello : IReturn<HelloResponse>
{
    public string Name { get; set; }
}

public class HelloResponse
{
    public string Result { get; set; }
}

[Route("/greetings/{Name}")]
public class Greetings : IReturn<GreetingsResponse>
{
    public string Name { get; set; }
}

public class GreetingsResponse
{
    public string Result { get; set; }
}
```

How it works...

AspNetWindowsAuthProvider works by looking at the OriginalRequest property on
ServiceStack's IRequest. Provided your ServiceStack application is running on IIS, this will,
as the property name suggests, return the original implementation of the request object
ServiceStack is using to construct its request. Information like LogonUserIdentity is
then accessible due to **Windows Authentication** being enabled on IIS. The authentication
provider then feeds this information into ServiceStack's session so that UserName and other
properties are available to work use.

If you try to use the **Hello World** sample text in the AngularJS template, you will be prompted for credentials, as follows:

The details required here are valid Windows user credentials, as they are challenging `/auth/windowsauth`, which is using `AspNetWindowsAuthProvider`. If provided with valid credentials, IIS can populate the identity information that ServiceStack uses to populate the session. Here's how your screen will look upon performing the aforementioned instructions:

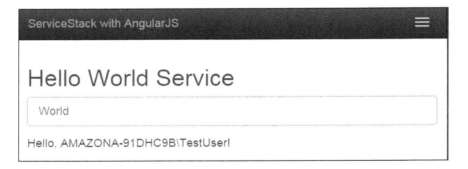

If we reload the page, everything still works the same. This is because we are using `ICacheClient` to persist session information in-memory, and your browser still has a valid session token. Any unauthenticated user will be unable to use the `Hello` service but will still be able to use the alternate `Greeting` service.

There's more...

Some corporate environments might have staff that are only working on a temporary basis, who are provided with domain credentials but are placed in a restricted group without other access. We might want the normal staff access to this application but not these restricted users. Instead of using the `AllowAllWindowsAuthUsers` flag, we can set the `LimitAccessToRoles` property to contain only the local Windows groups that users are members of and are allowed access to:

```
LimitAccessToRoles = new List<string> { "BUILTIN\\Users" }
```

The preceding code allows users that are a member of the service's local `Users` group to be able to authenticate. As this is a local machine group, this property would be more useful to system administrators.

Validating password complexity with a custom registration validator

Password complexity requirements for users creating a new account is a good place to encourage users to devise strong passwords. The `RegistrationFeature` plugin has default validations as it uses the `RegistrationValidator` built into ServiceStack. In this recipe, we will look at overriding this functionality to give you more control over registration validation.

Getting ready

First, we are going to need an application to integrate; we will start with a template from the ServiceStackVS Visual Studio extension. If you are using Visual Studio Express, please see *Creating your ServiceStack solution with Visual Studio and NuGet* section in *Appendix A, Getting Started*, and continue from the second instruction in the *How to do it...* section.

How to do it...

1. Create a new application using a template from the ServiceStackVS Visual Studio extension. For this example, we will use the AngularJS template.

2. Install `Servicestack.OrmLite.Sqlite.Windows` from NuGet, as follows:

   ```
   Install-Package ServiceStack.OrmLite.Sqlite.Windows
   ```

3. Initialize and register `ICacheClient`, `IDbConnectionFactory`, and `AuthFeature`:

   ```
   container.RegisterAs<MemoryCacheClient, ICacheClient>();
   container.Resolve<ICacheClient>().InitSchema();
   container.Register<IDbConnectionFactory>(
       new OrmLiteConnectionFactory(
   ```

```
        "~/App_Data/db.sqlite".MapHostAbsolutePath(),
        SqliteDialect.Provider)
    );

this.Plugins.Add(
    new AuthFeature(() =>
        new AuthUserSession(),
        new IAuthProvider[]
        {
          new CredentialsAuthProvider()
        })
    );
```

4. Create a custom registration plugin that contains a custom validation class inheriting from the existing `RegistrationValidator` class:

```
public class CustomRegistrationFeature : IPlugin
{
    public string AtRestPath { get; set; }

    public class CustomRegistrationValidator :
      RegistrationValidator
    {
        public CustomRegistrationValidator()
        {
            RuleSet(ApplyTo.Post, () =>
            {
                RuleFor(x => x.Password).Length(8, 50);
                RuleFor(x => x.Password)
                    .Matches("[a-z]")
                    .WithMessage(
                "Password must contain at least 1 lower case
                character");

                RuleFor(x => x.Password)
                    .Matches("[A-Z]")
                    .WithMessage(
                "Password must contain at least 1 upper case
                character");

                RuleFor(x => x.Password)
                    .Matches("[0-9]")
                    .WithMessage(
                "Password must contain at least 1 number");
              });
```

```
            }
        }

        public CustomRegistrationFeature()
        {
            this.AtRestPath = "/register";
        }

        public void Register(IAppHost appHost)
        {
            appHost.RegisterService<RegisterService>(AtRestPath);
            appHost.RegisterAs
                <CustomRegistrationValidator,
                IValidator<Register>>();
        }
    }
```

5. Register this feature instead of the standard `RegistrationFeature` class and initialize `IUserAuthRepository`, as follows:

```
this.Plugins.Add(new CustomRegistrationFeature());
```

```
container.Register<IUserAuthRepository>(
    new OrmLiteAuthRepository(
    container.Resolve<IDbConnectionFactory>()
));
container.Resolve<IUserAuthRepository>().InitSchema();
```

How it works...

The preceding technique seems a little strange when compared to creating other validators, and there are a couple of reasons for this. First, we want to keep the existing `RegistrationFeature` functionality and just override the validation. At first glance, it looks like we should be able to do the following:

```
container.Register<AbstractValidator<Register>>(
new CustomRegistrationValidator());
```

This method would leverage Funq to just replace the existing registration of the default `RegistrationValidator` class. This is exactly the reason this doesn't work. `RegistrationFeature` performs it's initialization during the `IPlugin` register function. This function is called *after* the configure method has completed its part.

Thankfully, the implementation of the `RegistrationFeature` plugin is small and easy to wrap, allowing us to replace it with very little code and injecting our own behavior as we see fit.

Migrating users from another system by overriding ServiceStack's credential-based authentication

If you're creating a new system and you want your users to move to the new system, it might make sense to want to move their authenticate information to your new system so that in the future, you don't have to maintain both systems. Ideally, we can make this as seamless as possible for end users. In this recipe, we will look at overriding `CredentialAuthProvider` to give it custom behavior, which in this case is to check whether the credentials are valid for a legacy system and migrate the user to the new one.

Getting ready

In this example, we are going to extend ServiceStack's `TextFileSettings` class to mock our external authentication system. This new class is just illustrating the custom behavior inside the `TryAuthenticate` method, which will be our new custom credential-based authentication provider, as follows:

```
public class UserMigrationStorage : TextFileSettings
{
    public UserMigrationStorage(
                string filePath,
                string delimiter = ":")
        : base(filePath, delimiter)
    {
    }

    public bool AuthenticateUser(string userName, string password)
    {
        var existingUser = Get<LegacyUser>(userName,null);
        if (existingUser == null)
        {
            return false;
        }

        return existingUser.Password == password
        && existingUser.Migrated == false;
    }
}

public class LegacyUser
{
    public string UserName { get; set; }
```

```
    public string Email { get; set; }
    public string Password { get; set; }

    public bool Migrated { get; set; }
}
```

The example also has a text file that populates these settings, called `exampleAuthMigration.txt`. The contents of the file are in the syntax used by ServiceStack's `DictionarySettings`, which can also populate complex objects such as `LegacyUser`:

```
TestUser1:{UserName:TestUser1,Password:password123,Email:user1@exa
mple.com}
TestUser2:{UserName:TestUser2,Password:password321,Email:user2@exa
mple.com}
```

Also, we are going to need an application to integrate; we will start with a template from the ServiceStackVS Visual Studio extension. If you are using Visual Studio Express, please see the *Creating your ServiceStack solution with Visual Studio and NuGet* section in *Appendix A, Getting Started*, and continue from the second instruction in the *How to do it...* section.

How to do it...

1. Create a new application using a template from the ServiceStackVS Visual Studio extension. For this example, we will use the AngularJS template.

2. Install `Servicestack.OrmLite.Sqlite.Windows` from NuGet, as follows:

    Install-Package ServiceStack.OrmLite.Sqlite.Windows

3. Register the `UserMigrationStorage` class shown in the *Getting ready* section of this recipe. The `UserMigrationStored` class should be declared in the `ServiceInterface` project and registered in the `AppHost` configure method. The following code shows you how this can be done:

    ```
    var existingUsers = new UserMigrationStorage(
        "~/exampleAuthMigration.txt".MapHostAbsolutePath());
    container.Register<UserMigrationStorage>(existingUsers);
    ```

4. Register and initialize `ICacheClient` and `IDbConnectionFactory` using the Sqlite provider, as follows:

    ```
    container.RegisterAs<MemoryCacheClient, ICacheClient>();
    container.Resolve<ICacheClient>().InitSchema();

    container.Register<IDbConnectionFactory>(
        new OrmLiteConnectionFactory(
            "~/App_Data/db.sqlite".MapHostAbsolutePath(),
            SqliteDialect.Provider)
        );
    ```

5. Create a custom credential-based authentication provider called `MyAuthProvider` overriding the `TryAuthenticate` method with the following logic; this class should be placed in the `ServiceInterface` project:

```
public class MyAuthProvider : CredentialsAuthProvider
{
    public override bool TryAuthenticate(IServiceBase
    authService, string userName, string password)
    {
        //Try authenticate with current system
        bool authenticated =
        base.TryAuthenticate(authService, userName,
        password);
        //If returns true, continue
        if (authenticated)
        {
            return true;
        }

        var userRepository =
        authService.TryResolve<IUserAuthRepository>();
        var userAuth =
        userRepository.GetUserAuthByUserName(userName);
        //User found but failed to authenticate
        if (userAuth != null)
        {
            return false;
        }

        //Potentially user of legacy system yet to be
        migrated.
        var existingUsers =
        authService.TryResolve<UserMigrationStorage>();
        //Try to authenticate with legacy system
        if (!existingUsers.AuthenticateUser(userName,
        password))
        {
            return false;
        }

        //Successful authentication with legacy system,
        create new user and migrate information
        var user = existingUsers.Get<LegacyUser>(userName,
        null);
        var newUser =
                userRepository.CreateUserAuth(
                ToUserAuth<UserAuth>(user), password);
        if (newUser != null)
```

```
        {
            //Flag used as migrated so current password is
            not used again to create a user.
            user.Migrated = true;
            existingUsers.Set(userName,user);
        }
        //Authenticate with current system
        return base.TryAuthenticate(
                    authService,
                    userName,
                    password);
    }


    /// <summary>
    /// Migrate and information into the UserAuth type used
    by your system
    /// </summary>
    /// <typeparam name="TUser"></typeparam>
    /// <param name="legacyUser"></param>
    /// <returns></returns>
    private TUser ToUserAuth<TUser>(LegacyUser legacyUser)
    {
        return legacyUser.ConvertTo<TUser>();
    }
}
```

6. Register a new `AuthFeature` plugin utilizing our new `MyAuthProvider` class in the `Configure` method of your AppHost, as follows:

```
this.Plugins.Add(
    new AuthFeature(() =>
        new AuthUserSession(),
        new IAuthProvider[]
        {
            new MyAuthProvider()
        })
    );
```

7. Register and initialize `RegistrationFeature` and `IUserAuthRepository` implemented as `OrmLiteAuthRepository`; this will be in the `Configure` method of your `AppHost`, as follows:

```
this.Plugins.Add(new RegistrationFeature());

container.Register<IUserAuthRepository>(new
OrmLiteAuthRepository(container.Resolve<IDbConnectionFactory>()));
container.Resolve<IUserAuthRepository>().InitSchema();
```

How it works...

`MyAuthProvider` inherits from `CredentialAuthProvider`, which handles simple credential-based authentication. By overriding the `TryAuthenticate` method, we can inject custom logic as to how the username and password are handled; in this case, we check them against an external system.

When a user tries to log in, we assume they are a current user and try to log them in. If this fails, we check if the username they are using is present in our current system. If it is, they have been migrated, and we don't need to check our external/legacy system. If both these conditions don't result in an authentication result, we can then check whether the user can successfully authenticate with the legacy system, and create a new login for them with the same credentials if they can. All this can be brought about by the following code:

```
var user = existingUsers.Get<LegacyUser>(userName, null);
var newUser =
userRepository.CreateUserAuth(ToUserAuth<UserAuth>(user),
password);
if (newUser != null)
{
    //Flag used as migrated so current password is not used again
    to create a user.
    user.Migrated = true;
    existingUsers.Set(userName,user);
}
```

There's more...

In this example, we aren't handling conditions for new users registering with the current system that have the same usernames. One way of handling this would be to use a custom registration validation that checks the old system, preventing people from taking usernames of users yet to be migrated. How to do this is shown in the recipe *Validating password complexity with a custom registration validator* in this chapter.

Writing your own OpenID authentication provider

A lot of different services on the Internet offer ways for their users to authenticate with third-party applications. In this recipe, we will look at implementing a custom OpenID authentication provider by using Steam as an example.

Steam is a platform for game distribution and social gaming. Like a lot of social, Internet-based applications, you can add friends, see their status, and message each other. Steam also keeps track of game statistics for certain games. If you were creating a web application centered around computer games or with a large cross-over audience, adding functionality that would allow your users to sign in with their Steam account might be a welcome feature.

Getting ready

First, we are going to need an application to integrate, we will start with a template from the ServiceStackVS Visual Studio extension. If you are using Visual Studio Express, please see the *Creating your ServiceStack solution with Visual Studio and NuGet* section in *Appendix A, Getting Started*, and continue from the second instruction in the *How to do it...* section.

Also, to authenticate with Steam, we will need to have a Steam account and sign up for an APIKey. Since this will be an OpenID provider, we will only need an APIKey and don't need to create a separate *application* with Steam.

Full documentation on Steam's API can be found at `http://steamcommunity.com/dev` and to register for an API, visit `http://steamcommunity.com/dev/apikey`. If you already have an APIKey, it will be listed here. If you don't have one, you will be asked for a domain of your application. At the time of writing, local development with the Steam API worked without the need to fake hostnames. Here's how your screen will look after the aforementioned actions have been performed:

How to do it...

1. Create a new application using a template from the ServiceStackVS Visual Studio extension. For this example, we will use the AngularJS template.

2. Install the `ServiceStack.OrmLite.Sqlite.Windows` package from NuGet, as follows:

   ```
   Install-Package ServiceStack.OrmLite.Sqlite.Windows
   ```

3. Install the OpenId ServiceStack NuGet package so that we can extend `OpenIdOAuthProvider`:

   ```
   Install-Package ServiceStack.Authentication.OpenId
   ```

4. Create a new class called `SteamAuthProvider` that inherits from `OpenIdOAuthProvider`, as follows:

```
public class SteamAuthProvider : OpenIdOAuthProvider
{
    public const string Name = "steam";
    public static string Realm = "http://steamcommunity.com/
openid";

    public SteamAuthProvider(IAppSettings appSettings)
        : base(appSettings, Name, Realm)
    {

    }
}
```

5. Override the `LoadUserAuthInfo` method to handle the fetching of Steam user information, as follows:

```
protected override void LoadUserAuthInfo(AuthUserSession
userSession, IAuthTokens tokens, Dictionary<string, string>
authInfo)
{
    base.LoadUserAuthInfo(userSession,tokens,authInfo);
    try
    {
        if (tokens.UserId != null)
        {
            var json =
            DownloadSteamUserInfo(tokens.UserId);

            SteamPlayerResponse steamResponse = null;
            using (new ConfigScope())
            {
                steamResponse =
                json.FromJson<SteamPlayerResponse>();
            }
            if (steamResponse != null &&
                steamResponse.Response != null &&
                steamResponse.Response.Players != null &&
                steamResponse.Response.Players.Count > 0)
            {
                var player =
                steamResponse.Response.Players[0];
                tokens.DisplayName = player.PersonaName;
                tokens.State = player.LocStateCode;
                tokens.FullName = player.RealName;
```

```
                    tokens.Items[AuthMetadataProvider.ProfileUrlKey] =
                    player.AvatarFull;
                    tokens.Items["SteamId"] = player.SteamId;


                }
            }
        }
        catch (Exception ex)
        {
            Log.Error("Could not retrieve Steam user info for
            SteamId '{0}'".Fmt(tokens.UserId), ex);
        }
}


private const string SteamUrl =
"https://api.steampowered.com/ISteamUser/GetPlayerSummaries
/v0002/?key={0}&steamids={1}";
private string DownloadSteamUserInfo(string userId)
{
    string steamId;
    //Extract steamId from openid url
    steamId = userId.Substring(userId.LastIndexOf("/",
    System.StringComparison.Ordinal) + 1);
    var finalUrl = SteamUrl.Fmt(base.ConsumerKey, steamId);
    var webReq =
    (HttpWebRequest)WebRequest.Create(finalUrl);
    webReq.Accept = MimeTypes.Json;
    using (var webRes = webReq.GetResponse())
    {
        return webRes.ReadToEnd();
    }
}
```

Create classes to represent response from Steam's ISteamUser interface.

```
public class SteamUserProfile
{
    public string SteamId { get; set; }
    public int CommunityVisibilityState { get; set; }
    public int ProfileState { get; set; }
    public string PersonaName { get; set; }
    public int LastLogoff { get; set; }
    public int CommentPermission { get; set; }
    public string ProfileUrl { get; set; }
    public string Avatar { get; set; }
    public string AvatarMedium { get; set; }
```

```
              public string AvatarFull { get; set; }
              public int PersonaState { get; set; }
              public string RealName { get; set; }
              public string PrimaryClanId { get; set; }
              public int TimeCreated { get; set; }
              public int PersonaStateFlags { get; set; }
              public string GameServerIp { get; set; }
              public string GameServerSteamId { get; set; }
              public string GameExtraInfo { get; set; }
              public string GameId { get; set; }
              public string LocCountryCode { get; set; }
              public string LocStateCode { get; set; }
              public int? LocCityId { get; set; }
         }


         public class SteamPlayerSummary
         {
              public List<SteamUserProfile> Players { get; set; }
         }


         public class SteamPlayerResponse
         {
              public SteamPlayerSummary Response { get; set; }
         }
```

6. Create a class with `JsConfigScope` to handle different naming conventions coming
    back from the Steam service:

```
public class ConfigScope : IDisposable
{
     private readonly WriteComplexTypeDelegate typeStrategy;
     private readonly JsConfigScope jsConfigScope;

     public ConfigScope()
     {
         jsConfigScope = JsConfig.With(
                 dateHandler: DateHandler.UnixTime,
                 propertyConvention:
                 PropertyConvention.Lenient,
                 emitLowercaseUnderscoreNames: true,
                 emitCamelCaseNames: false);

         typeStrategy =
         QueryStringSerializer.ComplexTypeStrategy;
         QueryStringSerializer.ComplexTypeStrategy =
         QueryStringStrategy.FormUrlEncoded;
```

```
    }

    public void Dispose()
    {
        QueryStringSerializer.ComplexTypeStrategy =
        typeStrategy;
        jsConfigScope.Dispose();
    }
}
```

7. Within `SteamAuthProvider`, override the `LoadUserOAuthProvider` function and update the user session with details from Steam, as follows:

```
public override void LoadUserOAuthProvider(IAuthSession
authSession, IAuthTokens tokens)
{
    var userSession = authSession as AuthUserSession;
    if (userSession == null) return;

    userSession.PopulateWith(tokens);
}
```

8. Register the new `SteamAuthProvider` class with the `AuthFeature` plugin, along with backing Sqlite `IUserAuthRepository`, as follows:

```
var authProviders = new List<IAuthProvider>();
var appSettings = new AppSettings();
authProviders.Add(new SteamAuthProvider(appSettings));

var authFeature = new AuthFeature(
    () => new AuthUserSession(),
    authProviders.ToArray());
this.Plugins.Add(authFeature);

container.Register<IDbConnectionFactory>(
        new OrmLiteConnectionFactory(
            "~/App_Data/db.sqlite".MapHostAbsolutePath(),
            SqliteDialect.Provider));

container.Register<IUserAuthRepository>(
    new OrmLiteAuthRepository(
    container.Resolve<IDbConnectionFactory>()
));
container.Resolve<IUserAuthRepository>().InitSchema();

container.Register<ICacheClient>(new MemoryCacheClient());
```

9. In the `_Layout.cshtml` page, create a login button and preview the user picture, as follows:

```
<ul class="nav navbar-nav">
    <li class="active"><a href="#">Home</a></li>
    @if (!IsAuthenticated)
    {
        <li>
         <a href="/auth/steam">
          <img src="http://steamcommunity-
          a.akamaihd.net/public/images/
          signinthroughsteam/sits_small. png" />
         </a>
        </li>
    }
    else
    {
        var user = (SessionAs<AuthUserSession>());
        <li>
            <a href="https://steamcommunity.com/id/@user.
DisplayName">
    <img src="@user.GetProfileUrl()" />@user.DisplayName
            </a>
        </li>
        <li><a href="/auth/logout">Logout</a></li>
    }
</ul>
```

The following screenshot shows how your resultant screen will look:

10. Update your `web.config` file to specify `RedirectUrl`, `CallbackUrl` and `ConsumerKey`, which will be your Steam APIKey:

```
<appSettings>
    <add key="webPages:Enabled"
        value="false" />
    <add key="oauth.RedirectUrl"
        value="http://localhost:26888/"/>
    <add key="oauth.CallbackUrl"
        value="http://localhost:26888/auth/{0}"/>
    <add key="oauth.steam.ConsumerKey"
        value="{YourSteamAPIKey}"/>
</appSettings>
```

How it works...

Although OpenID is an older form of authentication, many sites still use it. ServiceStack's base class `OpenIdOAuthProvider` implements the plumbing for communicating with OpenID services and allows extension points to handle the parts that are different between different services.

If we did not want any of the details from the Steam API, we would only have to provide APIKey, Name, and Realm for the authentication to work. Overriding the `LoadUserAuthInfo` method gives us the chance to update the user's details from the external provider, which in this case is Steam, bring back up-to-date information on the user, and present it in our application.

Update specific token information, such as `tokens.Items[AuthMetadataProvider.ProfileUrlKey]`, with data from the Steam services allowing us to use existing extension methods like `user.GetProfileUrl()` from our Razor pages to make this consistent across authentication providers. Here's how our screen looks after performing the preceding instructions:

The name of the authentication provider, which in this case is Steam, specifies where on our routes this provider will listen for requests. The `AuthFeature` plugin registers these providers at `/auth/{Name}`. We also use this name in `web.config` to specify our settings for the Steam authentication provider, as follows:

```
<add key="oauth.steam.ConsumerKey" value="{YourSteamAPIKey}"/>
```

Once the authentication completes, we populate the user session with the information now present in `IAuthTokens`, as follows:

```
public override void LoadUserOAuthProvider(IAuthSession authSession,
IAuthTokens tokens)
{
    var userSession = authSession as AuthUserSession;
    if (userSession == null) return;

    userSession.PopulateWith(tokens);
}
```

8
Working with Redis

In this chapter, we will look at the different ways in which we can use Redis. We'll also look at the different types of data we can store and how to work with those types in the following recipes:

- ▶ Getting started with ServiceStack.Redis
- ▶ Using Redis as a cache with the ServiceStack client
- ▶ Using ServiceStack.Redis for publish/subscribe
- ▶ Using the ServiceStack.Redis client to access a Redis list
- ▶ Using Redis hash data structures in ServiceStack
- ▶ Using Redis Set data structures in ServiceStack
- ▶ Using typed data structures with ServiceStack and Redis
- ▶ Scripting Redis with Lua

Introduction

Often, when scaling a web application, at some point it starts to make sense to include a distributed-memory cache. While this can sound exotic, and it can introduce some complexity, the basic idea is very simple. At its most basic, what a cache allows you to do is store a bit of information any way you want, optimized for nearly immediate retrieval.

For instance, you might have a product catalog in a database containing tens of thousands of **stock keeping units** (**SKUs**). You query this database fairly often to get the list of the top 100 items that are actually available for sale right now. Your database is pretty well optimized, and that query runs fairly quickly, but it still puts a fair amount of load on your database servers to do it on every page load.

What a cache could allow you to do is create a `List<Product>` that contains this often-needed list and then refer to it easily in code. The cache server stores the list in-memory, not on disk, which means that retrieval is much faster than from the database. Also, whether you have one web server or twenty, they all benefit from that record being cached in the cache server.

In Redis, you could model this problem fairly easily with simple logic:

```
topProducts = redisClient.Get<List<Product>>("top-products");
if (topProducts == null)
{
    topProducts = fetchTopProductsFromDatabase();
    redisClient.Set("top-products", topProducts);
}
```

If the cache has an item named `top-products`, `redisClient` will fetch that value and try to create an object of the type provided by deserializing the value it finds to the type provided. If the cache doesn't have an item named `top-products`, this logic will go and fetch that list from the database and then store the result before continuing, which ensures that next time we'll get the result from cache, not from the database.

While basic cache servers allow the basic key/value pattern shown previously, Redis goes much further than this. Redis is often referred to as a data structure server since Redis can store values in strings, hashes, lists, sets, ordered sets, bitmaps, and much more. Redis also provides transactions, a publish/subscribe system, scripting, and keys that automatically expire based on time-to-live, frequency of access, and other algorithms.

Getting started with ServiceStack.Redis

Redis is a powerful tool with performance as its main focus. In this recipe, we will look at how to use different aspects of the ServiceStack.Redis client to help take full advantage of integrating with Redis.

Getting ready

Let's use Redis to enhance `GreetingService`. We'll store each greeting created in the Redis cache. We'll need Redis installed and running in order to store and retrieve values, which we can do by performing the following steps:

1. Download the Redis `.zip` file from the Redis site at `http://redis.io/download`.

   For this example, it is easiest to run the Redis server on Windows. Although Windows is not officially supported, MSOpenTech on GitHub does maintain a repository for Redis on Windows. This can be found at `https://github.com/MSOpenTech/redis/`. At the time of writing, a zip of the latest can be found in `/bin/release` of the repository.

2. Extract the `.zip` file.

3. Start the `redis-server.exe` binary, as follows:

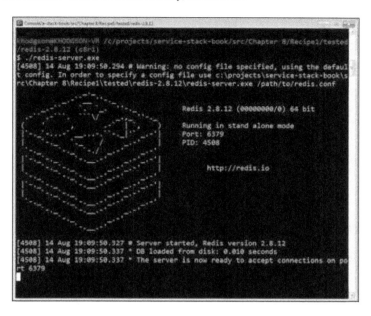

4. After Redis is running, we'll also need the `ServiceStack.Redis` package installed in our solution, as shown in the following line of code; we can use NuGet for this:

```
Install-Package ServiceStack.Redis
```

Once that's complete, we'll have access to the `ServiceStack.Redis` package that includes `RedisClient`. We'll use `RedisClient` to enable the caching features in our code.

How to do it...

Given that we want to store the results of `GreetingService` in a cache, it makes sense to store a response for each possible request. We can imagine that instead of concatenating two strings, `GreetingService` has to connect to databases or other remote resources, possibly do some processing, and we want to cache the result so that we don't have to do this over and over. To do that, perform the following steps:

1. Let's start with a basic solution that doesn't do anything with Redis for now:

```
public object Any(Greeting request)
{
   GreetingResponse response;
```

```
        response = new GreetingResponse
        {
          Response = "Hello {0}!".Fmt(request.Name)
        };

        return response;
}
```

The preceding code is pretty basic. Let's say you called the service with a request /
`hello/world`; we're going to get back a JSON response like this:

```
{"Response":"Hello World!"}
```

2. Next, let's add some basic code that will store the results in the cache:

```
public object Any(Greeting request)
{
   GreetingResponse response;
   using (var redisClient = new RedisClient())
   {

      response = new GreetingResponse
      {
        Response = "Hello {0}!".Fmt(request.Name)
      };
      redisClient.Set("greetings:" + request.Name,
        response, TimeSpan.FromHours(1));
   }
   return response;
}
```

The `using` statement encapsulates our use of a new `RedisClient` class and
handles its disposal for us. A few lines later, we use this client to `Set` the value of the
key, which would be `greetings:World`, to contain the response we just created
so that we can fetch it later. We can see the result using `redis-client` at the
command prompt:

```
C:\redis-2.8.12>redis-cli.exe
127.0.0.1:6379> get greetings:World
"{\"Response\":\"Hello World!\"}"
127.0.0.1:6379>
```

3. While we can see that Redis has JSON serialized and stored our object, we haven't started making use of that in our code yet. Next, let's add a conditional that checks to see whether a required response has been stored in the cache and uses it if it has. If not, we'll compute the response as we normally would. The following code shows just how we can do this:

```
public object Any(Greeting request)
{
  GreetingResponse response;
  using (var redisClient = new RedisClient())
  {
    response = redisClient.Get<GreetingResponse>(
      "greetings:" + request.Name);
    if (response == null)
    {
      response = new GreetingResponse
      {
        Response = "Hello {0}!".Fmt(request.Name)
      };
      redisClient.Set("greetings:" + request.Name,
        response);
    }
  }
  return response;
}
```

Now, multiple trips through this method looking for the same Greeting will only result in calculating Greeting the first time. The subsequent trips would simply fetch the result from the cache. We can see this by enabling the monitor function in the Redis command-line client, as follows:

```
C:\redis-2.8.12>redis-cli.exe
127.0.0.1:6379> monitor
OK
1408219987.615931 [0 127.0.0.1:2003] "INFO"
1408219987.616907 [0 127.0.0.1:2003] "GET" "greetings:there"
1408219987.622767 [0 127.0.0.1:2003] "SET" "greetings:there"
"{\"Response\":\"Hello there!\"}"
1408219988.763392 [0 127.0.0.1:2004] "INFO"
1408219988.764368 [0 127.0.0.1:2004] "GET" "greetings:there"
1408219989.733118 [0 127.0.0.1:2005] "INFO"
1408219989.733118 [0 127.0.0.1:2005] "GET" "greetings:there"
```

How it works...

As you can see, we first GET the `greetings:there` key. The first time through, we get NULL, so we compute the response and store it with SET. Subsequent requests only use the value we fetched from the cache as the full response will be returned.

What `ServiceStack.Redis` is doing under the hood is leveraging the ServiceStack JSON serializer to serialize our response object. Then, it's sending it to Redis as a simple string. Since we use the typed `RedisClient.Get<T>` method, it knows what type we're expecting to deserialize the JSON string to.

There's more...

It's worth noting that what we're doing so far is *permanently* caching the value. This is fine as long as we don't run out of memory. If you add too many objects to your cache, you'll eventually run into that problem. If you do run out of memory, you'll see the following text in your Redis logs:

VirtualAlloc/COWAlloc fail!

VirtualAlloc/COWAlloc fail!

[2560] 22 Aug 20:03:55.627 # Out Of Memory allocating 1310727 bytes!

One basic way to control this is to add a time-to-live value, or TTL. `RedisClient.Set()` has two overloads that allow us to state how long a certain item will live in the cache. We can either provide a `DateTime` property that the value should be considered expired, or a `TimeSpan` property that indicates for how long the item should be kept. For instance, if we provided a one-hour `TimeSpan`, we would see that Redis would add an expires argument to the cache set, as shown in the following code:

```
redisClient.Set("greetings:" + request.Name,
    response, TimeSpan.FromHours(1));

1408753464.817608 [0 127.0.0.1:9235] "GET" "greetings:Kyle"
1408753464.826397 [0 127.0.0.1:9235] "SET" "greetings:Kyle"
    "{\"Response\":\"Hello Kyle!\"}" "EX" "3600"
```

Now, after 3,600 seconds (one hour), the object will be removed from the cache, reducing the amount of memory in use. By default, there is no sliding window applied: reads to this value and even updates to the value won't extend the expiry. You'll have to do that in code if you want it to happen. Simply add code that extends the TTL to code that reads the values that need a sliding expiry.

Also, the previous code purposefully mixes concerns up all in one place to show the flow through the various steps. You'd want to refactor this code to be more expressive and more maintainable. For instance, it might be better to push some of this code down into a layer that understands how to deal with the caching logic. The next recipe goes into more detail about a better practice for how to use caching whereas this recipe was meant to show the basics. It's also a good idea *not* to build out our cache key over and over again. At a minimum, that should be refactored out to a method to reduce the chances of mistakes.

Using Redis as a cache with the ServiceStack client

In the previous recipe, we focused on using low-level Redis features directly to hand roll our own caching functions. While this is useful, we can also let ServiceStack's extension methods on the `Service` class do some of the work for us.

Getting ready

ServiceStack's `Service` class provides a method named `ToOptimizedResultUsingCache()`, which can help. The way it works is that we'll pass in an implementation of `ICacheClient`, a string that represents a cache key, and a function that knows how to generate our response in the event that there isn't a value at the location in the cache at that cache key.

This functionality can improve performance for expensive queries that don't need to be performed every time the service is hit. A common example would be a service that runs a query to give back statistics that require a large number of joins across database tables. This query might be calculating yesterday's statistics—something that isn't going to change and, therefore, can be cached with a time-to-live until the end of the day. The expensive query only has to run once, and the result is stored in Redis for future requests, saving viewers time in that they don't have to wait and database resources.

How to do it...

1. First, we'll register `PooledRedisClientManager`, and a cache client based on it that our application can use in the `Configure` method of our `AppHost` class:

```
public override void Configure(Container container)
{
  container.Register<IRedisClientsManager>(
    c => new PooledRedisClientManager("localhost:6379"));

  container.Register(c =>
    c.Resolve<IRedisClientsManager>().GetCacheClient());
}
```

2. Next, let's create a method that holds the logic to generate our response just in case the cached value isn't yet present. To show the cache as functioning, we'll added `Thread.Sleep(3000)` to simulate a long-running query, as follows:

```
private GreetingResponse GreetingGenerator(
GreetingRequest request)
{
  Thread.Sleep(3000);
  return new GreetingResponse
  {
    Response = "Hello {0}!".Fmt(request.Name)
  };
}
```

3. Next, we'll create a method that can create our cache key. Since our requests and responses are so simple, this is quite easy. Make sure your cache key can safely represent a unique response; if the server finds this cache key present, it won't generate a new response. Here's how we create the method:

```
private string GreetingCacheKey(GreetingRequest request)
{
  return "greetings:" + request.Name;
}
```

4. Next, we'll call `ToOptimizedResultUsingCache` and pass in our instance of `ICacheClient`, our cache key, and the function that can generate a new request:

```
public object Any(GreetingRequest request)
{
  return base.Request.ToOptimizedResultUsingCache(
    base.Cache,
    GreetingCacheKey(request),
    () => GreetingGenerator(request));
}
```

At this point, our caching layer is enabled. If a response can be found in the cache, it will be taken from there. If not, the service will run the `GreetingGenerator` method to generate a new one, and the simulated delay will be seen.

How it works...

If we watch the Redis monitor while we call the service, we can see what it's doing behind the scenes. Here's the first request for `/hello/World`:

```
$ ./redis-cli.exe monitor
OK
```

```
1408453514.226550 [0 127.0.0.1:6477] "INFO"

1408453514.229479 [0 127.0.0.1:6477] "GET"
"greetings:World.json.deflate"

1408453514.307114 [0 127.0.0.1:6478] "INFO"

1408453514.307114 [0 127.0.0.1:6478] "SET" "greetings:World"
"{\"Response\":\"Hello World!\"}"

1408453514.314438 [0 127.0.0.1:6478] "SET" "greetings:World.json"
"\"{\\\"Response\\\":\\\"Hello World!\\\"}\""

1408453514.321762 [0 127.0.0.1:6478] "SET"
"greetings:World.json.deflate" "\xabV\nJ-
.\xc8\xcf+NU\xb2R\xf2H\xcd\xc9\xc9W\b\xcf/\xcaIQT\xaa\x05\x00"
```

As you can see, `ICacheClient` first checks to see if there is an existing cached response for `greetings.World.json.deflate`. That's not exactly the cache key we provided though you'll probably recognize the `greetings.World` part as our `GreetingsCacheKey` logic concatenates the prefix `greetings` with the `Name` property passed in on the request.

Next, we'll see that `ICacheClient` sets three values: `greetings.World`, which is a serialized version of our object; `greetings.World.json`; and `greetings.World.json.deflate`, which is a compressed version of the serialized object. If we call the service again, we'll see `GET` only for the compressed version. Here's the code for the explanation provided in this paragraph:

```
1408586691.937421 [0 127.0.0.1:6772] "INFO"

1408586691.939621 [0 127.0.0.1:6772] "GET"
"greetings:World.json.deflate"
```

There's more...

We can optionally provide a TTL value to instruct Redis as to how long it should hold on to the optimized result. Simply construct a `TimeSpan` object and pass it in after the cache key, as follows:

```
return base.Request.ToOptimizedResultUsingCache(base.Cache,
  GreetingCacheKey(request),
  TimeSpan.FromHours(1),
  () => GreetingGenerator(request));
```

Using ServiceStack.Redis for publish/ subscribe

Background processing of the CPU or resource intensive tasks should leverage asynchrony and can add to both scalability and performance when done correctly. Tasks that don't need to be done *while the user waits* are particularly good candidates for asynchronous execution.

Consider, for instance, a user logging in to a website. It may be true that several systems need to be involved on each login: a security audit, a Big Data sensor, and the actual authentication system with the correct usernames and passwords—a task that fetches the user's preferences concerning e-commerce purchases. You might find that while the authentication system needs to be involved to properly log in a user, several of the other tasks could be processed in the background.

Redis models this with the concepts of channels, publishers, and subscribers. A *subscriber*, a system that needs to be alerted of events, might create a subscription to a specific *channel*. *Publishers* publish messages on the correct channels as they happen. For instance, when a user logs in, the website might publish a message on the user-login channel. After the message on that channel is published, subscribers are notified asynchronously. The benefit to the overall system is that subscribers still receive the information they need in near real time in most circumstances, but the publisher's responsibility ends after the event is published to a queue, and processing can continue for the web server.

This has several benefits:

▶ The user's experience is improved, as the site can return content more quickly

▶ If the subscribing systems become backlogged processing events, the publisher doesn't need to be slowed down waiting for that processing to complete

▶ The subscribing systems and publisher can be scaled out separately. For instance, if the message queue that represents the user-login channel is constantly filling up, the system can simply start more processes that subscribe to that channel and process those messages

This concept can be a bit tricky to grasp at first for developers used to synchronous processing, but once understood, the concept can greatly simplify the process of scaling a high-volume system.

Getting ready

We'll need a few things before we can create a system that leverages this technique, which is sometimes referred to as pub/sub. Installing Redis and creating a basic ServiceStack app are required and are covered in previous recipes.

Let's imagine that a social network needs to allow users to quickly post statuses to their timeline, but several tasks need to take places for each status being posted. We'll create the service that receives the post and publishes the event, and separately, we'll create a command-line process that subscribes to the channel and performs the background processing.

Given that we're using the Redis components, it's important to make sure that the `ServiceStack.Redis` Nuget package is installed, as follows:

```
PM> install-package servicestack.redis
```

How to do it...

1. First, we'll create a project in our solution to contain the ServiceModel components, such as the `TimelineStatus` class, as follows:

```
[Route("/timeline/{User}/{Status}")]
public class TimelineStatus
{
  public DateTime Date { get; set; }
  public string Status { get; set; }
  public string User { get; set; }
  public Guid Id { get; set; }

  public TimelineStatus()
  {
    Id = Guid.NewGuid();
    Date = DateTime.Now;
  }
}
```

2. Next, we'll create a project in our solution for the web service itself. This project will need a reference to the ServiceModel project in order to have access to the `TimelineStatus` class. We'll start with a basic service:

```
public class TimelineStatusService : Service
{
  public object Any(TimelineStatus request)
  {
    using (var redisClient = new RedisClient())
    {
      redisClient.PublishMessage(
        "timeline", request.ToJson());
    }
    return request.Id;
  }
}
```

3. This method serializes any incoming requests to JSON and then publishes them to the timeline channel. Next, we'll create a console app project that subscribes to the same channel:

```
public class StatusConsumer
{
  public void StartProcessor()
  {
    using (var redisClient = new RedisClient())
    {
      using (var subscription =
        redisClient.CreateSubscription())
      {
        subscription.OnMessage =
          (channel, msg) =>
          {
            var status = msg.FromJson<TimelineStatus>();
            Console.WriteLine(
              "[" + channel + "] : " + status.Status);
            StatusRepository.AddStatus(status);
            Console.WriteLine("Added.");
          };
        subscription.SubscribeToChannels("timeline");
      }
    }
  }
}

public static class Program
{
  public static void Main(string[] args)
  {
    Console.WriteLine("Starting Status Processor.");
    (new StatusConsumer()).StartProcessor();
  }
}
```

4. Lastly, we'll augment our service to handle timeline access requests to display messages after they arrive, as follows:

```
public class TimelineService : Service
{
  public StatusAccess StatusAccess { get; set; }

  public object Any(NewStatusRequest request)
```

```
    {
        StatusAccess.AddStatus(request);
        return request.Id;
    }

    public object Get(AllTimelineRequest request)
    {
        return StatusAccess.GetTimeline();
    }

    public object Get(TimelineRequest request)
    {
        return StatusAccess.Recent(request.Quantity);
    }
}
```

How it works...

If we have the `redis-cli monitor` running in the background, we'll see the console app subscribe to the timeline channel as it starts:

```
C:\TimelineService\TimelineService.StatusProcessor\bin\Debug>Timeline
Service.StatusProcessor.exe
Starting Status Processor.
```

```
$ ./redis-cli monitor
OK
1408681222.539628 [0 127.0.0.1:8198] "INFO"
1408681222.543088 [0 127.0.0.1:8198] "SUBSCRIBE" "timeline"
```

If we access the service and add a status message for a user, we'll see that it shows up in the command-line app and monitor as the events fire `http://localhost/timeline/Kyle/Hello%20world`.

We see that the message is published on the channel in the `redis-cli monitor` as it's published:

```
1408681402.242832 [0 127.0.0.1:8208] "PUBLISH" "timeline"
"{\"Date\":\"\\/Date(1408681402237-0400)\\/\",\"Status\":\"Hello
world\",\"User\":\"Kyle\",\"Id\":\"ed7c6aede4af4249bb2963e88b681ce6\"
}"
```

The command-line app shows the new message arriving and prints out the name of the channel it arrived on:

```
[timeline] : Hello world
Added.
```

The `StatusConsumer` app runs the `OnMessage` function when the event is raised, notifying us that the event has arrived. Then it adds the status to our backend storage using the `StatusRepository` service. We see this in the `redis-cli monitor` as we'd expect:

```
1408681402.431309 [0 127.0.0.1:8209] "INFO"
1408681402.432285 [0 127.0.0.1:8209] "RPUSH" "timeline-statuses"
"{\"Date\":\"\\/Date(1408681402237-0000)\\/\",\"Status\":\"Hello
world\",\"User\":\"Kyle\",\"Id\":\"ed7c6aede4af4249bb2963e88b681ce6\"
}"
```

We kept this example simple on purpose to illustrate the concept. Your system could easily add more processing logic to the command-line app. Users will be able to post status messages to their timeline very rapidly even as we add longer-running workflows and other processing to the command-line app.

Using the ServiceStack.Redis client to access a Redis list

We've seen already that Redis can act as a key-value store, allowing us to temporarily store objects at a specific location from where we can retrieve them later. Redis also has other data structures it can store, including a list structure. Redis implements the list as a linked list. Accessing linked lists randomly is less efficient; however, they have excellent performance characteristics to add elements to the beginning or the end of the list, as well as fetch elements at the beginning or end of the list.

Getting ready

Let's try to use the Redis list to implement a status timeline suitable for a social network. We'll build a basic service that can accept new statuses and retrieve the last *n* statuses from the timeline. We'll create a service layer that handles the details of dealing with the client and an access layer that handles the specifics of dealing with the Redis list.

How to do it...

1. First, let's build a basic service that can accept new status requests. We'll need some request DTOs and a basic service, as follows:

```
[Route("/status/{User}/{Status}")]
public class NewStatusRequest
{
  public Guid Id { get; set; }
  public string User { get; set; }
  public string Status { get; set; }
  public DateTime Posted { get; set; }

  public NewStatusRequest()
  {
    Id = Guid.NewGuid();
    Posted = DateTime.Now;
  }
}

[Route("/timeline","GET")]
public class AllTimelineRequest
{}

[Route("/timeline/{Quantity}","GET")]
public class TimelineRequest
{
  public int Quantity { get; set; }
}

public class TimelineService : Service
{
  public object Any(NewStatusRequest request)
  {
    return request.Id;
  }
}
```

2. Next, let's model what it looks like to add our new status to a Redis list so that we can persist our timeline events. We'll create a class `StatusAccess` that serves to access the Redis list. We'll start with a method that adds new requests to our list, as follows:

```
public class StatusAccess
{
  private const string TimelineStatuses =
    "timeline-  statuses";

  public void AddStatus(NewStatusRequest status)
  {
    using (var redisClient = new RedisClient())
    {
      var typedClient = redisClient.As<NewStatusRequest>();
      typedClient.Lists[TimelineStatuses].Add(status);
    }
  }
}
```

When we call the `typedClient.Lists[TimelineStatuses].Add()` method, the `RedisClient` method will have the Redis server add the new status entry to the list on the server.

3. Now, we can wire that into our `Service` method that creates new statuses:

```
public class TimelineService : Service
{
  public StatusAccess StatusAccess { get; set; }

  public object Any(NewStatusRequest request)
  {
    StatusAccess.AddStatus(request);
    return request.Id;
  }
}
```

4. Next, add the `StatusAccess` IoC registration in the configure block so that Funq will auto-wire the service to have a `StatusAccess` object:

```
public override void Configure(Container container)
{
  container.Register(new StatusAccess());
}
```

5. Next up, we'll focus on a simple method to pull all of the timeline statuses at once. This won't be the normal case, and as our list grows, it won't be performant, but it's an easy place to start:

```
public class StatusAccess
{
  private const string TimelineStatuses = "timeline-statuses";

  public void AddStatus(NewStatusRequest status)
  {
    using (var redisClient = new RedisClient())
    {
      var typedClient = redisClient.As<NewStatusRequest>();
      typedClient.Lists[TimelineStatuses].Add(status);
    }
  }
  public IList<NewStatusRequest> GetTimeline()
  {
      using (var redisClient = new RedisClient())
      {
        var typedClient = redisClient.As<NewStatusRequest>();
        return typedClient.Lists[TimelineStatuses].ToList();
      }
  }
}
```

6. Now that we have the access layer in place, we can wire it up for the service layer. We'll create a new `Service` method that will return all of the timeline at once. It's not very performant at web scale, but it'll get us started:

```
public class TimelineService : Service
{
  public StatusAccess StatusAccess { get; set; }

  public object Any(NewStatusRequest request)
  {
    StatusAccess.AddStatus(request);
    return request.Id;
  }
  public object Get(AllTimelineRequest request)
  {
    return StatusAccess.GetTimeline();
  }
}
```

7. Now, what if we wanted to only access the last ten statuses on the timeline? Users are mostly interested in the recent posts after all. From the service perspective, we could model that like this:

```
public class TimelineService : Service
{
  public object Any(NewStatusRequest request)
  {
    StatusAccess.AddStatus(request);
    return request.Id;
  }

  public object Get(AllTimelineRequest request)
  {
    return StatusAccess.GetTimeline();
  }

  public object Get(TimelineRequest request)
  {
    return StatusAccess.Recent(request.Quantity);
  }
}
```

8. From here, we now need to implement the `Recent` method. We could just take the last *n* entries from the timeline after fetching the whole thing from Redis, but that wouldn't make use of Redis list's capabilities or solve the problem. Redis has a function `LRANGE` that can fetch an arbitrary range of elements from its list. Since `ServiceStack.Redis` does expose this function, if we want to only grab the last *n* elements of our list, we can do it with the `GetRange` method, as shown in the following code:

```
public class StatusAccess
{
  private const string TimelineStatuses =
    "timeline-statuses";

  public void AddStatus(NewStatusRequest status)
  {
    using (var redisClient = new RedisClient())
    {
      var typedClient = redisClient.As<NewStatusRequest>();
      typedClient.Lists[TimelineStatuses].Add(status);
    }
  }

  public IList<NewStatusRequest> Timeline
```

```
          {
            get
            {
              using (var redisClient = new RedisClient())
              {
                var typedClient =
                redisClient.As<NewStatusRequest>();
                return typedClient.Lists[TimelineStatuses].ToList();
              }
            }
          }
          public List<NewStatusRequest> Recent(int quantity)
          {
            using (var redisClient = new RedisClient())
            {
              var typedClient = redisClient.As<NewStatusRequest>();
              var list = typedClient.Lists[TimelineStatuses];
              return list.GetRange(list.Count - quantity, list.Count -
              1);
            }
          }
        }
```

How it works...

If we watch the Redis monitor while hitting the service, we see that it's using the LRANGE function as we expect when accessing the service:

```
1408331465.388382 [0 127.0.0.1:5836] "INFO"

1408331465.389847 [0 127.0.0.1:5836] "LLEN" "timeline-statuses"

1408331465.391312 [0 127.0.0.1:5836] "LLEN" "timeline-statuses"

1408331465.391312 [0 127.0.0.1:5836] "LRANGE" "timeline-statuses" "2"
"3"
```

We are also utilizing IRedisTypedClient in this recipe to interact with our list and to add new values:

```
    using (var redisClient = new RedisClient())
    {
      var typedClient = redisClient.As<NewStatusRequest>();
      typedClient.Lists[TimelineStatuses].Add(status);
    }
```

The As<T> method when called gives us a strongly typed client to add our strongly typed request to the list. The Lists property is being used with our key to access the correct list, and the Add function is persisting our request to the Redis instance:

Using Redis hash data structures in ServiceStack

If you're familiar with the hash data structure, then working with the Redis implementation won't surprise you. A hash in Redis is roughly analogous to a C# dictionary—a collection of key/value pairs.

If you're just serializing objects to be stored, it's easy enough to store them as Redis strings. Where the hash can be useful is that it can allow you to update a given property on an object without fetching and changing the whole object at once.

Getting ready

For this example, we'll model the idea of allowing a user to change certain properties of their profile. We'll provide a service that accepts requests to update a given property of the user's profile, and which updates only that property.

The service interface might look something like this:

```
curl -d "NewEmail=newemail@company.com"http://myserver/user/Kyle/Email
```

We'll provide a POST including the new e-mail address to a route /user/Kyle/Email and expect the service to update only the e-mail property.

How to do it...

1. We can model the user simply like this, providing a route that creates new users:

```
public enum UserProperties
{
  UserName,
  FirstName,
  LastName,
  Email
}

[Route("/user","POST")]
public class User
{
  public string UserName { get; set; }
  public string FirstName { get; set; }
  public string LastName { get; set; }
  public string Email { get; set; }
}
```

The `enum` type will help us later when we're saving things to Redis.

2. We can construct a repository object that knows how to work with our hash storage. Creating a new user is a bit of a process: we will have to map our object as a collection of `KeyValuePair<string, string>` that contains the property name and current value, as follows:

```
public class UserRepository
{
  public void SaveNewUser(User user)
  {
    user.ToKeyValuePairs().Each(
    keyValuePair =>
    {
      using (var redisClient = new RedisClient())
      {
        redisClient.Hashes[user.UserName].Add(keyValuePair);
      }
    });
  }
}
```

3. That `ToKeyValuePairs` method is a simple extension method on `User` in our repository which knows how to extract `KeyValuePair` for saving to Redis, as follows:

```
public static IEnumerable<KeyValuePair<string, string>>
  ToKeyValuePairs(this User user)
{
  return new Dictionary<string, string>
  {
    {UserProperties.UserName.ToString(),
      user.UserName},
    {UserProperties.FirstName.ToString()
      user.FirstName},
    {UserProperties.LastName.ToString()
      user.LastName},
    {UserProperties.Email.ToString()
      user.Email}
  };
}
```

4. Updating only the e-mail address is a simple matter of accessing the correct hash and then updating the value to the new one provided, as follows:

```
public class UserRepository
{
  public void SaveNewUser(User user)
  {
    user.ToKeyValuePairs().Each(
      keyValuePair =>
      {
        using (var redisClient = new RedisClient())
        {
          redisClient.Hashes[user.UserName]
            .Add(keyValuePair);
        }
      });
  }

  public void UpdateUserEmail(
    string userName, string newEmail)
    {
      using (var redisClient = new RedisClient())
      {
        redisClient.Hashes
        [userName]
```

```
        [UserProperties.Email.ToString()]
        = newEmail;
    }
}
```

5. We'll need a request DTO to express to ServiceStack where to expect these requests, as follows:

```
[Route("/user/{UserName}/Email", "POST")]
public class ChangeUserEmail
{
    public string UserName { get; set; }
    public string NewEmail { get; set; }
}
```

6. We'll need a `Service` method to process these:

```
public object Post(ChangeUserEmail request)
{
    UserRepository.UpdateUserEmail(
        request.UserName, request.NewEmail);
    return "OK";
}
```

7. The end result can be observed by monitoring the Redis server as we run the cURL command, as follows:

```
1408981432.410329 [0 127.0.0.1:11087] "INFO"

1408981432.411306 [0 127.0.0.1:11087] "HSET" "Kyle" "Email"
"newemail@company.com"
```

How it works...

When we create the `User` object, we're storing it as a hash using the `RedisClient.Hashes` object. It acts like an indexed accessor. We can first access the instance of `User` we want to update by providing the hash key associated with that user—`UserName` in this case. That simply selects the specific hash associated with this user. After that, we're accessing that hash directly. Here's what it looks like:

```
var userHash = redisClient.Hashes[user.UserName];
```

Once we have access to `userHash`, we can easily update the e-mail address just like we would do when updating a value in a dictionary, as follows:

```
userHash[EmailProperty] = newEmail;
```

There's More...

ServiceStack's `RedisClient` doesn't have a clean way to retrieve a hash and instantiate an object. We can apply a similar technique to the one that we used in this recipe when it came time to save an object as a hash. Let's add one more method to our `UserExtensions` class to convert a hash into `User`:

```
public static User ToUser(this Dictionary<string,string> entries)
{
  return new User
  {
    Email = entries[UserProperties.Email.ToString()],
    FirstName = entries[UserProperties.FirstName.ToString()],
    LastName = entries[UserProperties.LastName.ToString()],
    UserName = entries[UserProperties.UserName.ToString()]
  };
}
```

The code to retrieve the hash and do the conversion is similar—we'll use a method `GetAllEntriesFromHash` provided by ServiceStack's `RedisClient`:

```
public User GetUser(string userName)
{
  using (var redisClient = new RedisClient())
  {
    return redisClient
        .GetAllEntriesFromHash(userName)
      .ToUser();
  }
}
```

Using Redis Set data structures in ServiceStack

Sets in Redis are what you might expect—unordered, unique lists, similar to the `HashSet` class in .NET. You can try to add the same thing to Sets twice, but Redis will silently discard subsequent requests. Sets have some nice features in Redis: you can ask for the *union* of two sets to find out what unique values are present across multiple Sets, or you can ask for the *intersection* of two Sets to only see what values are shared. Sets are good at modeling the relationships between things, and tagging systems are often implemented in Sets for this reason.

Getting ready

For this example, we'll model the idea of allowing users our timeline service to tag people on to statuses. For instance, if I post **Hello world!** I might want to specify that two other people are involved. I can tag them on to my post.

A simple service interface might look something like the following:

```
curl -d
"UserNames=Kyle&UserNames=Layoric&StatusId=b377c7c7013c47fdb726665760
28210a" http://myserver/tag
```

This POST allows us to indicate that users *Kyle* and *Layoric* were both involved with the status b377c7c7013c47fdb72666576028210a.

How to do it...

1. We'll need a DTO and a route to model the preceding POST:

```
[Route("/tag", "POST")]
public class TagUser
{
  public string StatusId { get; set; }
  public List<string> UserNames { get; set; }
}
```

2. We'll create a repository object to access our Set members:

```
public class TagRepository
{
  public void Tag(string statusId, List<string> userNames)
  {
    using (var redisClient = new RedisClient())
    {
      userNames.ForEach(user =>
      redisClient.Sets[statusId].Add(user));
    }
  }
}
```

3. `TimelineService` could simply leverage this repository object to add tags as they arrive, as follows:

```
public object Post(TagUser request)
{
  TagRepository.Tag(request.StatusId, request.UserNames);
  return "OK";
}
```

4. Accessing the tags later is simple. We'll create another DTO to model the concept of accessing the tags:

```
[Route("/tags/{StatusId}")]
public class StatusTags
{
  public string StatusId { get; set; }
}
```

5. We'll amend our repository to create an ability to retrieve the tags for a specific status, as follows:

```
public class TagRepository
{
  public void Tag(
    string statusId, List<string> userNames)
  {
    using (var redisClient = new RedisClient())
    {
      userNames.ForEach(user =>
        redisClient.Sets[statusId].Add(user));
    }
  }

  public object GetTagsForStatus(string statusId)
  {
    using (var redisClient = new RedisClient())
    {
      return redisClient.Sets[statusId].GetAll();
    }
  }
}
```

6. Now, it's a simple matter of connecting the two in our service:

```
public object Get(StatusTags request)
{
  return TagRepository.GetTagsForStatus(request.StatusId);
}
```

How it works...

If we send a list of users to our tag service, our `TagRepository` will use Redis `SET` commands to assign anything we provide to Set for this status.

For instance, we could send the following cURL command and check the Redis monitor to see what it shows:

```
curl -d
"UserNames=kylehodgson&UserNames=layoric&StatusId=3c7038f77d1f43cdb6a
b62717990ccfc" http://myserver/tag?format=json
```

As expected, the monitor shows that Redis receives two `SADD` commands, one per user we want to tag on the status, as follows:

```
1409021127.881600 [0 127.0.0.1:12483] "INFO"

1409021127.882674 [0 127.0.0.1:12483] "SADD"
"3c7038f77d1f43cdb6ab62717990ccfc" "kylehodgson"

1409021127.883748 [0 127.0.0.1:12483] "SADD"
"3c7038f77d1f43cdb6ab62717990ccfc" "layoric"
```

Now, if we hit the `/tags` service and specify `statusId`, we'll be presented with a JSON representation of the two users associated with this status post:

```
curl
http://myserver/tags/3c7038f77d1f43cdb6ab62717990ccfc?format=json
["layoric","kylehodgson"]
```

We could easily show the group of all people who have posted on a series of posts using a union, as shown in the following code:

```
public static object UnionTagsForStatuses(string status1,
   string status2)
{
  using (var redisClient = new RedisClient())
  {
    var status1Tags = redisClient.Sets[status1];
    var status2Tags = redisClient.Sets[status2];
    return status1Tags.Union(status2Tags);
  }
}
```

This results in Redis using the `Union` command to fetch the union of the two Sets:

```
1409022184.221843 [0 127.0.0.1:12605] "INFO"

1409022184.223796 [0 127.0.0.1:12605] "SUNION"
"b377c7c7013c47fdb72666576028210a" "3c7038f77d1f43cdb6ab62717990ccfc"
```

This, as advertised, returns the super Set of the two:

```
curl
http://myserver/union/b377c7c7013c47fdb72666576028210a/3c7038f77d1f43
cdb6a

b62717990ccfc?format=json
["KyleHodgson","layoric","Layoric","Kyle","kylehodgson"]
```

Using typed data structures with ServiceStack and Redis

We learned about using Redis hash data structures in a previous recipe. In that explanation, as with others, we used the ServiceStack client to directly manipulate the Redis data structures on the server. If you want a higher level of abstraction, you can use the Redis client's typed approach. Instead of directly dealing with strings and other primitives, you can tell the Redis client the type you want to store and then let it handle some of the details. In this recipe, we'll make use of this approach.

Getting ready

If we continue with our social network theme, we can begin to model the concept of a comment. For our service, a comment is a reply on a status:

Kyle's status: **Hey guys what movie should we see?**

▸ Darren's comment: **How about Guardians of the Galaxy?**

▸ Kyle's comment: **That works!**

We saw in the previous recipe how we can store our statuses in a list. We could store our comments now in a hash. The hash key could be the `StatusId` of the status itself.

How to do it...

Let's imagine that we had a service that received requests from the client to store new comments. It would need access to a repository that would know how to persist them:

1. Start by creating a class to represent our status request, as follows:

```
public class Status
{
  public string Message { get; set; }
  public DateTime Date { get; set; }
  public Person Poster { get; set; }
  public Guid StatusId { get; set; }
}
```

2. We can model a comment in a similar way. Let's create a class for comments, as shown in the following code:

```
public class Comment
{
  public string Message { get; set; }
  public DateTime Date { get; set; }
  public Person Commenter { get; set; }
  public string ParentStatus { get; set; }
}
```

3. Calls to our timeline service can return timeline entries, combinations of statuses, and associated comments. Let's create a class to store the comments for our timeline, as follows:

```
public class TimelineEntry
{
  public Status Status { get; set; }
  public List<Comment> Comments { get; set; }
}
```

4. Next, our service would accept new status requests and store them via a repository service, as illustrated by the following code:

```
public object Post(Status request)
{
  StatusAccess.CreateStatus(request);
  return "OK";
}
```

5. First we'll add a `Guid` if this is a new status that doesn't have one established yet. Under the cover, we would store the status in the Redis list for easy access, as follows:

```
if (status.StatusId.Equals(Guid.Empty))
{
   status.StatusId = Guid.NewGuid();
}
redisClient.As<Status>()
   .Lists["timelineStatuses"].Add(status);
```

6. Also, our service would accept new comments and store them via a repository service, as shown in the following code:

```
public object Post(Comment request)
{
   StatusAccess.StoreComment(request);
   return "OK";
}
```

How it works...

So, what would `StatusAccess.StoreComment` look like?

First, we ask `RedisClient` to locate the hash that we'll be storing comments in, as follows:

```
var commentsHash = redisClient.As<List<Comment>>()
   .GetHash<Guid>("statusComments");
```

`RedisClient` provides the method `As<List<Comment>>` that allows us to specify that the type of the *value* we store will be `List<Comment>`. The method `GetHash<Guid>` specifies that the type of the *key* will be `Guid`.

Then, we get the list of comments for the `ParentStatus` message, as follows:

```
var parentStatus = new Guid(comment.ParentStatus);
var commentsList = commentsHash[parentStatus];
```

We don't know if the list has been initialized yet or not. If this is the first comment on that status, we'll get back `null` when we try to pull the list of comments. The following code depicts the procedure to be followed:

```
if (commentsList == null)
{
   redisClient.As<List<Comment>>()
      .GetHash<Guid("statusComments") [parentStatus]
      = new List<Comment>();
   commentsList = new List<Comment>();
}
```

What we've done is create the list on the server and also created an in-memory list as its proxy to replace the null we got back.

Now that we have our list, it's easy to add a new comment to it. This happens in memory on our application server, the command won't be sent to Redis just yet:

```
commentsList.Add(comment);
```

After we're ready to save the new list back to the servers, we can do that easily too. We'll access the server-side hash in much the same way as when we read the hash in the first place, as follows:

```
commentsHash[parentStatus] = commentsList;
```

If you put it all together, our method for storing comments looks like this:

```
void StoreComment(IRedisClient redisClient, Comment comment)
{
  var parentStatus = new Guid(comment.ParentStatus);
  var commentsHash = redisClient.As<List<Comment>>()
    .GetHash<Guid>("statusComments");

  var commentsList = commentsHash[parentStatus];
  if (commentsList == null)
  {
    redisClient.As<List<Comment>>()
    .GetHash<Guid(CommentsHash)[parentStatus]
    = new List<Comment>();
    commentsList = new List<Comment>();
  }

  commentsList.Add(comment);
  commentsHash[parentStatus] = commentsList;
}
```

This would be easy to refactor into something more expressive, but we'll leave the code together in this example to show the idea.

Now, if we wanted to fetch our timeline, we just need to grab the list of the most recent timeline entries from the linked list and then fetch the comments from the hash. This is borne out by the following code:

```
public IEnumerable<TimelineEntry> GetRecentTimeline(int entries)
{
  using (RedisClient)
```

```
    {
      var timelineList = RedisClient.As<Status>()
        .Lists["timelineStatuses"];
      var timelineCount = timelineList.Count;
      if (timelineCount < entries) entries = timelineCount;
      var recentStatuses = timelineList.GetRange(
        timelineCount - entries, timelineCount - 1);

      return recentStatuses.Select(status => new TimelineEntry
      {
        Status = status,
        Comments =
          RedisClient.As<List<Comment>>()
          .GetHash<Guid>(CommentsHash)[status.StatusId]
          ?? new List<Comment>()
      });
    }
  }
```

We're combining two powerful concepts in Redis: `LinkedList`, which we saw in the previous recipe can easily fetch the entries from the end or beginning of a list, and a `hash`, which can easily store items that can be fetched via a key.

When `GetRecentTimeline` starts its work, it goes to get the last *n* elements of the list. The `entries` parameter informs us how many we are expected to fetch. First we compare the length of the list with the number of entries we've been requested to make sure we're not asking for a value that's out of range. The following code helps us achieve what has been set out in this paragraph:

```
var timelineList =
  RedisClient.As<Status>().Lists["timelineStatuses"];
var timelineCount = timelineList.Count;
if (timelineCount < entries) entries = timelineCount;
```

Once we have the range, we use the `GetRange` method to ask Redis for the range we'd like, as follows:

```
    var recentStatuses = timelineList.GetRange(
      timelineCount - entries, timelineCount - 1);
```

The result is that Redis performs the `LRANGE` operation asking for the range starting ten entries back from the end and continuing until the end of the list, which in this case has 100 entries:

```
1410150522.115126 [0 127.0.0.1:5377] "LRANGE" "timelineStatuses" "91"
"100"
```

Once we have the most recent entries in the timeline, we can fetch the comments for them and construct the `TimelineEntry` objects that make up our timeline:

```
return recentStatuses.Select(status => new TimelineEntry
    {
      Status = status,
      Comments =
      RedisClient.As<List<Comment>>()
        .GetHash<Guid>("statusComments")
      [status.StatusId]
      ?? new List<Comment>()
    }).ToList();
```

If there aren't any comments, we'll return an empty list.

Scripting Redis with Lua

Many modern NoSQL data stores offer a way to evaluate scripts within the remote server, often by way of sending bits of code to the remote server for execution. Redis offers this capability too, using the popular Lua scripting language. This unlocks capabilities not currently offered by the official Redis API or the ServiceStack Redis client API. In the RDBMS world, this might be like creating a stored procedure.

Scripts evaluated will be compiled and cached on the Redis server. Calling them again in the future will simply execute the cached, compiled function. Scripts can be stored on the server and named so that they can be referenced without resending the full text of the script over the wire.

We'll cover some very basic concepts about how you can script Redis operations in Lua, without getting into the full language specification. Lua itself is a lightweight, multi-paradigm programming language designed as a scripting language. Based on C, it's portable across a wide variety of systems. Popular network tools Nginx and Nmap both also use Lua as a scripting language, as do a wide variety of video games.

[Note: More information on programming in Lua can be found at `http://www.lua.org`.]

Getting ready

For this example, we'll create a new service for storing links in our timeline service. When presented with a new link, we'll increment a counter to obtain an ID for this link, store the link in a global hash indexed by the link's ID, and then return the ID.

The evaluation of Lua scripts in Redis follows a specific pattern, which is as follows:

```
eval SCRIPT_TEXT KEYS_ACCESSED [KEYS] [ARGS]
```

`eval` tells Redis that we want to evaluate a script as the basic operation. `SCRIPT_TEXT` should contain the text of the Lua script we want to execute. `KEYS_ACCESSED` tells Redis how many keys we will be accessed, and the `[KEYS]` array contains the keys themselves. The `[ARGS]` array contains the arguments to the script.

In our example, `KEYS` would be the name of the counter we're going to increment and the name of the hash we're going to add the ID to, while `[ARGS]` would contain the actual link of the text that we want stored.

The keys could simply be passed in as part of the script text, of course. Passing in the keys specifically is important: it allows Redis to optimize the way it executes the query. In a clustered environment, in fact, it could be critical, as you can connect to one server to evaluate and execute your script, but the keys you want to operate on could be located on another server. Providing the `KEYS` explicitly allows Redis to make sure that the command is run on the cluster node that contains your data.

The simplest possible bit of Lua we could execute wouldn't require keys or arguments of course, but we'd still have to specify that there were zero keys. You can execute Lua scripts using the `redis-cli` tool by passing them in to the `eval` command, as follows:

```
127.0.0.1:6379> eval "return ('hello')" 0
"hello"
```

How to do it...

We'll create a new class that will handle accessing our links. Instead of using the Redis list, Set, or hash APIs, it will directly execute a Lua script that will directly perform what we need.

We'll start with the Lua script we want to execute:

```
private const string LuaScript = @"
  local link_id = redis.call(""INCR"", KEYS[1])
  redis.call(""HSET"", KEYS[2], link_id, ARGV[1])
  return link_id";
```

This line of C# code creates a new string constant called `LuaScript` that contains the script we'll want the server to evaluate.

The first line of the Lua script starts by defining a local variable `link_id` and assigns it a value; the value assigned will be the result of a `redis.call` operation:

```
local link_id = redis.call(""INCR"", KEYS[1])
```

The `redis.call` method is directly calling the Redis command `INCR`, which increments a counter. The counter isn't named yet, and we'll expect the caller to provide the name of the counter as the first `KEY` array.

The second line of the script performs another `redis.call` operation, this time an `HSET` operation that sets the value `ARGS[1]` on a hash key `link_id` of a specific hash `KEYS[2]`:

```
redis.call(""HSET"", KEYS[2], link_id, ARGV[1])
```

This might have looked like `Hashes["links:urls"][link_id] = "http://www.lua.org"` in C#, given that we provide `"links:urls"` for `KEYS[2]`, and `"http://www.lua.org"` for `ARGV[1]`. `link_id` is just the value set by the first line in the script.

The third line simply returns `link_id` to the caller as you might imagine:

```
return link_id
```

If we looked at this script with the keys filled in, it would be a bit easier to read, as follows:

```
local link_id = redis.call("INCR", "links:counter")
redis.call("HSET", "links:urls", link_id, ARGV[1])
return link_id
```

Now that we have this packaged into a Lua script, we can execute the script, provide the keys and values, and obtain the result:

```
public long StoreNewLink(string url)
{
  using (RedisClient)
  {
    var args = new[] { url };
    var keys = new[] { "links:counter", "links:urls" };
    return RedisClient.ExecLuaAsInt(LuaScript, keys, args);
  }
}
```

The `RedisClient` method `ExecLuaAsInt` will execute whatever script, keys, and arguments we pass in and then return the result to the caller. Despite its name, `ExecuteLuaAsInt` returns a `long` datatype, not an `int` datatype.

The `args` array that we pass in contains the arguments to the script—the URL to store in this case. The `keys` array then contains the names of the keys that we want Redis to use. The first key that our script uses, `KEYS[1]`, is the counter; the index for that is `links:counter`. The second key our script uses is the URL hash, which should be `links:urls` in this case.

How it works...

Under the covers, `RedisClient` is passing the script to the Redis server and requesting that it evaluate the script with the given keys and arguments provided. The Redis server then passes the script to the Lua instance on the server, executes the script, and returns the result as requested.

It's important to note that while the script is executing, this specific Redis server won't do anything else. Redis stops the world to execute your script. Luckily, the ServiceStack Redis client provides a few handy helper methods, such as `KillRunningLuaScript()`, which will stop execution.

9
Integrating with Other Technologies

In this chapter, we will go through an example of integrating and using ServiceStack with different technologies as well as existing projects. We will look at introducing ServiceStack into existing projects as well as introducing technologies like MongoDB, AngularJS, and others in the following recipes:

- ▶ Integrating with ServiceStack using the C# client and NativeTypes
- ▶ Using ServiceStack with WebForms applications
- ▶ Using ServiceStack with ASP.NET/MVC applications
- ▶ Broadcasting ServiceStack services with SignalR hubs
- ▶ Using ServiceStack with MongoDB
- ▶ Using ServiceStack with Elasticsearch
- ▶ Working with ServiceStack and AngularJS resources

Introduction

One of ServiceStack's strengths is its modular design that assists when it comes to using ServiceStack with different technologies. Through the recipes in this chapter, we will look at integrating with popular technologies on both the server and clients. We will look at the AngularJS and **Windows Presentation Foundation** (**WPF**) clients to show how these can be used with your ServiceStack web services. Then we will look at SignalR to update connected clients of other requests made to ServiceStack web services. We will also discuss the use of MongoDB and Elasticsearch from the ServiceStack host and integration options with ASP.NET WebForms and MVC projects.

Integrating with ServiceStack using the C# client and Native Types

When you're looking to integrate a ServiceStack service with a .NET project, often the first place to start is the ServiceStack C# client. Flexible and easy to use, it's the best way to drop in a connection to your service. The end result is a strongly typed connection. We will also use ServiceStack's Native Types feature so that our client is a separate application with generated references to improve integration.

Getting ready

Before we start, it's important to have your project laid out in a way that's convenient for the client to pick up your custom types. If you use any of the templates from ServiceStackVS, your project will be laid out in the recommended way from the start. To make it clear in this example, we are going to call the main project `TimelineService.Hosting`. This project will be a part of the `TimelineService` solution that will be our server application:

- `TimelineService.Hosting`: This contains our `AppHost` class, and `Global.asax` and `Web.config` files
- `Timeline.DataModel`: This contains our Redis repository
- `TimelineService.Tests`: This contains our unit and integration tests
- `Timeline.ServiceInterface`: This now contains our service implementation
- `Timeline.ServiceModel`: This contains our contracts

This decoupled design makes it easy to re-host the service outside of IIS by implementing a new hosting project, keeping all the ASP.NET details in one project. It would be simple to remove this implementation of the hosting project and replace it with one that self-hosts as a console application or a Windows service for instance.

We will also need a client application that will talk to our server. This application will not have direct dependencies on any of the server DLLs; it will use only ServiceStack's `JsonServiceClient` to integrate with our server by taking advantage of ServiceStack's Native Types. Native Types are an out-of-the-box feature of ServiceStack V4 that generates code base on metadata of the types running on the server. At the time of writing, ServiceStack already supports C#, F#, VB.Net, and TypeScript for generated clients via the ServiceStackVS extension.

How to do it...

1. First we will create `TimelineService`. Create the request and response for `TimelineService`:

```
[Route("/timeline", "GET")]
public class Timeline : IReturn<TimelineResponse>
{ }

public class TimelineResponse
{
  public List<TimelineEntry> Entries { get; set; }
}
```

2. Create an interface and implementation to access status information from our locally running Redis instance, as follows:

```
public interface IStatusAccess
{
  List<TimelineEntry> GetTimeline();
}

public class RedisStatusAccess : IStatusAccess
{
  private RedisClient RedisClient { get; set; }
  const string CommentsHash = "statusComments";
  const string TimelineList = "timelineStatuses";

  public RedisStatusAccess(RedisClient client)
  {
    RedisClient = client;
  }

  public List<TimelineEntry> GetTimeline()
  {
    return GetRecentTimeline(10);
  }

  public List<TimelineEntry> GetRecentTimeline(int entries)
  {
    using (RedisClient)
    {
      var timelineList =
          RedisClient.As<Status>().Lists[TimelineList];
```

```
var timelineCount = timelineList.Count;
if (timelineCount < entries) entries = timelineCount;
var recentStatuses = timelineList.GetRange(
  timelineCount - entries, timelineCount - 1);
return recentStatuses.Select(status => new
TimelineEntry
{
  Status = status,
  Comments = RedisClient.As<List<Comment>>()
  .GetHash<Guid>(CommentsHash)[
  status.StatusId]
  ?? new List<Comment>()
}).ToList();
    }
  }
}
```

3. In `TimelineService`, we will handle our new `Timeline` request object. This should use the injected `IStatusAccess` interface to get the latest timeline. Here's how we handle `Timeline` request:

```
public object Get(Timeline request)
{
  return new TimelineResponse
  {
    Entries = StatusAccess.GetTimeline().ToList()
  };
}
```

4. Register `RedisClient` and `IStatusAccess` in the `Configure` method of the `AppHost` class, as follows:

```
public override void Configure(Container container)
{
  var redisClient = new RedisClient();
  container.Register(redisClient);
  container.RegisterAutoWiredAs<
  RedisStatusAccess,IStatusAccess>();
}
```

Now that our server is set up, we can run the service and add the ServiceStack reference to our desktop application.

5. Create a new WPF project, and while the server is running, use ServiceStackVS. Right-click on your project in **Solution Explorer** and click on **Add ServiceStack Reference...**, as follows:

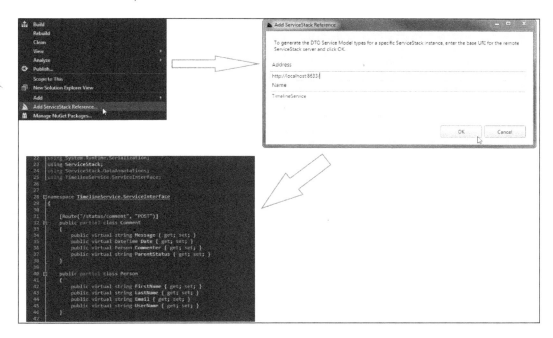

In the preceding image, we used ServiceStackVS to add a reference to our service. The server responds with the generated code, and the file is added to our project. The generated types, by default, use `IReturn<T>` statements for all the clients to facilitate easy integration with `JsonServiceClient`.

If you aren't using ServiceStackVS, you can get access to the same generated code by simply navigating to `/types/csharp` in a browser. This will generate C# types using the server's default settings for client type generation.

6. Create a simple client wrapper that uses `JsonServiceClient` and the generated types to make a request, as follows:

```
public class TimelineClient
{
  public string GetTimeline()
  {
    var client = new
    JsonServiceClient("http://localhost:8633/");
    TimelineResponse response = client.Get(new Timeline());

    return PrintTimeline(response);
```

```
      }

      static string PrintTimeline(TimelineResponse
      timelineResponse)
      {
        string output = "";
        timelineResponse.Entries.ForEach(
          entry => output += entry.Print() + "\n");
        return output;
      }
    }
```

7. On initialization of a new WPF window, use the client to update some text, as follows:

```
    public partial class MainWindow : Window
    {
      public MainWindow()
      {
        InitializeComponent();
        TimelineDisplay.Text = new
        TimelineClient().GetTimeline();
      }
    }
```

How it works...

To create the desktop client, we simply created a new project within our solution. In this case, we chose a WPF project, but this could just as easily be WinForms, ASP.NET, MVC, or WCF. In the WPF project, in the initial window provided, drop a large `TextBox` property on the screen, and change its name to `TimelineDisplay`, as follows:

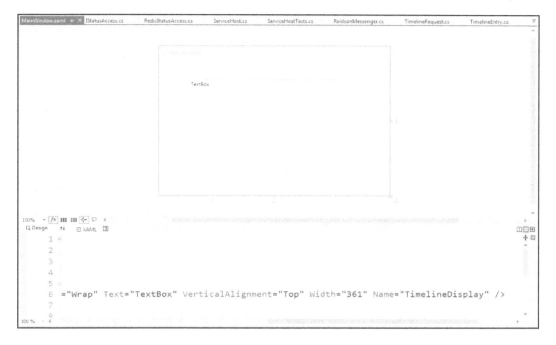

```
="Wrap" Text="TextBox" VerticalAlignment="Top" Width="361" Name="TimelineDisplay" />
```

Then we'll open up the `MainWindow.xaml.cs` file and add some logic to pull in the feed from `TimelineService`.

We'll start with a class that deals with `TimelineService`, called `TimelineClient`:

```
public string GetTimeline()
{
    var client = new JsonServiceClient("http://myserver/");
    var response = client.Get(new Timeline());
    return PrintTimeline(response);
}
```

We instantiate a `JsonServiceClient` first, passing in the base URL of our service. This component of the C# client connects to a remote ServiceStack endpoint for us.

Our new `client` object provides a helper method `Get` that accepts a `Timeline request` object. `JsonServiceClient` works out the return type by looking at the type used to make the request, which in this case is `Timeline`, and if it implements `IReturn<T>`, the method signature return type is `T`. The generated classes by default will add the `IReturn<T>` interface to request objects even if the server is only inferring them by naming convention. The server only has to name the request `Timeline`, and the response type is inferred to be `TimelineResponse` if it exists.

The following code does what is required to achieve the objective outlined in this paragraph:

```
[Route("/timeline","GET")]
public class Timeline : IReturn<TimelineResponse>
{ }
```

If your service doesn't specify the return type this way, you can move that responsibility to the client using an alternative API. The client call would simply need to specify the return type, as follows:

```
var response = client.Get<TimelineResponse>(new Timeline());
```

From here, it's fairly simple to have our WPF application print out the timeline it receives from `TimelineClient`:

```
public partial class MainWindow : Window
{
  public MainWindow()
  {
    InitializeComponent();
    TimelineDisplay.Text = new TimelineClient().GetTimeline();
  }
}
```

Thanks to our `PrintTimeline` formatting helper and some simple extension methods, the end result is that our timeline result will appear in our desktop client, as shown in the following screenshot:

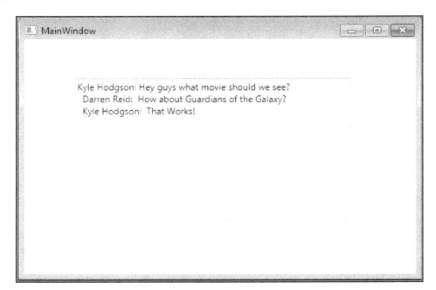

What's happening under the covers is that `JsonServiceClient` is crafting an HTTP request and sending it to the web service.

As a reminder, our `Timeline` class specifies `/timeline` as the route for `GET` requests:

```
[Route("/timeline","GET")]
public class Timeline : IReturn<TimelineResponse>
{ }
```

So, we instantiate a client and send a `Timeline` to the `Get` method like this:

```
var client = new JsonServiceClient("http://localhost:8633/");
var response = client.Get(new Timeline());
```

`JsonServiceClient` will craft `GET http`, as shown in the following code:

```
GET http://localhost:8633/timeline HTTP/1.1
Accept: application/json
User-Agent: ServiceStack .NET Client 4.032
Accept-Encoding: gzip,deflate
Host: myserver
Connection: Keep-Alive
```

The request specified that we want JSON back with the `Accept` header—given that we used the `JsonServiceClient`, this is convention.

The result is what you'd expect: a JSON rendering of `TimelineResponse` with entries that our service returns.

The `JsonServiceClient` doesn't provide raw JSON to our application, however. Our client has access to the proper object handling JSON serialization and deserialization for us.

This comes in handy in our formatting method `PrintTimeline`:

```
private static string PrintTimeline(TimelineResponse timeline)
{
  string output = "";
  timeline.Enties.ForEach(entry => output += entry.Print() +
  "\n");
  return output;
}
```

When the result of the `JsonServiceClient Get` method is passed in, it has already been deserialized into `TimelineResponse` and can be treated like any other .NET object.

Using ServiceStack with WebForms applications

There are a great many ASP.NET WebForms applications in production environments of enterprises today. Many of them are still maintained and augmented with new features, bug fixes, and integrations with other systems. It can be useful to run ServiceStack side by side with these legacy applications. You might want to create a new service on the existing code base to leverage existing data models and expose application data, but you might not want to use the traditional ASMX, WCF, or even Web API to share this data.

Getting ready

In this recipe, we'll discuss how to run ServiceStack services side by side with ASP.NET WebForms applications. We'll start with a basic WebForms application to illustrate this concept. Largely generated from the **ASP.NET WebForms New Project** template, this example should look familiar to many:

```
<%@ Page Title="Greeting Generator" Language="C#" MasterPageFile="~/
Site.Master" AutoEventWireup="true" CodeBehind="Default.aspx.cs"
Inherits="WebFormsApp._Default" %>

<asp:Content runat="server" ID="FeaturedContent"
ContentPlaceHolderID="FeaturedContent">
    <section class="featured">
        <div class="content-wrapper">
            <hgroup class="title">
                <h1><%: Title %>.</h1>
                <h2>Greetings and salutations,
                at your command.</h2>
            </hgroup>
            <p>
            </p>
        </div>
    </section>
</asp:Content>
<asp:Content runat="server" ID="BodyContent"
ContentPlaceHolderID="MainContent">
<asp:TextBox runat="server" ID="tbName"
Text="Dummy"></asp:TextBox>
    <asp:TextBox runat="server" ID="tbGreeting"/>
    <asp:Button runat="server" Text="Make Greeting"/>
</asp:Content>
```

Let's imagine we have one basic data model, a familiar `GreetingAccessor` class, as follows:

```
public class GreetingAccessor
{
  public string GetGreeting(string name)
  {
    return "Hello, " + name + "!";
  }
}
```

We'd also have a simple code behind in our `View` folder that would leverage the `GreetingAccessor` server side, which is shown in the following code:

```
protected void Page_Load(object sender, EventArgs e)
{
  tbGreeting.Text = new GreetingAccessor()
  .GetGreeting(tbName.Text);
}
```

At this stage, we should have a very simple WebForms app, as shown in the following screenshot:

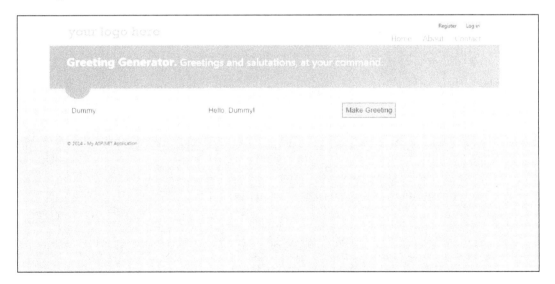

What we'll do is add a ServiceStack service to this application, use it to extend the GreetingAccessor, and then wire up our application to talk to the service to show the full life cycle.

How to do it...

1. First we need to add ServiceStack by NuGet, as usual:

```
Install-Package ServiceStack
```

2. Next, we'll add **New Project** to our existing WebForms site. It's *OK* to just use a class library in this case. Let's call it App.ServiceInterface. We'll create a GreetingService class that lives in our ServiceInterface project and that extends the ServiceStack.Service class, and an AppHost class that extends the AppHostBase class, as shown in the following code:

```
public class GreetingService : Service
{ }

public class AppHost : AppHostBase
{
    public AppHost() : base("GreetingService",
    typeof(GreetingService).Assembly)
    { }

    public override void Configure(Container container)
    { }
}
```

3. Next, we'll make sure the application boots by editing Global.asax.cs from our WebForms app, as shown in the following code:

```
void Application_Start(object sender, EventArgs e)
{
    new AppHost().Init();
    RegisterRoutes(RouteTable.Routes);
}

private static void RegisterRoutes(RouteCollection routes)
{
    routes.Ignore("api/{*pathInfo}");
}
```

At this stage, we have the basics of a ServiceStack service. We can go back in and add the Service code to handle Greeting request just as we normally would.

We'll add a request DTO. Note that we don't need to specify /api/ in front of the route; our request DTO doesn't know that we're being hosted on an application root.

4. Create our `request` and `response` objects with the desired `Route` path, as shown in the following code:

```
[Route("/hello/{Name}")]
public class Greeting
{
  public string Name { get; set; }
}
public class GreetingResponse
{
  public string Greeting { get; set; }
}
```

5. Create a simple service to integrate with our WebForms application, as follows:

```
public object Get(Greeting request)
{
  return new GreetingResponse
  {
    Greeting = new GreetingAccessor()
    .GetGreeting(request.Name)
  };
}
```

6. Now that we have all of the pieces of the service, we'll head to the `Web.config` file to configure ASP.NET. We'll insert the following XML under the `<configSections>` element of the `<configuration>` block, as follows:

```
<location path="api">
<system.web>
  <httpHandlers>
    <add path="*"
    type="ServiceStack.HttpHandlerFactory, ServiceStack"
        verb="*" />
  </httpHandlers>
</system.web>

<!-- Required for IIS 7.0 -->
<system.webServer>
 <modules runAllManagedModulesForAllRequests="true" />
  <validation
          validateIntegratedModeConfiguration="false" />
  <handlers>
    <add path="*"
        name="ServiceStack.Factory"
```

```
          type="ServiceStack.HttpHandlerFactory,
          ServiceStack"
          verb="*" preCondition="integratedMode"
          resourceType="Unspecified" allowPathInfo="true" />
    </handlers>
  </system.webServer>
</location>
```

How it works...

With all of the preceding pieces in place, the original WebForms project that handled the hosting details is still in charge of responding to web requests. However, with the new changes in place in the `Global.asax` and `Web.config` files, it will also start our ServiceStack service when our WebForms app starts and hand off any requests to the `/api/` URL to ServiceStack. In fact, our ServiceStack service is even reusing the data model from the WebForms app.

If we connect to `/api/hello/World?format=json`, we'll get back a JSON object shaped like our `GreetingResponse` type containing the expected string:

```
C:\>curl http://localhost:26512/api/hello/World?format=json
{"Greeting":"Hello, World!"}
```

There's more...

Now that our service is up and running, we can start to make use of this new API in our WebForms app. This might help with developing new features; for instance, if you wanted to start to add a JavaScript-rich client-user interface to an existing WebForms application. Let's go ahead and add some simple HTML to the WebForms app that uses the JavaScript API—we'll replace our old server-side form with a client-side one that leverages the new REST endpoint:

```javascript
<script type="text/javascript">

    var renderGreeting = function(name) {
        $.getJSON("/api/hello/" + name, function(data) {
            $("#generated_greeting").text(data.Greeting);
        });
    };

    $(document).ready(function () {

        renderGreeting($("#greeting_name").val());

        $("#render_greeting").click(
```

```
        function() {
            renderGreeting($("#greeting_name").val());
        });
    });

</script>
<p><input type="text" name="name_to_greet" id="greeting_name"
value="Dummy"/> <br/>
<a id="render_greeting">Click me</a></p>
<div id="generated_greeting"></div>
```

Then, we can remove the code from our `Page_Load` in the code behind too.

The astute reader will note that the previous technique isn't refactoring safe. If we refactor the `Greeting` class to expose a different route than `"/hello"` or rename the `GreetingResponse.Greeting` property, the preceding JavaScript code won't work as those are hardcoded as strings. Let's tackle these problems one at a time.

In the WebForms application that generates the JavaScript `renderGreeting` function, we can write code to specify the correct URL, as follows:

```
$.getJSON(
  "<%= ServiceStackHost.Instance.Config.HandlerFactoryPath %>" +
  "<%= new Greeting().ToGetUrl() %>", {'Name': name},  //continued...
```

Now, instead of constructing our URL from bare strings that could change, we'll fetch the values we need from `ServiceStackHost.Instance.Config.HandlerFactoryPath` and `Greeting.ToGetUrl()`. We'll also need to change the way we pass in the data—instead of passing it in on the URL, we will construct a JavaScript object to pass to the service, which `getJSON` will provide to ServiceStack on the query string:

http://myserver/api/hello/?Name=Dummy

Now, we have created a new refactoring difficulty for ourselves in that we compose the JavaScript object using the raw string `Name`, which refers to the `Greeting.Name` property. We can solve that by creating a new attribute that will allow us to inquire for the name of the property instead of hardcoding it as a string, as follows:

```
public static class Extensions
{
  public static string GetPrimaryPropertyName(this object obj)
  {
    var primaryProperty =
      obj.GetType()
      .GetProperties()
      .FirstOrDefault(
```

```
            x => x.HasAttribute<PrimaryPropertyAttribute>());

        return primaryProperty != null
                ? primaryProperty.Name
                : String.Empty;
    }
}

public class PrimaryPropertyAttribute : Attribute
{ }

[Route("/hello/", "GET")]
[Route("/hello/{Name}", "GET")]
public class Greeting
{
  [PrimaryProperty]
  public string Name { get; set; }
}
```

A simple update to our JavaScript code allows us to fix the problem:

```
$.getJSON(
  "<%= ServiceStackHost.Instance.Config.HandlerFactoryPath %>" +
  "<%= new Greeting().ToGetUrl() %>",
  {'<%= new Greeting().GetPrimaryPropertyName() %>': name},
```

We can use the same attribute with the response property name. If we put it all together, it would look like this:

```
<% var request = new Greeting(); %>
<% var response = new GreetingResponse(); %>
var renderGreeting = function(name) {
  $.getJSON(
  "<%= ServiceStackHost.Instance.Config.HandlerFactoryPath %>" +
  "<%= request.ToGetUrl() %>",
  {'<%= request.GetPrimaryPropertyName() %>': name},
    function (data) {
      $("#generated_greeting").text(data.<%=
      response.GetPrimaryPropertyName() %>);
  });
};
```

Of course, we could have used AngularJS, BackboneJS, or KnockoutJS to do the same thing instead of raw JQuery. Now, we can begin to replace our old WebForms application bit by bit with something more modern instead of needing to rewrite it entirely.

Using ServiceStack with ASP.NET/MVC applications

ASP.NET/MVC has arguably improved the lives of .NET web developers who are serious about creating really great web apps. While not as clean and low-level as ServiceStack, ASP.NET/ MVC (often just called MVC by .NET programmers) was a radical improvement in the lives of many developers previously stuck with WebForms—its lower level of abstraction was vastly preferred over its older sibling. MVC is much closer to writing straight, static HTML that makes it easier than WebForms to build and maintain as well.

A great many sites have been developed using MVC. While MVC provides the WebAPI system to develop services, integrating ServiceStack side by side with MVC applications is easy and very useful.

Getting ready

In this recipe, we'll discuss how to run ServiceStack services side by side with ASP.NET MVC applications. This would be a common scenario to enhance a legacy ASP.NET MVC application with a ServiceStack service. We'll use the **ServiceStackVS MVC4** template to create our example and initial MVC application but will walk through the different points of integration in an existing application as though ServiceStack were not yet introduced.

How to do it...

1. First we need to add `ServiceStack` via NuGet, as follows:

   ```
   Install-Package ServiceStack
   ```

   Just as when integrating with WebForms, we'll begin by creating a new class library project within our solution. Following the convention, we'll name it `[AppName].ServiceInterface`. Let's call it `Mvc4Application.ServiceInterface`.

2. We'll also create `GreetingService` that lives in our `Mvc4Application.ServiceInterface` project and extends `ServiceStack.Service`, as shown in the following line of code:

   ```
   public class GreetingService : Service
   { }
   ```

3. We will also create an `AppHost` class that extends the `AppHostBase` class that is added to the MVC project as that is where it's being hosted. Here's how:

   ```
   public class AppHost : AppHostBase
   {
     public AppHost() : base("GreetingService",
   ```

```
                                    typeof(GreetingService).Assembly)
  { }

  public override void Configure(Container container)
  {
      SetConfig(new HostConfig {HandlerFactoryPath =
      "api"});
  }
}
```

The `SetConfig` line in `Configure` is different than what we'd normally do; we're
going to have our ServiceStack service appear only under the application root `/api/`.
In this way, components of ServiceStack know that the hosted path start with `"api"`.
This affects things like the Native Types generation and the metadata generated on
the server. ASP.NET knows this path is being used by `web.config` in the `<location
path="api">` section. ASP.NET then knows to send anything that starts with `/api/` to
ServiceStack and everything else to the normal ASP.NET MVC app.

4. We also need to register the `"api"` path as an ignored route with MVC. This should
    be done on `Application_Start` in the `Global.asax.cs` file, as follows:

```
void Application_Start(object sender, EventArgs e)
{
    new AppHost().Init();
    RegisterRoutes(RouteTable.Routes);
}

private static void RegisterRoutes(RouteCollection routes)
{
    routes.Ignore("api/{*pathInfo}");
}
```

If you are already using the `WebActivator` library, you keep your `AppHost` class
and MVC route registrations separate by registering a static method to fire on
application start. The following code shows you just how to do that:

**[assembly:WebActivator.PreApplicationStartMethod(
typeof(Mvc4Application.AppHost), "Start")]**

At this stage, we have the basics of a ServiceStack service. We can go back in and
add the `Service` code to handle `Greeting request`.

5. We'll add a request DTO. Note that we don't need to specify `/api/` in front of the
    route; our Request DTO doesn't know that we're being hosted on an application root.
    This is how we add a request DTO:

```
[Route("/hello")]
[Route("/hello/{Name}")]
```

```
public class Greeting : IReturn<GreetingResponse>
{
    public string Name { get; set; }
}
```

6. We'll add a simple response DTO, as follows:

```
public class GreetingResponse
{
    public string Result { get; set; }
}
```

7. And then, we can fill out our service as usual:

```
public class GreetingService : Service
{
    public object Any(Greeting request)
    {
        return new GreetingResponse
        {
            Result = "Hello, {0}!".Fmt(request.Name)
        };
    }
}
```

8. Now that we have all of the pieces of the service, we'll head to the `Web.config` file to configure ASP.NET. We'll insert the following XML under the `<configSections>` element of the `<configuration>` block:

```
<location path="api">
    <system.web>
      <httpHandlers>
      <add path="*"
      type="ServiceStack.HttpHandlerFactory, ServiceStack"
      verb="*" />
      </httpHandlers>
    </system.web>

    <!-- Required for IIS 7.0 -->
    <system.webServer>
      <modules runAllManagedModulesForAllRequests="true" />
      <validation validateIntegratedModeConfiguration="false" />
      <handlers>
        <add path="*" name="ServiceStack.Factory"
        type="ServiceStack.HttpHandlerFactory,
        ServiceStack" verb="*"
        preCondition="integratedMode"
        resourceType="Unspecified" allowPathInfo="true" />
```

```
      </handlers>
    </system.webServer>
  </location>
```

9. Next, if WebAPI is present in our application we'll need to remove it from the
    `Application_Start` method of the `Global.asax` file, and we'll also need to
    instruct ASP.NET MVC to ignore our `/api/` route. When that's all done, our new
    `Application_Start` method looks like this:

```
protected void Application_Start()
{
    AreaRegistration.RegisterAllAreas();

    FilterConfig.RegisterGlobalFilters(GlobalFilters.Filters);
    RouteTable.Routes.Ignore("api/{*pathInfo}");
    RouteTable.Routes.Ignore("{*favicon}",
    new {favicon =
    @"(.*/)?favicon.ico(/.*)?"});
    RouteConfig.RegisterRoutes(RouteTable.Routes);
    BundleConfig.RegisterBundles(BundleTable.Bundles);
    new AppHost().Init();
}
```

> Note that we've removed the `WebApiConfig.`
> `Register(GlobalConfiguration.Configuration)`
> line and added lines just above where the `RouteTable` is
> added to `RouteConfig`.

```
RouteTable.Routes.Ignore("api/{*pathInfo}");
RouteTable.Routes.Ignore("{*favicon}",
    new {favicon =
    @"(.*/)?favicon.ico(/.*)?"});
```

10. In our new `AppHost` class, we can register Funq as `ControllerFactory` so that all
    our IoC-registered dependencies are accessible from our MVC controllers, provided
    they inherit from the ServiceStack provided `ServiceStackController` in our
    `AppHost` class's `Configure` method:

```
ControllerBuilder.Current.SetControllerFactory(
new FunqControllerFactory(container));
```

How it works...

With all of the previous code pieces in place, the original ASP.NET MVC project that handled the hosting details is still in charge of responding to web requests. However, with the new changes in place in the `Global.asax` and `Web.config` files, it will also start our ServiceStack service when our app starts and hand off any requests to the `/api/` URL to ServiceStack.

If we connect to `/api/hello/World?format=json`, we'll get back a JSON object shaped like our `GreetingResponse` type containing the expected string:

```
C:\>curl http://localhost:26512/api/hello/World?format=json
{"Result":"Hello, World!"}
```

We are also enabling the existing MVC controllers to access ServiceStack services and other injected resources. We changed `HomeController` to now inherit from `ServiceStackController` and used the `GreetingService` service class from within a controller method called `"Hello"`:

```
public class HomeController : ServiceStackController
{
    //Injected via Funq
    public GreetingService MyService { get; set; }

    public ActionResult Index()
    {
        ViewBag.Message = "Modify this template to jump-start your
        ASP.NET MVC application.";

        return View();
    }

    public ActionResult About()
    {
        ViewBag.Message = "Your app description page.";

        return View();
    }

    public ActionResult Contact()
    {
        ViewBag.Message = "Your contact page.";

        return View();
```

```
    }

    public ActionResult Hello()
    {
        var response =
          (GreetingResponse)MyService.Any(
          new Greeting {Name = "World"});
          ViewBag.Message = response.Result;
        return View();
    }
}
```

The following screenshot depicts the example of this recipe:

Any injected resource can now be accessible just as on a normal ServiceStack service. Services themselves are also available to be resolved and used within the controller. This allows us to build isolated functionality related to our MVC application and reuse that same logic and resources used by the isolated services on our existing MVC controllers.

There's more...

After following the instructions in an existing MVC site, you might have two different IoC containers. ServiceStack is making use of Funq, while you might be using Castle Windsor, Unity, Ninject, StructureMa, or some other framework to resolve MVC controllers. If you want, you can simplify this by having Funq take over the job. Given Funq's speed and easy configuration, it's not a bad idea.

All you need to do is create an object that adheres to `IControllerFactory`. The `ServiceStack.mvc` package contains `FunqControllerFactory` that fills this role. Simply pass it in your container object in `AppHost.Configure` and pass the result to `ControllerBuilder.Current.SetControllerFactory`, as follows:

```
//Set MVC to use the same Funq IOC as ServiceStack
   ControllerBuilder.Current.SetControllerFactory(
   new FunqControllerFactory(container));
```

When we're doing this, you might find that you need to move the `ServiceHost` method to the same project that contains your controllers and work to eliminate circular dependencies; it won't work to have an `App.ServiceInterface` project that depends on `App` to find the controllers with `App` depending on `App.ServiceInterface` to find the service to start in the `Global.asax` file.

Also, it's important to begin registering your controllers in your `ServiceHost` method when making use of this technique. For instance, after making use of Funq throughout our example ASP.NET MVC application, our `ServiceHost.Configure` method now has the job of registering controller dependencies and the controllers themselves in order for MVC to find them. The following code shows how this is done:

```
public override void Configure(Container container)
{
   SetConfig(new HostConfig { HandlerFactoryPath = "api" });

   //Set MVC to use the same Funq IOC as ServiceStack
   ControllerBuilder.Current.SetControllerFactory(
   new FunqControllerFactory(container)
   );
}
```

In this example, we first register `GreetingAccessor` that `HomeController` depends on, and then we can register the controllers. As the controllers inherit from `ServiceStackController`, they are automatically discovered.

Broadcasting ServiceStack services with SignalR hubs

SignalR is a popular library for enabling real-time functionality to a web application. A simple use of this library with ServiceStack is to enable the requests or responses of our web services to SignalR clients that are listening to specific groups or methods.

Getting ready

First we are going to need an application to integrate; we will start with a template from the ServiceStackVS Visual Studio extension. If you are using Visual Studio Express, please see the *Creating your ServiceStack solution with Visual Studio and NuGet* section in *Appendix A, Getting Started*, and continue from the second instruction in the *How to do it...* section.

How to do it...

1. Create a new application using a template from the ServiceStackVS Visual Studio extension. For this example, we will use the **ServiceStack ASP.NET Empty** template. This is how the template for the new application will look:

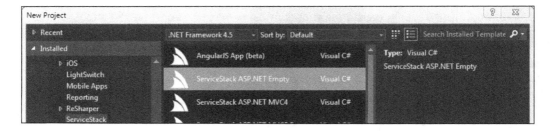

2. Install the SignalR NuGet package in both the main project and the `ServiceInterface` project on your new solution:

    ❑   For `ServiceInterface`, install `Microsoft.AspNet.SignalR. SystemWeb` with the following command in NuGet's **Package Manager Console**:

    `Install-Package Microsoft.AspNet.SignalR.SystemWeb`

    ❑   For the main project, install `Microsoft.AspNet.SignalR` with the following command in NuGet's **Package Manager Console**:

    `Install-Package Microsoft.AspNet.SignalR`

3. Add the required SignalR startup class that will map the `/signalr` route, as follows:

```
public class Startup
{
    public void Configuration(IAppBuilder app)
    {
        app.MapSignalR();
    }
}
```

4. Edit the `web.config` file to host the ServiceStack HTTP listener at `"api*"`. An example `web config` is shown as follows:

```
<configuration>
  <system.web>
    <compilation debug="true" targetFramework="4.5" />
    <httpRuntime targetFramework="4.5" />
    <pages controlRenderingCompatibilityVersion="4.0" />
  </system.web>
  <system.webServer>
    <modules runAllManagedModulesForAllRequests="true" />
    <validation validateIntegratedModeConfiguration="false"
    />
  </system.webServer>
  <location path="api">
    <system.web>
      <httpHandlers>
        <add path="*" type="ServiceStack.HttpHandlerFactory,
        ServiceStack" verb="*" />
      </httpHandlers>
    </system.web>
    <!-- Required for IIS 7.0 -->
    <system.webServer>
      <modules runAllManagedModulesForAllRequests="true" />
      <validation validateIntegratedModeConfiguration="false" />
      <handlers>
        <add path="*" name="ServiceStack.Factory"
        type="ServiceStack.HttpHandlerFactory, ServiceStack"
        verb="*" preCondition="integratedMode"
        resourceType="Unspecified" allowPathInfo="true" />
      </handlers>
    </system.webServer>
  </location>
</configuration>
```

5. Now that SignalR is hosted, we want to create a ServiceStack filter to give us the ability to broadcast or relay a request or a response to SignalR clients. First, let's create an outgoing relay:

```
public class OutgoingHubRelayAttribute :
ResponseFilterAttribute
{
    public string HubName { get; set; }
    public string MethodName { get; set; }

    public string GroupName { get; set; }
```

```
public HubTarget HubTarget { get; set; }

public override void Execute(IRequest req, IResponse
res, object responseDto)
{
    if (string.IsNullOrWhiteSpace(HubName))
    {
        throw new ArgumentNullException(
        "HubName required for OutgoingHubRelay");
    }

    if (string.IsNullOrWhiteSpace(MethodName))
    {
        throw new ArgumentNullException(
        "MethodName required for OutgoingHubRelay");
    }
    if (string.IsNullOrEmpty(GroupName) &&
    HubTarget == HubTarget.Group)
    {
        throw new ArgumentException(
        "GroupName is required if targeting a group");
    }

    var hub =
        GlobalHost.ConnectionManager.GetHubContext(HubName);
    if (hub == null)
    {
        throw new InstanceNotFoundException(
        "Hub not found with the name '" +
        HubName + "'.");
    }

    switch (HubTarget)
    {
        case HubTarget.AllUsers:
        hub.Clients.All.Invoke(MethodName,
        responseDto);
            break;
        case HubTarget.Group:
            hub.Clients.Group(GroupName)
            .Invoke(MethodName, responseDto);
            break;
        default:
```

```
                        throw new ArgumentOutOfRangeException();
            }
        }
    }

    public enum HubTarget
    {
        AllUsers,
        Group
    }
```

6. Next, we will create an incoming relay; this will broadcast the request to SignalR clients before being processed by the ServiceStack service. This can be used if the request doesn't have to be persisted or validated:

```
public class IncomingHubRelayAttribute :
RequestFilterAttribute
{
    public string HubName { get; set; }
    public string MethodName { get; set; }

    public string GroupName { get; set; }
    public HubTarget HubTarget { get; set; }

    public override void Execute(IRequest req, IResponse
    res, object requestDto)
    {
        if (string.IsNullOrWhiteSpace(HubName))
        {
            throw new ArgumentNullException(
            "HubName required for IncomingHubRelay");
        }

        if (string.IsNullOrWhiteSpace(MethodName))
        {
            throw new ArgumentNullException(
            "MethodName required for IncomingHubRelay");
        }
        if (string.IsNullOrEmpty(GroupName) &&
        HubTarget == HubTarget.Group)
        {
            throw new ArgumentException(
            "GroupName is required if targeting a group");
        }
```

```
var hub =
GlobalHost.ConnectionManager.GetHubContext(HubName);
if (hub == null)
{
    throw new InstanceNotFoundException(
    "Hub not found with the name '" +
     HubName + "'.");
}

switch (HubTarget)
{
    case HubTarget.AllUsers:
    hub.Clients.All.Invoke(MethodName, requestDto);
        break;
    case HubTarget.Group:
        hub.Clients.Group(GroupName)
                    .Invoke(MethodName, requestDto);
        break;
    default:
        throw new ArgumentOutOfRangeException();
}
    }
}
```

7. Now, we can use one of these filters on the existing `Hello` request inside `MyServices.cs`:

```
[IncomingHubRelay(HubName = "HelloHub", MethodName =
"HelloAll")]
public object Any(Hello request)
{
    return new HelloResponse { Result = "Hello,
    {0}!".Fmt(request.Name) };
}
```

8. Previously, we specified a `HubName` variable, we will need to declare the `Hub` class itself before we can use it:

```
[HubName("HelloHub")]
public class HelloHub : Hub
{

}
```

9. On the client, we can use SignalR's JavaScript client to register a connection with `HelloHub` and also listen for the `MethodName` variable specified on the `IncomingHubRelay` filter attribute. The following is a simple `index.html` file that listens to the `Hello` response from both ServiceStack and SignalR to show that both are being received:

```html
<!DOCTYPE html>
<html xmlns="http://www.w3.org/1999/xhtml">
<head>
    <title>Recipe4 Demo</title>
    <script src="Scripts/jquery-1.6.4.min.js"></script>
    <script src="Scripts/jquery.signalR-
    2.1.2.min.js"></script>
    <script src="signalr/hubs"></script>
</head>
    <body>
        <script type="text/javascript">
            var connection = $.hubConnection();
            var helloHubProxy =
            connection.createHubProxy('HelloHub');
            helloHubProxy.on('HelloAll', function (request)
{
              $('#output').append(
              '<span style="color:green;display:block">
              Hello, ' + request.Name + '! via
              SignalR</span>');
              });

            function sendRequest() {
                var name = $('#name').val();
                $.getJSON('/api/hello/' + name)
                    .success(function(response) {
                    //ServiceStack response response
                    $('#output').append(
                    '<span style="color:blue;display:block">' +
                    response.Result +
                    ' via ServiceStack response</span>');
                    });
            }
        </script>
        <div>
            <input id="name" type="text" name=""
            value="World" />
            <button onclick="sendRequest()">Send</button>
```

```
            <div id="output"></div>
        </div>
    </body>
</html>
```

How it works...

In this example, we separated ServiceStack and SignalR so that their routes do not conflict. This might not be practical if you are using ServiceStack's Razor views as the primary way of rendering pages. It is also worth noting that our session is also not being shared between the two technologies, so authentication using SignalR's `Authorize` attribute is not available to use in this situation.

The client is sending a normal HTTP GET request to our `Hello` service, which our `IncomingHubRelay` filter is picking up and redistributing to all clients registered to that hub. It invokes the `HelloAll` method, which is then called on the client.

Messages are broadcast from a SignalR `Hub` class. This represents a subscription that a client can get messages from. The client can subscribe to hub in JavaScript using the following lines:

```
var helloHubProxy = connection.createHubProxy('HelloHub');
helloHubProxy.on('HelloAll', function (request) {
    $('#output').append('<span
    style="color:green;display:block">Hello, ' + request.Name + '!
    via SignalR</span>');
});
```

These proxies register their connection with the SignalR `Hub` class and then listen for methods to be invoked. When the server invokes the `HelloAll` method, clients listening for that method will run a function and receive arguments passed on the server. Here's the line of code showing how it's done:

```
hub.Clients.All.Invoke(MethodName, requestDto);
```

The request DTO is passed as an argument that is used in the JavaScript function registered to the `HelloAll` event. Since we are invoking this method on `All` clients, the client sending the original request is also invoked. If you open multiple browsers, we can see how the other clients receive the messages relayed via our filter and SignalR:

World1	Send		World2	Send
Hello, World1! via SignalR			Hello, World1! via SignalR	
Hello, World1! via ServiceStack response			Hello, World2! via SignalR	
Hello, World2! via SignalR			Hello, World2! via ServiceStack response	

A situation like a live poll or votes is a good application for this integration—basically, where the current state of simple objects needs to be distributed and losing a message doesn't have an effect on what data is presented to the client.

There's more...

To illustrate this, we can make a simple example of moving a block around the screen and showing the block in the same position on all clients regardless of when they started listening to the hub.

We will need to create the same components for which we have the `Hello` service:

- A `Request/Response` object for ServiceStack services
- A SignalR `hub`
- The ServiceStack service and the application of the filter
- A client listening for updates from the `Hub` class and sending requests to the service

The `Request` object will simply ask to move a block up, down, left, or right:

```
[Route("/moveblock")]
public class MoveBlock
{
    public string Direction { get; set; }
}

public class Block
{
public long X { get; set; }
public long Y { get; set; }
}
```

The server will update the block stored using `ICacheClient`, and the resultant block position will be sent back to the client:

```
[OutgoingHubRelay(HubName = "MoveBlockHub", MethodName = "Move")]
public object Post(MoveBlock request)
{
    var block = Cache.Get<Block>("TheBlock");
    block = block ?? new Block {X = 0, Y = 0};
    switch (request.Direction)
    {
        case "Left":
            block.X--;
            break;
```

```
                case "Right":
                    block.X++;
                    break;
                case "Up":
                    block.Y--;
                    break;
                case "Down":
                    block.Y++;
                    break;
                default:
                    throw new ArgumentOutOfRangeException();
        }
        Cache.Replace("TheBlock", block);
        return block;
    }

    public object Get(MoveBlock request)
    {
        return Cache.Get<Block>("TheBlock");
    }
```

The `OutgoingHubRelay` filter will then notify all clients of the new position of the block via a `Hub` class:

```
[HubName("MoveBlockHub")]
public class MoveBlockHub : Hub
{

}
```

Clients listening to the hub `Move` event will update the local blocks position, as follows:

```
moveBlockProxy.on('Move', function (response) {
    var block = $('#block');
    block.css('left', (response.X * moveAmount) + 'px');
    block.css('top', (response.Y * moveAmount) + 'px');
    var blockPos = $('#blockPosition');
    blockPos.html('<span>' + response.Y + ', ' + response.X +
    '</span>');
});
```

All clients listening will have an up-to-date representation of the block as of their last notification. It is possible for client messages not to have the effect of changing the server state successfully even with a successful request due to the small possibility of concurrent requests having edited the same version of the block in-memory on the server. The use of `ICacheClient` was for the simplicity of the example; the same services could be used with PostgresSQL or other more sophisticated storage mechanisms, where the updates could be handled in a way such that data of the request would affect the state in the database correctly during an update.

Special thanks to Filip W and his blog post on SignalR integration and ServiceStack; his article used the same pattern with ServiceStack V3.

Using ServiceStack with MongoDB

Inarguably the most popular of the NoSQL databases, MongoDB is fast, reliable, commercially supported, enterprise friendly, and widely considered to be scalable in a web context. Perhaps the biggest secret to its popularity, however, is just how easy it is to get started. Unlike its cousin the **Relational Database Management System** (**RDBMS**), when using MongoDB, one can simply store an object as in a collection of objects—no normalization, no entity diagrams, and no formal object relational mapping is required.

MongoDB is in a family of NoSQL databases referred to as a document store. Document stores build on the foundations of a key-value store that simply allow a developer to retrieve values based on a key—document stores commonly add the ability to *search* through documents for a particular document. For instance, if we had a collection called inventory in our MongoDB database, we could search it for `"snacks"` items with the following simple query:

```
db.inventory.find( { type: "snacks" } )
```

MongoDB would go through all of the documents in the inventory collection looking for a property called `type` containing the string `"snacks"`. It would build a collection (or iterator) containing all of the documents that matched that criteria. This might be like doing `SELECT * from INVENTORY WHERE type='snacks'` in a simple SQL database. However, in a production SQL database, the query would more likely be much more complicated, using `JOIN` statements to leverage foreign keys to aggregate multiple tables, whereas in MongoDB, the whole object is stored in a single document.

Getting ready

Before we can write code that accesses a MongoDB database, we need to start by installing MongoDB. Luckily, this is quite simple. Simply visit the MongoDB downloads page at `http://www.mongo.org/downloads`, and locate the `.zip` file containing the binary for your platform. After unzipping it, create a directory to hold the database. I created mine at `c:\mongo\data\db`. Then, you can start MongoDB from the command line:

```
c:\mongo\bin>mongod --dbpath c:\mongo\data\db --smallfiles
2014-09-15T18:18:37.050-0400 [initandlisten] MongoDB starting :
pid=3980 port=27017 dbpath=c:\mongo\data\db 64-bit host=DEVELOPMENT-
VM
2014-09-15T18:18:37.388-0400 [initandlisten] waiting for connections
on port 27017
```

Once MongoDB is up and running, it's simple to connect to it using the MongoDB client, as follows:

```
C:\mongo\bin>mongo
MongoDB shell version: 2.6.4
connecting to: test
>
```

Connecting your ServiceStack app to MongoDB will make use of the MongoDB C# client. You can install it with NuGet, as follows:

```
PM> Install-Package mongocsharpdriver
```

Our example will cover storing profiles in MongoDB. We'll create a `PersonAccess` class that can store objects of the type `Person` that represent our users.

How to do it...

Once we have `mongocsharpdriver` and the NuGet package is installed, we can begin storing users. Let's build a `Person` class to use as an entity:

```
public class Person
{
  public ObjectId Id { get; set; }
  public string FirstName { get; set; }
  public string LastName { get; set; }
  public string Email { get; set; }
  public string UserName { get; set; }
}
```

From here, we can build a `PersonAccess` service that can store and retrieve our users. We'll use the typed access provided by MongoDB C# Driver. Let's start with a method that can store people in a collection called `profile`. Remember, collections in MongoDB are collections of documents—so roughly equivalent to tables in an RDBMS. This is how we build a `PersonAccess` service:

```
public class PersonAccess
{
  public void StorePerson(Person person)
  {
    new MongoClient()
        .GetServer()
        .GetDatabase("timelineService")
        .GetCollection<Person>("profile")
        .Insert(person);
  }
}
```

Let's unpack our `StorePerson` method a little bit at a time. First, we instantiate a `MongoClient` object. We don't need to connect or disconnect it; the driver manages a connection pool for us, as follows:

```
new MongoClient()
```

Once we have `MongoClient`, we use `GetServer()` to access our server. Since we didn't provide a connection string, `MongoClient` defaults to connecting to `localhost`:

```
new MongoClient()
  .GetServer()
```

`GetServer` returns a server object. On that, we call `GetDatabase` and specify the name. It's a good idea to make sure that each application gets its own database, so let's name this one `timelineService` after our application:

```
new MongoClient()
  .GetServer()
  .GetDatabase("timelineService")
```

On the database object, we call `GetCollection<T>` and provide it with the name of the collection we'd like to use, which is `profile` in this case. Since `GetCollection` is typed, it knows how to serialize and deserialize entities that we store, which in this case are as objects of the type `Person`:

```
new MongoClient()
  .GetServer()
  .GetDatabase("timelineService")
  .GetCollection<Person>("profile")
```

`GetCollection` returns an object that refers to the specific collection we want to manipulate. From the collection, it's a simple matter of calling `Insert()` to insert our `person` document into the `profile` collection, as shown in the following code:

```
new MongoClient()
  .GetServer()
  .GetDatabase("timelineService")
  .GetCollection<Person>("profile")
  .Insert(person);
```

Now, let's write an integration test for our `StorePerson` method. We'll provide it with `testPerson`:

```
var testPerson = new Person
{
  Email = "abc@def.ghi",
  FirstName = "Abc",
  LastName = "Def",
  UserName = "AbcDef"
};
```

Once we have `testPerson` created, we can instantiate a `PersonAccess` object and use it to store our test object:

```
var service = new PersonAccess();
service.StorePerson(testPerson);
```

`StorePerson` didn't return an `Id` field, but what `MongoClient` has done under the hood is initialized the `Id` field for us, so we can now reference it if needed, as follows:

```
var testPersonId = testPerson.Id;
```

Now that we can store users, it might be nice if we could retrieve them later. Let's develop a method on our `PersonAccess` service that can do that for us.

Let's call the method `GetPersonByUserName`. It will have one argument—the `userName` we want to retrieve:

```
public Person GetPersonByUserName(string userName)
{
  return new MongoClient()
    .GetServer()
    .GetDatabase(Db)
    .GetCollection<Person>(Profile)
    .FindOne(
    Query<Person>.EQ(p => p.UserName, userName));
}
```

Just as with the `StorePerson` method, we begin by instantiating `MongoClient`, calling `GetServer`, `GetDatabase`, and `GetCollection`. Next up, we'll call the MongoDB method `FindOne`. `FindOne` expects an argument of the type `IMongoQuery`. The MongoDB driver provides a helper method `Query<T>.EQ` that returns `IMongoQuery` for us based on the arguments that we pass in. We'll pass in a lambda to specify the document property that we want to match, which in this case is `p => p.Username`. The second parameter is the string that we want to match it against, which is the variable `userName` in this case:

```
.FindOne(
    Query<Person>.EQ(
    p => p.UserName, userName));
```

`FindOne(Query<Person>.EQ(p => p.UserName, userName))` returns the first `Person` object that has a property `UserName` matching the string passed in to `GetPersonByUserName`.

How it works...

The `MongoClient` driver passes the query generated to the MongoDB server. MongoDB runs MongoDB's `db.collection.findOne()` method with the query provided. MongoDB returns a JSON result, which the MongoDB driver deserialized into a `Person` object. If there is more than one document in the datastore, the method will return the first document according to the natural order of documents on the disk.

None of the code shown previously is particular to ServiceStack—we're simply leveraging MongoDB C# Driver.

We can do more than just retrieve single documents. We can illustrate more about how you can query MongoDB with some simple integration tests. We can begin by creating an entity type and a test collection that contains a few simple objects, as follows:

```
class TestEntity
{
    public ObjectId Id { get; set; }
    public string Name { get; set; }
    public DateTime Birthday { get; set; }
    public int Rank { get; set; }
    public string Stripe { get; set; }
}
var testCollection = new MongoClient()
    .GetServer()
    .GetDatabase("tests")
    .GetCollection("tests");

testCollection.Drop();
```

```
testCollection.Insert(new TestEntity
{
  Name = "test one",
  Rank = 1,
  Birthday = new DateTime(2001, 1, 1),
  Stripe = "Blue"
});
testCollection.Insert(new TestEntity
{
  Name = "test two",
  Rank = 2,
  Birthday = new DateTime(2002, 2, 2),
  Stripe = "Blue"
});
testCollection.Insert(new TestEntity
{
  Name = "test three",
  Rank = 3,
  Birthday = new DateTime(2003, 3, 3),
  Stripe = "Green"
});
```

It's easy to count the number of items in a collection, as follows:

```
Assert.That(testCollection.Count().Equals(3));
```

Likewise, we can count items that have Rank greater than 2:

```
Assert.That(testCollection.Count(
Query.GT("Rank", 2)).Equals(1));
```

Comparing dates is just as simple:

```
Assert.That(testCollection.Count(
Query.GT("Birthday",
new DateTime(2001, 1, 1)))
.Equals(2));
```

If you actually want to return a group of documents, you can do that too. For instance, you might want to get all of the documents that have the Stripe property set to "Blue". The simplest way is to use the FindAs<T> method, and the way we've been working with the Query<T> helper still applies. Here's the code for this course of action:

```
var list = testCollection.FindAs<TestEntity>(
  Query<TestEntity>.EQ(e=>e.Stripe, "Blue"));
```

`FindAs<TestEntity>` specifies that each document MongoDB finds in the collection should be deserialized as a `TestEntity` object. `Query<TestEntity>` allows us to use the strongly typed query syntax `e=>e.Stripe` to specify the document property we want to match against, as follows:

```
Assert.That(list.All( e=>e.Stripe.Equals("Blue")));

Assert.That(list.Count().Equals(2));
```

There's more...

ServiceStack does have some specific integration with MongoDB in the form of `ServiceStack.Authentication.MongoDB`. This allows you to build applications that store the authentication credentials in MongoDB instead of an OrmLite database as we've shown in other recipes. Installing it is easy with NuGet, as follows:

PM> Install-Package ServiceStack.Authentication.MongoDB

With that package installed, you can register the MongoDB auth to take advantage of the feature:

```
var authDatabase = new MongoClient()
  .GetServer()
  .GetDatabase("mongoAuth");

  container.Register<IUserAuthRepository>(
  new MongoDbAuthRepository(authDatabase, true));
```

Using ServiceStack with Elasticsearch

A sort of specialized category within NoSQL is search engines. These services specialize in *indexing* data and are often used in concert with an application database. For instance, you might be building an e-commerce website. You could query your product database when a visitor wants to search products, but you'd have to take on much of the work of figuring out partial searches, relevancy, boosting, multi-field search, and other challenges.

Many people start out thinking of search engines as being associated with search crawlers—Google and Bing have crawlers that visit websites and index content, titles, links, and other relevant data. With most NoSQL search engines, they don't include a crawler mechanism. Instead, we'll insert documents for indexing as they are created, giving us greater control over how they are indexed and reducing the complexity and computing overhead involved in building a search crawler.

In fact, many application development teams consider using these indexes as primary data stores in their own right and sometimes end up doing just that. Solr and Elasticsearch both, for instance, have many (but not all) of the same features as a document store like MongoDB or RavenDB.

Elasticsearch is essentially a wrapper around Lucene. By default, Elasticsearch uses Lucene to return results in the order of relevance, specifically using a TF/IDF algorithm.

- **Term Frequency** (**TF**): This is what it sounds like—the more often a term appears in a document, the more likelihood of it's being relevant.

- **Inverse Document Frequency** (**IDF**): This attempts to correct for terms that appear very frequently in all documents. Terms that appears in many documents have a lower weight than more uncommon ones.

- The field length norm is also considered. A term appearing in a short field, for instance, a title, might have more relevance than a term appearing in a longer field like an article body.

Note that for more information on Elasticsearch, its website at http://www.elasticsearch.org contains great documentation. For more information on Lucene, which provides much of the infrastructure for Elasticsearch, check out the Lucene website at http://lucene.apache.org/.

Getting ready

For this example, we'll set up Elasticsearch to index the different profiles in our application so that we can quickly search for them by name or e-mail, returning UserName and Id. We'll use MongoDB as our primary datastore. It is possible to use Elasticsearch as the index and as the primary datastore—but teams often find themselves using a NoSQL store like MongoDB for the advanced features, while Elasticsearch excels at natural language text search.

Elasticsearch depends on Java, and the JAVA_HOME environment variable must be set before you can start the service. On Windows, once you have Java installed, you can check the **Configure Java** control panel to see where Java is installed. Click on the **Java** tab and then the **View** button. You should see a list of the Java environments installed on this machine—choose the most recent and then grab the contents of the **Path** column. Then, in your command prompt, you can make sure that JAVA_HOME is set. The following screenshot shows how the objective set out in this paragraph can be achieved:

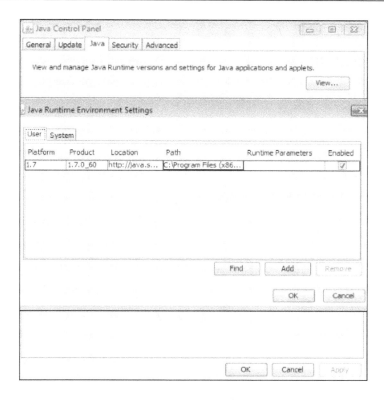

For instance, in my case, the Path field is set to `C:\Program Files (x86)\Java\jre7\bin\javaw.exe`, and `JAVA_HOME` should point to the folder that contains the `bin` folder, so I'll set `JAVA_HOME` like this:

```
C:\>set JAVA_HOME=C:\Program Files (x86)\Java\jre7\
```

We'll also need Elasticsearch installed. Obtaining the latest stable build of Elasticsearch is easy as Elasticsearch maintains downloads of the latest stable builds at `http://www.elasticsearch.org/download/`. Download the `.zip` file with the correct binaries, making sure `JAVA_HOME` is set properly. Once they're unzipped, you can start Elasticsearch at the command line:

```
C:\elasticsearch-1.3.2\bin>elasticsearch
```

We'll also make use of a strongly typed client for Elasticsearch called `NEST`. It's an officially supported Elasticsearch driver. You can install it easily using NuGet, as follows:

```
PM > Install-Package NEST
```

How to do it...

1. Once we have the service running, we can begin the work of indexing data. Let's say that for each new user created in the future, we want to store them in MongoDB and also submit them for indexing in Elasticsearch. We could alter our `PersonAccess` service class to do that, as follows:

```
public void StorePerson(Person person)
{
  new MongoClient()
      .GetServer()
      .GetDatabase("timelineService")
      .GetCollection<Person>("profile")
      .Insert(person);

  var elasticSettings = new ConnectionSettings(
      new Uri("http://localhost:9200"),
      "timelineservice");

  new ElasticClient(elasticSettings)
      .Index(person);
}
```

2. We saw how `MongoClient` worked in a previous recipe, but let's start unpacking the Elasticsearch specific stuff. We create a new `ConnectionSettings` object to configure our connection to the server. Elasticsearch uses HTTP and by default is exposed on `localhost` on port number `9200`. We'll also need to specify the name of the index we want to use. In Elasticsearch, the index is roughly analogous to a database in other systems. Each application should get its own index, so we'll call ours `timelineservice`. We can't CamelCase the name as Elasticsearch won't create indexes that contain uppercase letters. Here's the code for our purposes:

```
var elasticSettings = new ConnectionSettings(
new Uri("http://localhost:9200"),
"timelineservice");
```

3. Now that we have our Elasticsearch `ConnectionSettings` object, we can create an `ElasticClient` object, pass it the `Settings` object, and then call `Insert` to index our `person` object, as follows:

```
new ElasticClient(elasticSettings)
  .Index(person);
```

As we said before, NEST is strongly typed. It's going to check the type of the object we present and notice it's a `Person` object.

4. It's worth noting that NEST uses Newtonsoft JSON.NET under the hood to serialize and deserialize objects. Since our `Person` object has a MongoDB `ObjectId` field on it, there's actually going to be trouble deserializing the `Person` object later unless we change around our `Person` object a little bit. Let's take a look at one way to handle that:

```
public class Person
{
  [BsonRepresentation(BsonType.ObjectId)]
  public string Id { get; set; }

  public string FirstName { get; set; }
  public string LastName { get; set; }
  public string Email { get; set; }
  public string UserName { get; set; }
}
```

JSON.NET handles strings just fine, but MongoDB needs the `Id` field to be `BsonType.ObjectId`. So, what we'll do is annotate the `Id` field to tell MongoDB how to serialize and deserialize the object, but let JSON.NET (and thereby NEST) handle the field like a plain string to remediate the issue with deserialization.

5. Now that we've indexed our `Person` object, we can search for it on the command line using cURL, as follows:

```
curl -XGET
'http://localhost:9200/timelineservice/person/_search?pretty'
-d '{
  "query" : { "match": {"firstName": "jkl"}},
  "from": 0,
  "size": 10,
  _source": ["email","lastName"]
}'
```

Elasticsearch provides a default REST implementation for queries. You can see from this example that our URL is constructed first from the name of the index we passed in, `timelineservice`, and then the type (`Person`) of the object we indexed. The `_search?pretty` URL handle tells Elasticsearch that the data submitted is a search request, and that we'd like the results pretty printed.

The `query` parameter of the request contains a request that we match documents with a `firstName` field of `jkl`. It's worth pointing out that Elasticsearch converted our `FirstName` field to `firstName`, preferring that the first character not be uppercase. The `from` parameter tells Elasticsearch where to start; if this were the second page of results, and we were getting `10` results per page, we might have said `10` here. `Size` tells Elasticsearch how many records we want back. The `source` argument allows us to specify what parts of the source document we want back, in this case `email` and `lastName` only.

Coming back to our `PersonAccess` service, let's see what it might look like to search the index by `UserName` and get back the MongoDB `ObjectId` property of our user.

6. First, let's model our search request. Much like the cURL command shown previously, we'll provide `From`, `Size`, and `MatchQuery`. Also, we'll still need to remember to lowercase the first character of the field, specifying `userName` instead of `UserName`. Here's how we model our search request:

```
var searchRequest = new SearchRequest
{
    From = 0,
    Size = 10,
    Query = (QueryContainer)new MatchQuery
    {
      Field = "userName",
      Query = userName
    }
};
```

7. Next, we'll create our `Settings` object and connect to Elasticsearch just as we did before. We'll also pass in the `searchRequest` class we created to the strongly typed `Search<T>` method and specify the type as `Person`. The following code shows how this is done:

```
var elasticSettings = new ConnectionSettings(
new Uri("http://localhost:9200"),
"timelineservice");

var results = new ElasticClient(elasticSettings)
      .Search<Person>(searchRequest);
```

8. As long as we've ensured that `UserNames` are unique somehow, Elasticsearch will only return one document. We'll use the `Id` field of that document to query MongoDB for the profile we need, as follows:

```
var firstUser = results.Documents.First();
```

9. Once we have it, we can query Mongo to get the right user, as follows:

```
return new MongoClient()
  .GetServer()
  .GetDatabase("timelineService")
  .GetCollection<Person>("profile")
  .FindOne(
  MongoDB.Driver.Builders.Query<Person>
  .EQ(p => p.Id, firstUser.Id));
```

10. After specifying the correct server, database, and collection, we'll call MongoDB's FindOne function and pass in a Query specifying that we want the person's Id to be the one we found in Elasticsearch. If we put the whole thing together, the code might look like this:

```
public void StorePerson(Person person)
{
  new MongoClient()
  .GetServer()
  .GetDatabase("timelineService")
  .GetCollection<Person>("profile")
  .Insert(person);

    var elasticSettings = new ConnectionSettings(
    new Uri("http://localhost:9200"),
    "timelineservice");

  new ElasticClient(elasticSettings)
  .Index(person);
}

public Person GetPersonByUserName(string userName)
{
  var searchRequest = new SearchRequest
  {
    From = 0,
    Size = 10,
    Query = (QueryContainer)new MatchQuery
    {
      Field = "userName",
      Query = userName
    }
  };

    var elasticSettings = new ConnectionSettings(
```

```
                new Uri("http://localhost:9200"),
                "timelineservice");

            var results = new ElasticClient(elasticSettings)
            .Search<Person>(searchRequest);
            var firstUser = results.Documents.First();
            return new MongoClient()
            .GetServer()
            .GetDatabase("timelineService")
             .GetCollection<Person>("profile")
            .FindOne(
            MongoDB.Driver.Builders.Query<Person>
            .EQ(p => p.Id, firstUser.Id));
        }
```

How it works...

Under the hood, the NEST client is converting the `searchRequest` object we create to a REST call that connects to the Elasticsearch service running on our machine. Since we inserted our `Person` object into Elasticsearch and MongoDB upon creation, when we query Elasticsearch, we'll find the user and then be able to pull up the user from our MongoDB server.

In larger systems, the main datastore often grows in size and complexity until searching it becomes more and more difficult and more slow; using a search engine like Elasticsearch can provide search capabilities in this situation.

There's more...

It would be better, of course, to use **Dependency Injection** (**DI**) to create the `MongoClient` and `ElasticClient` objects. Doing that with Funq is a snap. In `ServiceHost`, we'll register the components we need so that we can resolve them later.

First we'll register a default `MongoClient` object, as follows; `MongoClient` manages our connection pool for us:

```
var mongoClient = new MongoClient();
container.Register(mongoClient);
```

Next we'll create the `elasticSettings` object and create an `ElasticClient` object, as follows:

```
    var elasticSettings = new ConnectionSettings(
    new Uri("http://localhost:9200"), "timelineservice");
var elasticClient = new ElasticClient(elasticSettings);
container.Register(elasticClient);
```

It's important to register our `PersonAccess` object after its dependencies so that Funq can locate them:

```
container.RegisterAutoWiredAs<PersonAccess, IPersonAccess>();
```

Once we've done that, we can clean up our `PersonAccess` service quite a bit:

```
public interface IPersonAccess
{
  void StorePerson(Person person);
  Person GetPersonByUserName(string userName);
}

public class PersonAccess : IPersonAccess
{
  private const string Db = "timelineService";
  private const string Profile = "profile";
  private const string TimelineIndex = "timelineservice";

  private MongoCollection<Person> ProfileCollection;
  private ElasticClient Elastic;
  private MongoClient Mongo;

  public PersonAccess(ElasticClient elastic, MongoClient mongo)
  {
    Mongo = mongo;
    Elastic = elastic;

    ProfileCollection = Mongo
    .GetServer()
    .GetDatabase(Db)
    .GetCollection<Person>(Profile);
  }

  public void StorePerson(Person person)
  {
    ProfileCollection.Insert(person);
    var index = Elastic.Index(person);
    if (!index.Created) throw new Exception("Failed to index
    person " + person);
  }

  public Person GetPersonByUserName(string userName)
  {
    var searchRequest = new SearchRequest
```

```
    {
      From = 0,
      Size = 10,
      Query = (QueryContainer)new MatchQuery
      {
        Field = "userName",
        Query = userName
      }
    };
    var results = Elastic.Search<Person>(searchRequest);
    var firstUser = results.Documents.First();
    return ProfileCollection.FindOne(
    MongoDB.Driver.Builders.Query<Person>
    .EQ(p => p.Id, firstUser.Id));
  }
}
```

Working with ServiceStack and AngularJS resources

AngularJS is a JavaScript-based frontend MVC web framework that makes quite a number of things easier when building complex web applications. Large JavaScript applications can get harder and harder to maintain as they grow, AngularJS is structured in such a way that it helps keep the applications, complexity isolated in separate modules. AngularJS itself is separated into several modules to make the framework easier to manage if you don't need all of its functionality. One of these modules is called NgResource. This module can help when you are dealing with server-side domain objects (resources) that can be viewed, created, updated, and deleted, but it does come with its own assumptions and conventions. In this recipe, we will look at a simple example of how you utilize, extend, and consume the AngularJS resource module to make it easier to handle server-side updates.

Getting ready

AngularJS is quite a large framework that has a number of interrelated concepts. This recipe is not intended as an introduction to AngularJS, rather an expansion on how it can be used with ServiceStack to avoid writing a lot of duplicate code on the client to interact with web services.

How to do it...

We are going to start from an empty ASP.NET ServiceStack host and add our client-side dependencies from NuGet. To keep this focused on how to interact with our ServiceStack services via AngularJS, we will desist from using ServiceStack Razor views unlike previous recipes. We will also reuse some of the `PlacesToVisit` services from previous chapters as an example of a resource we will be viewing and updating. Perform the following steps to achieve the objectives set out in this paragraph:

1. Create a new project using the **ServiceStack ASP.NET Empty** project template in ServiceStackVS, or follow the guide in *Appendix A, Getting Started*.

2. Install AngularJS Core, Route, and Resource from NuGet using the following commands:

   ```
   Install-Package AngularJS.Core
   ```

   ```
   Install-Package AngularJS.Route
   ```

   ```
   Install-Package AngularJS.Resource
   ```

3. Install Bootstrap from NuGet using the following command:

   ```
   Install-Package Twitter.Bootstrap
   ```

4. We will create the following folder structure for our AngularJS application under the `scripts` folder inside the main project:

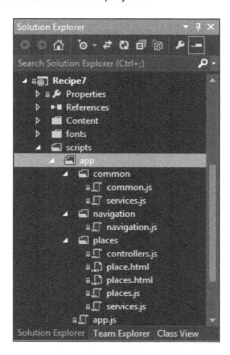

5. Create an `app.js` file that initializes the main module, specifies our dependencies, and a default client-side route:

```
angular.module('myApp', [
    'ngRoute',
    'myApp.navigation',
    'myApp.places',
    'myApp.common'
]).
    config(['$routeProvider', function ($routeProvider) {
    $routeProvider.otherwise({ redirectTo: '/places' });
}]);
```

6. Create a `places.js` file in a new `places` folder under the `app` folder. The `places` folder will contain the logic to get and update a place resource, as follows:

```
var app = angular.module('myApp.places',
    [
        'myApp.places.controllers',
        'myApp.places.services'
    ]);


app.config([
    '$routeProvider', function($routeProvider) {
    $routeProvider.when('/places/:placeId', {
    templateUrl: 'scripts/app/places/place.html',
    controller: 'PlaceCtrl'
        });
    $routeProvider.when('/places', {
    templateUrl: 'scripts/app/places/places.html',
    controller: 'PlacesCtrl'
        });
    }
]);
```

7. Create AngularJS controllers to list all places as well as edit a single place. This will be in the `app/places/controllers.js` file inside its own module called `myApp.places.controllers`. The following is the code that will help you achieve the objectives set out in this paragraph:

```
var app = angular.module('myApp.places.controllers',
['ngRoute', 'ngResource', 'myApp.places.services']);


app.controller('PlaceCtrl', ['$scope', 'Place',
'$routeParams', '$location', function ($scope, Place,
$routeParams, $location) {
```

```
      Place.get({ Id: $routeParams.placeId }, function
      (place) {
        $scope.currentPlace = place;
      });

      $scope.updatePlace = function () {
      $scope.currentPlace.$save();
      }

      $scope.cancel = function() {
      $location.path('/places');
      }
}]);

app.controller('PlacesCtrl', ['$scope', 'Places', function
($scope, Places) {
    Places.get(function (places) {
    $scope.places = places;
    });
}]);
```

8. Create a custom `resource` wrapper to let us customize how the HTTP requests are sent to our ServiceStack services. These will be common to our application and so can be isolated within their own module. Here's how:

```
var app = angular.module('myApp.common.services',
['ngResource']);

//Extend $resource to provide defaults
app.factory('PlacesToVisitResource', ['$resource', function
($resource) {
    return function (url, params, methods) {
        var defaults = {
            update: { method: 'put', isArray: false },
            create: { method: 'post' },
        };

        methods = angular.extend(defaults, methods);

        var resource = $resource(url, params, methods);

        resource.prototype.$save = function () {
            if (!this.Id) {
                return this.$create();
```

```
            }
            else {
                return this.$update();
            }
        };

        return resource;
    };
}]);
```

9. Create a `Place` and `Places` factory to keep our resource URLs within one location, as shown in the following code; this will be located in the `myApp.places.services` module and will depend on `myApp.common`:

```
var app = angular.module('myApp.places.services',
['ngRoute', 'myApp.common']);

app.factory('Place', [
    'PlacesToVisitResource', function
    (PlacesToVisitResource) {
      return PlacesToVisitResource('places/:Id', { Id:
      '@Id' });
    }
]);

app.factory('Places', [
    'PlacesToVisitResource', function
    (PlacesToVisitResource) {
        return PlacesToVisitResource('places', null,
            {
                get:
                {
                    method: 'get', isArray: true
                }
            });
    }
]);
```

10. Create `places.html` within the `app/places` directory, as shown in the following code; this will be our template for listing all places from our services:

```
<div>
    <ul>
        <li ng-repeat="place in places">
            <a href="#/places/{{place.Id}}">{{place.Name}}</a>
```

```
        </li>
      </ul>
   </div>
```

11. Create a `place.html` file to view and edit an existing place resource, as follows:

```
<div class="row">
    <div class="col-lg-12 col-md-12">
        <form name="placeForm" role="form" class="form-
        horizontal" >
            <fieldset>
                <legend>Place</legend>
                <div class="form-group" ng-show="!isNew">
                <label for="inputId" class="control-
                label">Id</label>
                    <div>
                      <input type="text" class="form-
                      control" name="inputId"
                      value="{{currentPlace.Id}}" disabled>
                    </div>
                </div>
                <div class="form-group">
                    <label for="Name" class="control-
                    label">Name</label>
                    <div>
                        <input type="text" class="form-
                        control" name="Name"
                        placeholder="Place name..."
                        required ng-
                        model="currentPlace.Name">
                    </div>
                </div>
                <div class="form-group">
                    <label for="Description"
                    class="control-
                    label">Description</label>
                    <div>
                        <input type="text" class="form-
                        control" name="Description"
                        placeholder="Description..."
                        required ng-
                        model="currentPlace.Description">
                    </div>
                </div>
                <div class="form-group">
```

```
                              <div>
                                  <button type="submit" ng-
                                  click="updatePlace()" class="btn
                                  btn-primary">Save</button>
                                  <button type="button" class="btn"
                                  ng-click="cancel()">Cancel</button>
                              </div>
                          </div>
                      </fieldset>
                  </form>
              </div>
          </div>
```

How it works...

First we will look at the three services our frontend is interacting with so that we can see what we are getting back, as follows:

```csharp
public class PlaceService : Service
{
    public IPlacesToVisitRepository PlacesToVisitRepository { get;
    set; }

    public PlaceToVisitResponse Get(PlaceToVisit request)
    {
        if (!PlacesToVisitRepository.PlaceExists(request.Id))
        {
            throw HttpError.NotFound("Place not found");
        }
        return
        PlacesToVisitRepository.PlaceById(request.Id)
        .ConvertTo<PlaceToVisitResponse>();
    }

    public List<Place> Get(AllPlacesToVisitRequest request)
    {
        return PlacesToVisitRepository.AllPlaces();
    }

    public PlaceToVisitResponse Put(UpdatePlaceToVisit request)
    {
        if (!PlacesToVisitRepository.PlaceExists(request.Id))
        {
            throw HttpError.NotFound("Place not found");
```

```
            }
            var place =
            PlacesToVisitRepository.UpdatePlace
            (request.ConvertTo<Place>());
            return place.ConvertTo<PlaceToVisitResponse>();
        }
    }
```

Although we don't have to, we are specifying the return type from our services here to clearly show what is being returned and what the AngularJS $resource is expecting from the server. In the PlaceToVisit GET request, we are returning a PlaceToVisit response, which is a response DTO that matches the Place type in our database. We are using the ConvertTo<T> extension method to automatically map the properties from one to the other.

Now that we can see what our services are returning, we can have a look at the AngularJS factory we made to wrap the built-in $resource service, PlacesToVisitResource:

```
app.factory('PlacesToVisitResource', ['$resource', function
($resource) {
    return function (url, params, methods) {
        var defaults = {
                update: { method: 'put', isArray: false },
                create: { method: 'post' },
        };

        methods = angular.extend(defaults, methods);

        var resource = $resource(url, params, methods);

        resource.prototype.$save = function () {
                if (!this.Id) {
                    return this.$create();
                }
                else {
                    return this.$update();
                }
        };

        return resource;
    };
}]);
```

In the preceding wrapper, we are creating some defaults that can be overridden, but these defaults should match the conventions followed by your ServiceStack services to reduce the code on the client. The `$save` method has been created to again create sensible behavior that follows the conventions of your web services. In this case, we are checking for the presence of an `Id` property on the model calling the `$save` method to decide whether the call to our web services should be a `POST` or a `PUT`. If `Id` is present, we are going to use `PUT` to update the whole resource. If `Id` is not present, we will use a `POST` call to create a new resource.

The idea behind `PlacesToVisitResource` is that these defaults will be across a domain, which will more than likely have multiple resources within it. We will need to match the URL paths of these resources to a single object, so for maintainability, we want to keep that URL in one place:

```
app.factory('Place', [
    'PlacesToVisitResource', function (PlacesToVisitResource)
    {
        return PlacesToVisitResource('places/:Id', { Id: '@Id' });
    }
]);
```

While in an application this small, it might be considered overkill to illustrate a technique that helps keep your app "DRY" (don't repeat yourself)—we have wrapped our domain `PlacesToVisitResource` in another, albeit very small, `factory` that can be injected into our controllers or directives so that we don't have to use the URL in various different places. To get a `Place` now from a controller, we can use the following code:

```
Place.get({ Id: 1 }, function (place) {
    //'place' with Id 1 is our place resource from the server
});
```

The `place` resource we get back now has methods like `$save` accessible from it that allow us to edit the resource, for example, change the description and perform a save. In the case of the example, we are using ng-model and two-way binding to our input fields to handle the updating of our `currentPlace` object. Once the user is done with updating the input fields, we can call `$scope.currentPlace.$save()`, and this will call the appropriate `POST` or `PUT` method to create or update our `Place` resource. The following code shows how this can be acomplished in our example:

```
$scope.updatePlace = function ()
    {
        $scope.currentPlace.$save();
    }
```

To give an example of overriding how our `PlacesToVisitResource` factory handles requests, we can create a `Places` factory that will handle getting all places back from the server. For this example, we are using a service that specifically returns an array; generally, it might be easier to just have a response object that has a property for the results, for example:

```
public class PlacesToVisitResponse
{
  public List<Place> Places { get;set; }
}
```

However, if you do prefer to return an array from the service, the AngularJS `factory` can be overridden, as follows:

```
app.factory('Places', [
    'PlacesToVisitResource', function (PlacesToVisitResource) {
        return PlacesToVisitResource('places', null,
            {
                get:
                {
                    method: 'get', isArray: true
                }
            });
    }
]);
```

The last parameter passed to the `PlacesToVisitResource` function is an object that represents methods and their options that we want to use instead of the defaults. In this case, we are overriding the `get` function specifying that we will use the `GET` HTTP method/verb and that we will be expecting an array back from the server.

Again, this is so that in other areas in our AngularJS application, we don't have to worry about managing these conventions, and we can just use the following code to retrieve all places:

```
Places.get(function (places) {
        //'places' returned from the server
    });
```

This allows us to handle our resources in a consistent way from our controllers and directives as well as allowing us to write very simple code that is easy to read and easy to override when required.

A
Getting Started

Creating a ServiceStack solution with Visual Studio and NuGet

We'll use Visual Studio in the examples within this book. If you don't have access to Visual Studio 2013 Professional or higher, it's highly recommended that you use Microsoft's new free version of Visual Studio, Visual Studio Community Edition 2013. The community edition enables the use of extensions. ServiceStack has its own Visual Studio extension called ServiceStackVS, which is available from within Visual Studio or via the Visual Studio Gallery.

If you are currently stuck with a Visual Studio Express version or an earlier version of Visual Studio, such as Visual Studio 2010, this appendix will walk you through the steps to get you started from an empty project. Everything in this appendix can be done from a ServiceStackVS project template. Check out the Visual Studio 2013 Community Edition at the Visual Studio website at `http://www.visualstudio.com/products/visual-studio-community-vs`.

Once you have Visual Studio installed, run it, and click on **New Project**. You'll be prompted to choose a project type, respond by selecting **Web** and then **ASP.NET Web Application**. Name the solution. The following screenshot depicts the actions to be performed to set up the project in Visual Studio:

Once you click on **OK**, your solution will be created. Choose the **Empty** project type. Don't check the **Add Unit Tests** checkmark; we'll be adding NUnit with NuGet later. The following screenshot depicts the actions explained in this paragraph:

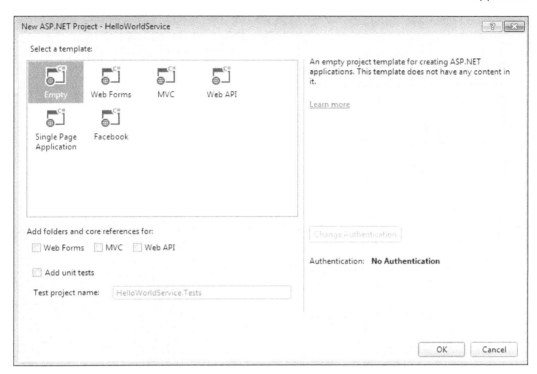

The next thing you need to do is pull in the ServiceStack framework via Nuget. To do that, find **Package Manager Console** in Visual Studio and enter the following command:

```
Install-Package ServiceStack
```

NuGet will download the ServiceStack binaries and add references to them to our project. You should see messages of the form **Successfully added ServiceStack. <version number> to <SolutionName>** in the output if this succeeded.

Integrating NUnit

The next step is to integrate a testing framework. We'll make use of the NUnit library in the examples in this book, though ServiceStack does work with almost any testing framework. First, add a new project to our solution. Call it `<SolutionName>.Tests`, substituting in the name of the package that you will test. Choose **Class Library** as the type. In **Package Manager Console**, choose `<SolutionName>.Tests` from the **Default Project** dropdown, and then type `Install-Package nunit`. You'll need to add a reference to ServiceStack from the test project as well—you can do that by typing `Install-Package servicestack` in **Package Manager Console**, as you did previously.

Now that you have a test project, you can start adding test classes. Generally, the idea is to create a test class for each grouping of tests—often, this means one test class per object under test. Create a new class inside your test project, then place the annotation [TestFixture] above the class declaration. Make sure you add the using declaration for NUnit.Framework, then add the annotation. If you were creating a test fixture to test GreetingService for instance, your code until now should look like this:

```
[TestFixture]
public class GreetingServiceTest
{

}
```

Then, you can add a method ShouldHaveWorkingTests, for instance, which proves your test environment is working. We'll decorate the method with the [Test] annotation like this:

```
[TestFixture]
public class GreetingServiceTest
{
  [Test]
  public void ShouldHaveWorkingTests()
  {
    Assert.AreEqual(false, true, "Can make assertions");
  }
}
```

Note on NUnit and Visual Studio Express:

Visual Studio Express can easily help you to write NUnit tests, but the popular NUnit Test Adapter extension to run NUnit tests doesn't work with the Express version at the time of writing. To work around this, download either nunit-gui.exe or nunit-console.exe. Once you compile your tests, you can find the test assembly with NUnit and run your tests that way. If you're using a non-Express version of Visual Studio, the extension is highly recommended.

When using AppSelfHostBase, you will need to run the **NUnit** GUI as administrator for the tests to have sufficient privileges to host an HTTP application on the local machine.

If you're using the **NUnit** GUI, the test assembly might look like this:

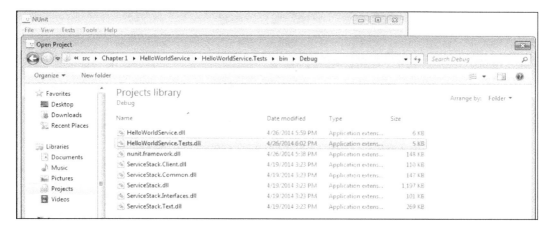

This test should fail of course, proving that your test environment works. You can correct that by simply changing `false` to `true`.

```
[TestFixture]
public class GreetingServiceTest
{
  [Test]
  public void ShouldHaveWorkingTests()
  {
    Assert.AreEqual(true, true, "Can make assertions");
  }
}
```

B
Testing Locally

This appendix shows a work around when dealing with external services that won't allow call-back URLs to specify localhost as a domain.

Testing external service callbacks locally using Fiddler2 and IIS Express

Some providers will not accept **localhost** as a callback URL, which can make testing external services difficult. Other problems with local networks could also cause various problems when trying to test callbacks locally. In this appendix, you are going to set up a workaround that can help when working with a specified call-back URL.

You want to provide either a URL for an existing development server/environment or a URL you are going to redirect to your local machine for testing. If you don't have a development server to deploy to, and want to test it locally, put it in `http://localdev.<websiteurl>/`, where `<websiteurl>` might be your production domain or a temporary name used only for testing. It can be any valid URL, but to avoid problems, you want to avoid locally redirecting a real URL.

The following instructions are for local development with IIS Express:

- If not already installed, download and install the Fiddler2 tool, which will be used to redirect, allowing you to test your local site as shown in the following screenshot:

- Go to **Tools | HOSTS** and tick **Enable remapping of requests**, specifically from the `localdev` URL provided to Twitter and `localhost` (of the example application), as shown in the following screenshot:

- Update IIS Express `applicationhost.config` file to accept requests pointing to any host name. The `applicationhost.config` file should be located in your local user's `My Documents/IISExpress/config` directory. Find the `<site>` entry in `applicationhost.config` for the example application. If it's missing, try running the application using IIS Express. Update HTTP's `bindingInformation` `*:<port>:*`. For example:

```
<site name="Recipe2" id="471">
  <application path="/"
  applicationPool="Clr4IntegratedAppPool">
```

```
        <virtualDirectory path="/"
        physicalPath="C:\projects\service-stack-
        book\src\Chapter
        7\Recipe2\Recipe2\Recipe2" />
    </application>
    <bindings>
        <binding protocol="http" bindingInformation="*:54511:*"
        />
    </bindings>
</site>
```

▸   Restart IIS Express and keep Fiddler2 running to handle remapping.

Index

custom headers
  adding, via response filter 218-222
custom queries
  mapping, to POCOs 163, 164
custom registration validator
  used, for validating password
    complexity 301-303

D

data
  streaming, from services 186-188
data transfer object (DTO)
  about 8, 55
  attributes, used for routing 18-22
database
  audit functionality, creating with
    OrmLite filters 144-148
  CRUD operations, performing on 148-156
  modeling, with attributes 130-138
  records, creating 153, 154
  records, deleting 155
  records, updating 154, 155
Debug Log 117
DELETE
  testing 111, 112
Dependency Injection (DI) 398
Distributed Current Version
    Systems (DCVS) 114

E

Elasticsearch
  ServiceStack, using 391-399
  URL 392
  URL, for downloading 393
Entity Framework
  installing 173, 174
  using, with ServiceStack 173-175
Error Logging Modules and
    Handlers (ELMAH) 117
EventLog 117

exceptions
  monitoring via email, with logger 121-128
external service call-backs
  testing, Fiddler2 used 417, 418
  testing, IIS Express used 417, 418

F

Facebook authentication
  creating 272-274
  starting with 269-271
  URL 270
Fiddler2
  used, for testing external service call-backs
    locally 417, 418
file uploads
  handling 186-188
  restricting by type, filters used 222-226
  testing 189-191
filters
  about 209-211
  used, for restricting file uploads
    by type 222-226
Flickr 84
Flickr API
  URL 85
FluentValidation
  URL 210
Fluent Validation syntax
  used, for creating static
    validation rules 211-213
form
  submitting, to service 202-207
functional contract tests
  ServiceStack services 105-109
functional tests 92
Funq
  used, for managing dependencies 37-49
Funq IoC
  used, for accessing configuration 49-53
  used, for sharing configuration 49-53

DELETE, testing 111, 112
form, submitting 202-207
functional contract testing 105-109
POST, testing 109, 110
PUT, testing 110, 111
ServiceStack solution
creating, with NuGet 411-413
creating, with Visual Studio 411-413
NUnit, integrating 413-415
sessions 254-258
SignalR hubs
ServiceStack services,
    broadcasting with 375-385
Single-Page Applications (SPA) 198
static validation rules
creating, Fluent Validation
    syntax used 211-213
Steam API
URL 309
stock keeping units (SKUs) 317
stored procedures
creating 160-162
OrmLiteSPStatement, using 159, 160
utilizing, with OrmLite 157-163

T

T4 templates
using 165-172
TeamCity
about 91, 114
build agents 114
installing 115
server process 114
URL 114
working with 116
Term Frequency (TF) 392
Testing pyramid
about 92
functional tests 92
integration tests 92
unit tests 93

Twilio
about 88
URL 88
Twitter authentication
creating 259-264
starting with 259
URL 259
typed data structures
using, with Redis 344-349
using, with ServiceStack 344-348

U

unit tests
about 93
ServiceStack applications 93-99
unit tests, approaches
classic style 93
mockist style 93
user actions
restricting by session details,
    validators used 244-247
user configurable HTTP callback service
creating, response filter used 227-236
user repositories 254-258

V

validators
about 209-211
used, for restricting user actions by session
    details 244-247
Visual Studio
used, for creating
    ServiceStack solution 411-413
Visual Studio 2013 Community Edition
URL 411
Visual Studio Express 414

W

WebForms applications
ServiceStack, using 362-368

Thank you for buying
ServiceStack 4 Cookbook

About Packt Publishing

Packt, pronounced 'packed', published its first book, *Mastering phpMyAdmin for Effective MySQL Management*, in April 2004, and subsequently continued to specialize in publishing highly focused books on specific technologies and solutions.

Our books and publications share the experiences of your fellow IT professionals in adapting and customizing today's systems, applications, and frameworks. Our solution-based books give you the knowledge and power to customize the software and technologies you're using to get the job done. Packt books are more specific and less general than the IT books you have seen in the past. Our unique business model allows us to bring you more focused information, giving you more of what you need to know, and less of what you don't.

Packt is a modern yet unique publishing company that focuses on producing quality, cutting-edge books for communities of developers, administrators, and newbies alike. For more information, please visit our website at www.packtpub.com.

About Packt Open Source

In 2010, Packt launched two new brands, Packt Open Source and Packt Enterprise, in order to continue its focus on specialization. This book is part of the Packt open source brand, home to books published on software built around open source licenses, and offering information to anybody from advanced developers to budding web designers. The Open Source brand also runs Packt's open source Royalty Scheme, by which Packt gives a royalty to each open source project about whose software a book is sold.

Writing for Packt

We welcome all inquiries from people who are interested in authoring. Book proposals should be sent to author@packtpub.com. If your book idea is still at an early stage and you would like to discuss it first before writing a formal book proposal, then please contact us; one of our commissioning editors will get in touch with you.

We're not just looking for published authors; if you have strong technical skills but no writing experience, our experienced editors can help you develop a writing career, or simply get some additional reward for your expertise.

Learning JavaScript Data Structures and Algorithms

ISBN: 978-1-78355-487-4   Paperback: 218 pages

Understand and implement classic data structures and algorithms using JavaScript

1. Learn how to use the most used data structures such as array, stack, list, tree, and graphs with real-world examples.

2. Get a grasp on which one is best between searching and sorting algorithms and learn how to implement them.

3. Follow through solutions for notable programming problems with step-by-step explanations.

Dart Cookbook

ISBN: 978-1-78398-962-1   Paperback: 346 pages

Over 110 incredibly effective, useful, and hands-on recipes to design Dart web client and server applications

1. Develop stunning apps for the modern web using Dart.

2. Learn how to store your app's data in common SQL and NoSQL databases with Dart.

3. Create state-of-the-art web apps with Polymer and Angular.

Please check **www.PacktPub.com** for information on our titles

Tizen Cookbook

ISBN: 978-1-78398-190-8   Paperback: 350 pages

Over 100 hands-on recipes to develop, deploy, and debug applications using the exciting Tizen platform

1. Discover new opportunities to develop and publish Tizen applications for cutting edge devices.

2. Create new or port existing Qt, PhoneGap, and Android applications to Tizen.

3. This book covers step-by-step recipes exploring Tizen's application development environment.

Mockito Essentials

ISBN: 978-1-78398-360-5   Paperback: 214 pages

A practical guide to get you up and running with unit testing using Mockito

1. Explore Mockito features and learn stubbing, mocking and spying dependencies using the Mockito framework.

2. Mock external dependencies for legacy and greenfield projects and create an automated JUnit safety net for building reliable, maintainable and testable software.

3. A focused guide filled with examples and supporting illustrations on testing your software using Mockito.

www.ingramcontent.com/pod-product-compliance
Lightning Source LLC
LaVergne TN
LVHW081328050326
832903LV00024B/1069

9 781783 986569